Mick Kinane

Mick Kinane
BIG RACE KING

The Authorised Biography

MICHAEL CLOWER

MAINSTREAM
PUBLISHING

EDINBURGH AND LONDON

First published in Great Britain in 1996 by
MAINSTREAM PUBLISHING COMPANY (EDINBURGH) LTD
7 Albany Street
Edinburgh EH1 3UG

This edition 1997
ISBN 1 84018 002 1

A catalogue record for this book is available from the British Library

Typeset in Sabon
Printed and bound in Finland by WSOY

Contents

Acknowledgements

I would like to thank all the very many people who so generously gave up their time to help me with this book – and also my wife, Tessa, who gave me the original idea and encouraged me to pursue it. In addition, my thanks to Tim Cox for checking the proofs.

Michael Clower
September 1996

1

The Kinanes

There is no family tree in the Kinane household. Details of ancestors are passed on from one generation to the next by word of mouth. Those sufficiently interested remember what they have been told.

Those interested ones can remember that the Kinanes came originally from Northern Ireland where they were farmers. They were also Catholics. They were therefore on the wrong side of the divide in that frequently troubled land where a person's religion can mean so much. Eventually they decided they would be better off in the South.

Many in the family can recall the story of the first of the Kinanes to have a passion for horses. The story is brief and nobody can even remember the man's Christian name. But he was the great-grandfather of Tommy Kinane and his addiction proved fatal. Literally. Out hunting one day near Galbally, just over the County Tipperary border into County Limerick, he took a crashing fall. He was kicked on the head and killed.

Ireland was a poor, frequently famine-ridden country in the last century and several of the next generation decided they would be better off in America, but Tommy's grandfather elected to return. He was the only one of five brothers to do so. It was his own son, James, who was to found a racing dynasty although he himself had little to do with horses. He worked for the Tipperary County Council as a stonemason and for most of his life he considered his most lasting achievement to be the building of the stone wall around the Rock of Cashel.

James and his wife Annie produced no less than 14 children at their home at Ballinahinch near Dundrum where the long-suffering Mrs Kinane worked from morning till night, not just feeding her huge brood but also milking a herd of cows and another of goats. Not surprisingly she and her husband eventually began to run out of Christian names and, three weeks after son Ned died at the age of 21, the latest boy was born and was also christened Ned. Tommy was the third youngest of nine brothers – he never met the eldest one, Jack, who left for America before Tommy was born on 3 October 1933 – and he was 14 when he left school to start work as a cowhand at a nearby farm. Some of his elder brothers were already working with horses and Tommy hankered to do the same. On the day of the local point-to-point he asked for a few hours off to go and watch the racing. He thought it a not unreasonable request. After all, he was at work each day at six milking every one of his charges by hand and the same task in the evening frequently saw him at it late into the night. But the farmer said no. Tommy's response was to walk out of the job but the prompt loss of his entire wealth – a ten shilling note – at the hands of a three-card trickster at the point-to-point quickly convinced him of the need to seek further employment.

He found it at Camas Park, just up the road from his home. Tim Hyde, who had won the 1939 Grand National on Workman and the 1946 Cheltenham Gold Cup on Prince Regent, was now training. His son, Timmy, who also became a jump jockey, was later to turn Camas Park into a successful stud. His phenomenal financial success at buying foals and selling them as yearlings has earned him the title of 'king of the pin-hookers'.

Tim Hyde senior paid the young Kinane a wage of £1 a week. It was not much even in those days but the rewards at the bottom of racing's ladder are poor. Christy, the next of the Kinane brothers, has for years entertained both himself (he is jovial fellow) and his listeners with stories of how he was paid four shillings (20p) a week when he started work for Vincent O'Brien at the age of 14 – 'Always two two-shilling pieces in a sealed brown envelope.'

But Tommy thought he was getting somewhere – he was officially apprenticed and therefore had a chance of riding in a flat race – until he accompanied his boss to a show at Clonakilty in County Cork. Hyde was showjumping at this stage but he broke his back in a freak fall. His wife took over the stable but some of the owners left the yard and Tommy was laid off.

Jim, another of the nine brothers, was working for Lord Harrington's trainer, Chally Chute, these days a frequent letter writer to *The Irish Field* on the wrongs of Irish racing. Tommy got a job with him, but Chute paid him only five shillings (25p) a week.

'Chally was not easy to get on with and I did not stay long,' is Tommy's wry comment. 'I took the boat to England.'

On the same ferry, making the same pilgrimage in search of work, was Johnny Kenneally who was to go so desperately close on Purple Silk in the 1964 Grand National. Tommy's first English job was with Tom Pettifer at Letcombe Regis, just outside Wantage, but after six months he moved to Tom Yates in the nearby village of Letcombe Bassett.

> At long last I got the chance to ride in a race. My first mount was on a two-year-old at Bath. Lester Piggott won the race. I had more rides, including some over hurdles, but no winners. Eventually I decided to leave racing. I went into Mr Yates's office and told him I was going. He said I was a fool, I had the ability to become champion jockey one day. I thought he was just trying to make me stay, so I took no notice and went off to London.

His Irish accent was as much of an advantage on the building sites of the capital as it was in the racing stables of Berkshire. He quickly found work as a scaffolder and, although he often went back to the Wantage-Lambourn area to ride out at weekends, there were two other interests that soon absorbed him.

The first was boxing. He trained at the Lyons Club in Cadbury Hall and boxed for Chiswick, mostly in the open air on Sunday afternoons on Clapham Common and in Battersea Park.

The second was an attractive dark-haired girl who first caught his eye in the Emerald Ballroom in Hammersmith. When he asked her to dance he was amused to discover that Frances O'Brien was from Knockavilla, not that far from Dundrum, and that they had met once in Ireland. Frances had also moved to London in search of work and was a check-out girl in one of the Express Dairy shops. They were married in St Thomas's Catholic Church in Fulham in 1956. Thomas was born the following year and the Kinanes returned to Ireland.

'I didn't marry a jockey but I knew Tommy had horses in his system,' Frances recalls. 'We decided that, as soon as the baby was old enough to stand up to the ferry journey, we would return to Ireland. Dan, the eldest of Tommy's brothers, was training at Mullinahone in County Tipperary and he was doing quite well. He suggested Tommy should join him. We said we would give it two years.'

Dan paid his younger brother the princely sum of £2 a week but there were rides, officially at £5 a time. Unofficially it was often half that.

> A lot of trainers made their own arrangements with the riding fee. You had to accept what they offered you otherwise the ride went to somebody else. It was a real struggle early on and we had no house. Frances and Thomas lived with my mother at Ballinahinch while I stayed in Mullinahone all week. On Sundays I cycled over to see them. The journey was 22 miles each way.

There were great celebrations when Tommy finally rode his first winner, on a horse called Trade Union in a handicap hurdle at Leopardstown in January 1958, not least on the part of his jockey who remembers Trade Union as 'a bit of a tricky bugger. He couldn't jump!'

A better horse was Kilmore, on whom Fred Winter was to win the 1962 Grand National, but Tommy's part in the horse's history was small. 'I rode him five times when he wasn't off and then Dan took over. The horse had one more run before the money went down at Mullingar. He was plunged on, started 7-4 favourite and won.'

Dan was not much more generous with the cash than he was with the rides. Tommy had finally managed to buy a house but he needed more than £2 a week. After a year at Mullinahone he asked for a small rise. Much to his younger brother's surprise, Dan said no. Tommy's reaction was much the same as it had been with the farmer who had said the same ten years earlier. He left. Fortunately Arthur Morris was looking for somebody who would act as his head man and help with the training at his stables beside Clonmel racecourse.

But a broken neck in a fall in a hurdle race at Clonmel proved a severe interruption to Tommy's progress as a jockey and he did not really begin to make the grade until May 1962 when Michael Purcell – one of the Purcell beef barons and the trainer of Trade Union – offered him the job as his head man at his Farney Castle stables near Holycross, between Cashel and Thurles.

There were some nice horses in the yard, I started to ride well and to hit the headlines. I rode mostly over jumps because I found it hard to get down to much below 8 st 11 lb. But I had quite a lot of winners and by May 1969 I had made enough money to buy a 90-acre farm at Killenaule, not far from where Edward O'Grady trains.

Mick, one of Tommy's brothers and now dead, used to be the driver of O'Grady's horsebox. Billy, like Dan, Christy and Jim all worked at various stages in their careers for Vincent O'Brien. Apart from Tommy, Christy was the most successful jockey, riding some 200 winners. He now trains at Cashel and survived a massive heart attack in 1992.

It was Tommy's association with Monksfield that brought him fame. This game little horse was a rarity in National Hunt racing, an entire. Few male horses do well over jumps unless they are gelded. Somewhat understandably, they are wary of hurting the most delicate part of their anatomy as they brush their way through the top of a hurdle or a fence. But Monksfield, who was kept to hurdles and flat racing before eventually being retired to stud, had no such qualms.

At the 1976 Cheltenham Festival Tommy rode him in the Daily Express Triumph Hurdle, the most sought-after four-year-old race of the season and, despite starting at an almost unconsidered 28-1, he finished second to the Jonjo O'Neill-ridden Peterhof. But Tommy was far from happy:

> I should have won but I was carried wide and I lodged an objection. I felt I was entitled to get the race but the stewards overruled me.

The pair were back at Cheltenham 12 months later, this time for the Champion Hurdle, and again they had to be content with second spot. They were beaten two lengths by Night Nurse who was winning the race for the second successive year. Once again Tommy believes he was robbed:

> I blame the instructions I was given. I wanted to hit the front after the second last and make my way home on the inside because further out it was wet and soggy. But I was told to wait until I neared the last. As a result Monksfield was forced

onto the bad ground and lost his momentum. The following
season I asked Des McDonogh and Dr Michael Mangan, the
horse's owner, not to give me any instructions. I told them
that, if they left it to me, I would win – and I did. I was 44 at
the time and I reckon I'm the oldest jockey ever to win a
Champion Hurdle.

He drove Monksfield to the front at the second last and they held
off Sea Pigeon by two lengths, with the gallant Night Nurse six
lengths further back in third. It was Tommy Kinane's greatest
moment. But it was not to last. Racing has a savage way of bringing
people down to earth and 12 days later tragedy struck. Riding
Kintai in the Irish Grand National, Tommy was brought down and
he crushed five vertebrae. He was still in hospital when Dessie
Hughes took his place on Monksfield at Aintree later the same week
to beat Night Nurse in the Templegate Hurdle. Indeed he was in bed
for three months. Few jump jockeys are still riding at the age of 44.
Those that are can seldom withstand the physical and mental
pounding of such a serious fall. It was widely assumed that he
would retire.

But Tommy, a small man with an elf-like face and a mischievous
twinkle in his eye, is a tough, determined character with on occasion
a fiery temper. He is made of stern stuff. He resolved to fight back.
After all, he had another Champion Hurdle to win on the best horse
he had ever ridden.

However the Erin Foods-sponsored Irish Champion Hurdle at
Leopardstown on 24 February 1979 proved a disaster. Monksfield
ran his first bad race over hurdles for 13 months. To be fair, he had
seldom really shone at Leopardstown and for this reason
McDonogh decided it would be best to hold him up longer than
usual. What the young County Meath trainer (he was only 32) had
not bargained for was that the early stages of the richest hurdle
race ever to take place in Ireland would be run at such a dreadfully
slow pace. Monksfield's renowned stamina could not be brought
into play and he finished a most disappointing sixth. In the
Champion Hurdle at Cheltenham Tommy was replaced by Dessie
Hughes.

He is still bitter about it:

Monksfield was not right that day at Leopardstown and he
ran like a hairy goat. I was told to ride him the opposite to

the way he was normally ridden. It was a well-organised conspiracy. I'm not mentioning names but I know who was behind it. What I will say is that it was nothing to do with Dessie Hughes. He and I were the closest of friends, and we still are. We are now virtual neighbours but we have never had a word about this matter – and we never will. Being jocked off is a part of life for a jockey. Not a pleasant part, but part of it all the same.

Monksfield's trainer said later that he had expected Tommy to use his initiative once he realised there was no pace, but he did not completely lose faith in him – 'Tommy had been a good friend to me in the early part of my career' – and he put him up on Stranfield in the Supreme Novices, the first race on Champion Hurdle day. Tommy won the race by five lengths but the famous roar that traditionally greets Irish winners at the Festival did not lift him in the same way that it had done a year earlier. Less than 90 minutes later Monksfield won his second Champion Hurdle, and his former jockey found it hard to take. But Tommy's age meant he was living on borrowed time – and there was no shortage of people to point this out to him.

> There were a lot of remarks passed. People kept telling me that, with three of my sons riding, it was time for me to move out of their way. I had taken out a trainer's licence in 1977 and eventually, at the end of 1980, I decided I should hang up my boots.

He then concentrated on training at his County Tipperary farm, but big race successes have been few – although he did win the 1982 PZ Mower Chase with Smoke Charger – and he has never been able to build up his string to a level that would enable him to compete with the fashionable names. In 1991, at Mick's suggestion, he moved his horses and his family to Pollardstown on the edge of the Curragh, only a short distance from Mick's home at Clunemore Lodge. There he built a smart house and a neat-looking yard but he is essentially a small-time trainer.

Tommy and Frances Kinane have three daughters but none has gone into racing. Susanne, the eldest, is a hairdresser. She is married to a prison officer and lives in Spalding in Lincolnshire. Katheryn is also married and lives in Naas where her husband works for Donnelly Mirrors while Janette, the baby of the family – she was born in January 1974 – moved to America with her boyfriend when she left college in 1995.

Their four brothers, though, have all chosen to follow in their father's footsteps. Only Mick has managed to stay light enough for the flat and the fame and fortune he has achieved have eluded the other three whose widely differing careers provide a pretty fair representation of the mixture of success, despair, injury and disappointment that make up the lot of the ordinary jump jockey.

Thomas is nearly two years older than Mick and of the four he is the one who seems the most content with life. He manages his younger brother's small farm and his busy Clunemore Equine Pool – it's behind Mick's house and is used by many of the Curragh trainers. Thomas lives in a small house alongside the pool with his wife and their two children. He is stockily built and in appearance a cross between his father and his famous brother. Some of Mick's humorous expressions – little seen by the public – come out in his face and he has the same white in the eyebrows. He also shared the same childhood passion for horses and he can vividly remember riding his first piece of fast work when he was only nine. He was also a keen boxer.

> I started boxing because my father said I should but I liked it and I became quite good. For four years I was Munster champion. I should also have been All-Ireland champion on two occasions but' – an amused grin spreads across his face – 'us country fellows were inclined to get raw treatment from the Dublin judges. In my first final I was up against Terry Christle whose brother Joe was later to knock out Frank Bruno when 'Know-what-I-mean-'Arry' was still an amateur. Terry hardly laid a glove on me and I knocked him down twice, yet he got a unanimous decision. I was robbed the following year too. I was convinced I had won but the judges decided otherwise.

Surprisingly Thomas finished up his schooldays with the idea of forsaking the racecourse to become an accountant:

> I went to Waterford Regional Technical College to study accountancy and I liked it but I was starting to do well as an

amateur. Four days before the end of the first year exams in 1976 I rode at Tramore. I had a heavy fall and crushed a vertebra. It meant I couldn't sit the exams and, by the time the repeats came round, I had gone off the whole idea of accountancy.

I turned professional in 1979 when I was nearly 22 and I managed to make a reasonable living. I rode about 120 winners in all, including the PZ Mower on my father's Smoke Charger, and I also won some good races for Uncle Christy when I was still an amateur. I won at Aintree on Grand National day on Multiple in 1977 and at the same meeting the following season I rode a double for him – on Multiple and Raleighstown.

The problem was that every four years I ended up in hospital. In 1980 I broke my shoulder and in 1984 it was my foot. But the 1988 one was far worse. I was riding Young Balladier for my father in a chase at the Thurles April meeting. The money was down, the horse was backed from 14-1 to 5-1 second favourite, and I had to go for everything at the last. If he had pinged it, he would have won. But he fell. I landed on my forehead and put my neck out of shape. I was only a millimetre away from spending the rest of my days in a wheelchair. I recovered alright but the doctors told me that if I had another bad fall I would do myself permanent damage. I didn't give up completely but I stopped riding seriously.

In October that year I moved from Killenaule to Clunemore. Mick had just bought the pool. We have been close all our lives and it was always on the cards that he would want me involved whenever he bought any sort of business. I enjoy running it, and working it.

Although Mick lives so close, I often only meet him for ten minutes in a week. People who don't know him might think he was a bit of a recluse and sometimes he hardly says much more than two words to me. He is always thinking, and often he is miles away in a world of his own. I pay no heed when he is like this but when he comes along with a frown on his face I know he is in bad form. Occasionally I can't resist it, and I deliberately try to rile him. It doesn't go down too well.

But on other occasions he will chat away quite happily

and occasionally the comedian he was as a child comes out. It's not often, though. He changed when he went to Liam Browne's to begin his apprenticeship. At Browne's the boys learned to keep their mouths shut. If they didn't, he would put them in their place. But I guess it came easy to Mick.

Paul is ten years younger than Thomas and, at five feet seven inches, the tallest of the four. He started off in style, rode his first winner when he was only 17 and finished up the following season as Ireland's leading claiming rider. He had beautiful hands – nothing to do with Fairy liquid but an expression conveying the sympathetic way his handling of his mounts carried its way down the reins to the horses' mouths – as well as sound judgment of pace, and above all that unmistakable mixture of flare and dash that marks out a future star.

His father still considers Paul to be the most naturally talented of any of his sons. But you need more than mere talent to make the grade as a jockey. One of the other qualities you need is confidence. The dark-haired Paul had this in abundance. But he had too much of it. In him it frequently came out as cockiness and trainers found him hard to take. As a result he failed to progress.

He moved to England to join Monica Dickinson at Harewood in Yorkshire but things did not work out and, after an unproductive spell back in Ireland, he went to New Zealand, Japan and Australia.

> When I was younger all I ever wanted was to become a jockey but, as I went round the world, I became very interested in the training side. I studied the different methods in the different countries and decided that I wanted to train. By the time this book comes out, I will have a licence.

He is married to Sue Smith, sister of flat race jockeys Wayne and David, but he admits that as a child there were times when he found his now famous elder brother hard to take.

> When we were playing hurling, he would come up behind me and trip me up. Then, when we were all sitting round the table having our evening meal, he would start pulling faces to make me laugh. My father wanted us to be quiet so he could watch the evening news. He would get mad with me and,

while Mick was sitting there like an angel, I would be sent to bed.

Of course, it's different now. I have nothing but respect for him and, contrary to what some people might think, I don't feel envious of his success. I would much rather it was him than somebody not in the family.

It's Jayo's story that is the most interesting. It's a sad story – one of heartache, disappointment and ambition dashed – and the man who tells it now lives with his wife and son on a new estate on the Dublin side of Newbridge with a railway line running behind the row of houses.

He was christened James Kevin but Mick, less than a year his senior, could not get his tongue round James when the new addition to the Kinane household was born on 2 June 1960. Jayo was the best he could manage, and it stuck.

The dark-haired Jayo, square-jawed with sharply defined features, has the same traces of white in his eyebrows as his two elder brothers but, unlike them, horses meant little to him in his early years.

What interested me was the farm but when I was 14 I took pity on the old pony Thomas and Mick had discarded. He had been turned out in a field and left there. I asked Dad for a stable for him and started riding him. Three years later I began riding on the flat but I didn't enjoy it. I found the horses difficult, basically because I wasn't strong enough. It was only when I started riding Smoke Charger over fences that I began to like it. He was fast over two miles – the main problem was holding him – and I had my first winner on him in a novice chase at Mallow on Easter Monday in 1979. Less than two months later I rode him to win the Connaught National.

After three years with his father, Jayo moved to the midlands town of Tullamore to join Guy Williams, brother-in-law of Grand National-winning rider Eddie Harty and who sent out Daletta to win the 1980 Irish Grand National. But the move was a mistake.

Guy was good with the words [he wrote a brilliant history of the Irish Derby in conjunction with bookmaker Francis

Hyland] but he proved weak on delivering horses for me to
win on. I'm not blaming him – it was my decision to join him
and therefore my fault – but most of my winners came from
outside stables.

In 1984 Jayo was introduced to Gordon Richards at the sales by
a man who recommended to the bluff North of England trainer that
he should take on the young jockey. The man was Timmy Hyde, son
of the trainer with whom Jayo's father had started in racing over 35
years earlier. What Jayo saw when he went to Greystoke, near
Penrith in Cumbria, filled him with a passion and enthusiasm that
he barely knew he possessed.

> To be there on schooling mornings would take your breath
> away. Forty or more superbly built jumpers coming out of
> the mist with Gordon at the head of affairs was just about
> the most magnificent sight you could wish for – and to be
> part of it was for me the ultimate.

A double at Southwell got him off to a flying start and at the end
of the season he returned to Ireland buoyed with success. At last he
knew where life was taking him. He filled in his 'holiday' by riding
at the summer meetings. One of the horses on whom he picked up
the ride was Star Of Coole and in the Rank Cup Chase at Killarney
the second favourite was just beginning to make ground as he
approached the fourth last.

> There were two horses on my outer. The one furthest from
> me came in and forced the other one across me. I was
> knocked straight through the wing and a steel bar went
> through my leg just below the knee. I was still in Tralee
> hospital when Gordon Richards rang my father to say he
> had a string of rides for me. For some reason Neale
> Doughty, his stable jockey, had temporarily parted with
> him. I was obviously in with a chance of being made first
> jockey. I had worked so hard to get into this position and
> not to be able to take it was sickening. Even more so when
> several of the horses won. Somehow I knew I would never
> get the same chance again and I felt I could not go back to
> a set-up as magnificent as the one at Greystoke as a semi-
> invalid. Indeed I never returned there. I see now I made a

terrible mistake. Gordon would have nursed me back.

I was out of action for 14 weeks. I should have stayed out a lot longer but I was impatient for success and, frankly, I needed the money – the middle of the road jump jockey barely makes a living. But I was not the same for ages afterwards. It even took me two years to recover my balance and every time I hit the ground I seemed to damage something. I had terrible pains in my shoulders and I had to ride with my reins knotted halfway up the horse's neck with one hand resting on the pommel of the saddle. It was not until I was operated on by Hugh Barber, the famous Carlisle surgeon, that I really recovered.

Jayo sued Killarney for negligence but, possibly because he had cut short his convalescence, the damages he was awarded amounted to only £12,000. For four years he struck up a reasonably successful partnership with Ken Oliver, the so-called 'benign bishop', at Hawick in Scotland but he was too far away from the Northern racing circuit and he managed only a handful of winners each year. It was a far cry from the heady expectations of the Greystoke days.

I grieved for years over the loss of my chance with Gordon. I'm not saying I would have been a brilliant jockey but I would still be hanging in there. Now I have to accept that my chances of making it back again are gone. Jump racing can be a cruel game when you reach your mid-thirties. Everybody thinks you are past it whereas I know I am as good as ever. Certainly I am as fit as I have ever been and my nerve is still there.

I am with Dermot Weld these days and I love nothing more than riding work alongside Mick. People say that this sort of adoration does not survive inside the family but it does with me and when he won the 1993 Derby on Commander In Chief on my birthday I cried and cried. The pleasure I get from watching him ride has largely taken away the pain and disappointment I have suffered in my own career. He is like a little ball of fire in the saddle and I get a great thrill from watching the expression on his face when he is heading for the winning post. Determination is too light a word for it. But he has always had that in him. I remember when he was small, he had a row with Dad and he finished up by saying 'I am going to be better than Lester Piggott' – and by God he meant it.

2

Hard Graft

The baby who would be champion was born in Cashel Hospital at 5.00 a.m. on Monday, 22 June 1959. He weighed just 5 lb 12 oz.

Less than five miles away the legendary Vincent O'Brien was about to put the finishing touches to the Irish Derby preparation of El Toro with whom he had already won the Irish 2,000 Guineas. But two days later – Ireland's premier classic was run on a Wednesday in those days – the colt flopped and finished with only one behind him.

However the high class horses of Ballydoyle were of little concern to the Kinane family. What Tommy and Frances were concentrating on was their move, just three weeks after the birth of their second child, to the first Irish home of their married life and Tommy's burgeoning career. The latter soon became disrupted by the new arrival.

> 'Why his father never strangled him I will never know,' Frances recalls. 'Tommy needed his sleep when he was riding the next day and Michael [she never calls him Mick] was a little devil. He was up to everything and he never slept more than two hours at a time.

In desperation she put brandy in his bottle. Elder brother Thomas took a great interest in the new baby but he was concerned about how small he was. The following April Tommy, planting potatoes, placed his two sons on a blanket on the lawn. Thomas did not need to be told to keep an eye on the baby but, when his father told him he was putting potatoes into the ground to make more and make them bigger, he was intrigued.

Two sweating hours later Tommy looked up from his labours and saw to his horror that the baby was missing. He rushed up to Thomas and asked him where he was. Tommy's elder son pointed to where his father had started planting. All that could be seen of the baby was a soil-plastered head sticking out of a pile of earth. His mother also has a painful early memory:

> His hair grew long. It was lovely and blonde. After Jayo was born I used to wheel him up the road in the pram with Thomas on one side of me and Michael on the other. A woman we passed took one look at Michael and said 'What a gorgeous little girl.' I was horrified. As soon as we got home I took out the scissors and cut off the lot.

Frances had five to cope with by the time Mick started his education at St Michael's School in Holycross. Like any mother, she was a little apprehensive about how his first day would go. She had planned to take him but, when a neighbour offered to lighten her load, she was only too happy to accept. However all day she worried. After all, he was very small.

It was not until he returned home with Thomas that she realised her fears were groundless. One of the more established pupils had decided to test the new boy. He began by giving him a sharp dig in the ribs and then a shove. When neither produced any response, he hit him. The would-be bully did not even have time to think he had found an easy target. A small fist hit him hard in the face and knocked him flat.

It was not long before the stables at Farney Castle began to prove an all‹compelling attraction for Mick and Thomas. They would cycle over after school and help with the feeding and cleaning. They were too small to be able to reach up and brush the backs of the horses, so they stood on upturned buckets when doing the grooming. On Saturdays there was a treat. Mick recalls:

> It's my earliest memory. I would muck out three or four stables and then run the two miles to the gallops. I was allowed to ride the quiet ones home as my reward. I was never afraid of horses even though I did get a bit of a fright one day when one of them tried to take off with me on the

road. I loved everything about them and I already wanted to become a jockey, a jump jockey like Dad. Lester Piggott was my idol. He was so good but, unless he was riding in a big race, I had no interest in the flat.

When I was eight I can remember Dad going off to Aintree to ride Reynard's Heir in the Grand National. He finished eighth – Brian Fletcher won the race on Red Alligator. Mum went with him for the meeting and so Thomas and I got up early to cycle over to Farney Castle, muck out and feed the horses in time to be at school by nine o'clock. I also used to go to the racemeetings with Dad. It was great.

He had been boxing competitively for some time when his father bought the farm at Crohane, and he switched to St Mary's National School in Killenaule. That was shortly before his tenth birthday and he continued to box until he left school as the holder of the Munster Juvenile Championship in the 6 st 7 lb category.

I had been messing around with the gloves on since I was tiny. Thomas and Jayo did the same so it was natural to get involved. I used to train a lot and I did not lose too often. But, on one of the occasions I was beaten, I got into a lot of trouble. I'd started smoking at school. Dad found out. He didn't smoke and he didn't like it, certainly not in kids, and he blamed my defeat on the fags. I was in the sin bin for a long time. There was no question of being the prodigal son then!

Mick had two other talents – sketching and making people laugh. 'He would sit in the corner of a room quietly drawing and he would come up with a superb likeness. At other times he would have everybody in stitches with his Stan Laurel impersonations. He was a real little comedian,' his father remembers. 'But now of course you can't get a word out of him.' However riding was his first love and he excelled on a pony his family named after the farm.

Crohane was bought by Uncle Mick, the one who drove Edward O'Grady's horsebox. We broke him in and he developed into a tremendous showjumper. I won a lot of competitions on him. Showjumping taught me a fair bit about horsemanship but it never occurred to me to take it up professionally. I was going to be a jockey.

There were two people in particular who were impressed by Mick's handling of Crohane. The first was his father – 'When I saw the way he rode that pony, it struck me that he just might become something special as a jockey. He had marvellous hands, particularly going into a jump.'

The other was the whipper-in for the County Tipperary Foxhounds. He had a fast pony and there was a race coming up at Ballinahone. It was an ordinary children's pony race – not one of the many run at flapper meetings where the horses are thoroughbreds and where so many of Ireland's future jockeys hone their craft – but the whipper-in felt his pony could win. He asked Tommy if he could borrow his showjumping son.

> I was 12. It was basically a fun race and I loved it. I won too. But there was no question of taking up pony racing proper – Dad didn't want me to get involved in that.

Mick then moved from the National School in Killenaule to the Presentation Convent – it was run by nuns but it was mixed – at nearby Ballingarry. When he was 14 he and Thomas moved up a rung and began riding out for Edward O'Grady on Saturday mornings and during the school holidays.

Among the trainers Tommy was riding for at this time was Larry Greene who was also a qualified vet and lived at Roscrea at the northern edge of County Tipperary. Tommy arranged for Mick to go there for part of the Christmas holidays. At the end of the following February, Greene spoke to Tommy. He was thinking of running a five-year-old called Muscari in a mile and a half apprentice handicap at Leopardstown on 19 March. Did he think Mick was sufficiently capable to ride him?

It was a good question. Muscari had never won a race. Tommy had ridden him a few times the previous year but it was not the gelding's lack of ability that concerned Greene – or Tommy who remembers:

> He was a difficult horse and he was a hard bugger to ride. He would try to take off with you. He only had one eye and he was nearly impossible to turn going right-handed. Leopardstown was left-handed but I still wasn't sure. I sent Mick up to Roscrea the next weekend to see how he would get on.

The 15-year-old schoolboy was not surprised to get the call. This was the moment he had been waiting for as long as he could remember. But what did surprise him was the horse chosen to begin his career.

> When I was at Larry Greene's at Christmas the one horse I was told I could not ride was Muscari because he was difficult. I was not frightened as such but I was extremely nervous. Your first ride in public is a big occasion. I knew how to ride but I also knew I didn't have the first clue about race-riding.

To ride in a flat race you have first to be apprenticed to a licensed trainer. Tommy, who had known Liam Browne since the early days when they were both struggling to get rides, had already agreed that his son should go to Browne at the end of the summer term. The papers were quickly signed. The Turf Club already had an M. Kinane registered as an apprentice – Martin, a son of Dan Kinane – and so the Browne apprentice was listed as M.J. Kinane. Martin also rode in the Firmount Apprentices Handicap and was later to ride over jumps in England.

Tommy watched the Leopardstown race from the stands but his nervously beating heart fell from his mouth to his stomach when he saw Muscari pull his head down almost to the ground and give a savage buck as he went to the start.

> I had him on a long rein and I sat still. He was the sort who would take off with you if you grabbed hold of him. But things were a bit complicated because I had been given two conflicting sets of instructions. Larry told me to hold the horse up but Tommy Carmody said I should make for the inside rail and not come off it. I did my best to do both. I held him up as long as I could but my arms eventually began to give way and he gradually got away from me. Then in the straight I had to move off the rails to pass a horse in front. But we won by three lengths. It was magic. A real dream come true.

Greene, who had not expected his 16-1 chance to win, was almost equally thrilled. He had already promised the young rider half-a-crown for every horse he beat. There were 27 of them! He then bought a gold pen, had it engraved and gave it to the boy as a memento.

The day after the race was the last of the spring term. None of the nuns at the Presentation Convent had any idea that one of the school's pupils had ridden a winner. The boy said nothing. Nor did he say goodbye. He thought he would be back the following term. In fact his schooldays were over. Tommy sent him to Liam Browne's for the Easter holidays but trainers ringing Browne to book his apprentices started to ask for the new boy. Browne told his father that there was no point in him going back to school. In any case, what use was passing an exam to a jockey?

Liam Browne was 37 when Mick joined him and was on his way to becoming one of the most successful producers of apprentices of all time. A small man with a lined face and short crinkly hair that has since gone grey, he was a tough character who believed it paid to be hard on his staff.

He served his own apprenticeship with Paddy Prendergast, a brilliant trainer who worked his way up from nothing to head the trainers' lists in England three years in succession in the 1960s even though he was based in Ireland. Browne became apprentice champion but, despite a year as first jockey to Mick Rogers and another as second jockey to Vincent O'Brien, his career rapidly went into decline. He soon could not even get rides and he was forced to move to England where he found work in a car components factory in Enfield in North London. The lure of the turf took him back into racing in Denmark but in 1969 Prendergast offered him a job. He returned to Ireland but once again the rides dried up. He decided to train. All he had was a house in Kildare town that had cost him £2,500 and a mortgage for the same amount. He did most of the work himself, not just with the horses but with the stables he built during his time off in the afternoons. But he prospered and by March 1975 he had 45 horses in three different yards – all of them rented. He also had a string of apprentices, notably Tommy Carmody and Stephen Craine. In addition to these two and Mick those whom he later turned into jockeys included Pat Gilson, Mark Dwyer, Warren O'Connor, Michael Fenton, David Parnell (first jockey to Kevin Prendergast when he was killed in a car crash in 1990) and Browne's own son Dermot who was twice champion amateur in England and a successful professional before tragically going off the rails, destroying his own career and nearly bringing his father to his knees in the process.

Browne's stable was the place to be for an aspiring apprentice but he imposed a hard regime more reminiscent of the previous century.

> We would start at 7.00 a.m. and, as I was not in a position to employ separate staff at each of the three yards, the lads would be on the go throughout the day and they would not finish until 7.00 p.m. They had to really work. There was no time for messing about and I was certainly not prepared to take any nonsense from any of them. I deliberately made them afraid of me. I firmly believe that, if they don't receive discipline on their way up and learn to respect who is paying them, they will not make the progress they should.

Tommy Carmody was Browne's first apprentice and one of the best. He came within a short head of winning the 1977 Irish Oaks shortly after his 21st birthday and, when he grew too heavy for the flat, he switched to jump racing with devastating effect. He twice won the Queen Mother Champion Chase at the Cheltenham Festival where he also won two Stayers' Hurdles and was twice successful in the Supreme Novices. For three years he was stable jockey to the powerful North of England Dickinson stable and each season won the King George VI Chase, the big race at Kempton's Boxing Day meeting. It was only when Michael Dickinson took over from his father Tony and insisted on giving too many of Carmody's mounts to the stable's good claiming riders that he decided to return to Ireland. He continued to do well, although he and his wife Tina suffered a terribly tragedy in February 1989 when their only son, Thomas, was thrown from his pony under an oncoming truck and killed. Now with his thinning hair having gone grey, he trains a small string on the Curragh and remembers his days under the stiff Browne regime as tough in the extreme:

> It was hard graft and at the end of each day I was utterly knackered. I was not fit to go out in the evenings even if I had the money which I didn't – I was paid 30 shillings a week [£1.50] pocket money and Liam footed the bill for my digs. You didn't even get weekends off. But you had to make a go of it. If you didn't, you would be shown the door. It was also a matter of survival of the fittest. You either stood up to all the work or you fell by the wayside. There were plenty who did just that. Looking back on it now, I can see

that it was all for my own good but at the time the only light
at the end of the tunnel was being able to go racing and ride
winners. For me there is nothing to compare with the thrill
and satisfaction you get from riding a winner. But the
winters were hell. No racing, just hard grind.

The arrival in the yard of the son of a well-known jockey cut little
ice with Carmody – 'He was pretty much what you would expect of
any new apprentice, certainly not cocky. He was obviously able to
ride and had been well tutored but I didn't take much notice of him.
I was more concerned with my own career.'
    Liam's wife Anne remembers Mick in his early days:

> He was a bit shy and very quiet. Later on you could get him
> talking a bit but even then he never said all that much. He
> was a bit of a greenhorn when it came to mixing with people.
> My favourite was Mark Dwyer because he was such a
> gentleman. All Mick ever wanted to do was win races. He
> learnt an awful lot very quickly. He had a good brain and he
> used it the right way. He was also very determined and you
> could tell that he was going to go places.

Mick settled into the hard-working routine surprisingly easily.
He had the advantage of having had plenty of experience with
racehorses and there were occasions when his boxing ability stood
him in good stead. Browne was furious when he found him putting
it to use one afternoon instead of getting on with his work.

> I drove into the Rathbride yard and there were he and Tommy
> Carmody having a real set-to. I beeped the horn at them but
> they took no notice. I beeped again. They carried on fighting.
> I was mad at them, as much for ignoring me as for fighting
> with each other. I marched over, grabbed Mick by the throat
> with one hand and Tommy with the other. I shook them until
> their teeth rattled.

What made the life both exciting and satisfying for Mick was that
the rides kept coming. Twelve days after that first winner he rode
Muscari again. It was at Mallow but this time he was beaten into
second.

I was even more nervous beforehand than I had been at Leopardstown, possibly because quite a lot was expected of me on this occasion – and Muscari started favourite. I wasn't happy about being beaten and I felt pretty low afterwards. All the elation of the first winner made the defeat even harder to take.

At Dundalk less than two months later he rode into the winner's enclosure for the second time but in this race he was up against senior jockeys. The horse was Irish Reports, trained by Tom Costello, who is perhaps best known for all the talented young jumpers he sells on to other trainers, particularly those in England. None of Mick's other mounts won in that first year but he kept getting rides to give some sense of purpose to the heavy workload in the stables.

It *was* hard work but in many ways it was fun. There was a fair bit of chatting and laughing in the yard, although you had to behave. I knew that if I did not discipline myself my career would be affected. I had to go straight from being a schoolboy to becoming a responsible adult.

I shared digs with Stephen Craine and we had to be up by 6.30 a.m. each day. We worked non-stop apart from 40 minutes for lunch. Often I was so tired by the end of the day that I went straight to bed. There was no such thing as a weekend off, just a few days at Christmas and that was under duress. But to get the bonus of race-riding, you had to do the work. On occasions it was murder, particularly with Liam having a go at you if you did something wrong. But, if I was to start my apprenticeship all over again, I would go back to him. All the hard work was worth it and Liam has his good points. He might really let you have it when he told you off but the next time you saw him there would be a laugh in him. Also I was no angel. I needed tough treatment to keep me in line, although that was not exactly the way I saw it at the time!

I had very little money and I normally went out only on Friday evenings but when I first went there I only had 50p left for the week after my digs had been paid for. Even later on, when I was sharing a flat with Tommy Carmody, I would often find myself with just a tenner to feed myself all week. I

would have starved if it hadn't been for my mother coming up
from Crohane periodically and bringing me some food. My
share of the riding fees and percentages went into my account
at the Turf Club and I wasn't allowed to touch them. Even so,
I was a long way from being well off when I eventually
finished my apprenticeship. I was extremely conscious of all
the competition for rides with the other lads in the yard. I'd
had quite a lot of experience when I first went there but
Stephen was nearly two years older and he was the better
rider. I felt that I had to get to his level to compete and,
frankly, I did not think I could compete with him – and I
knew I couldn't match Tommy.

This attitude changed significantly early the following April when
Des McDonogh ran Monksfield in an apprentice race at Naas. He
decided to put up the son of the man who had finished second on
the horse in the previous month's Triumph Hurdle. Monksfield was
given little chance and started an 8-1 shot. The race looked a
formality for Masqued Dancer who was ridden by Tommy
Carmody and started at 6-4 on. But Mick managed to beat the
favourite by a head.

I felt this win proved something in other people's eyes as well
as my own. Certainly it seemed to get me going. The winners
started to flow and by the end of the following month my total
was 12. I began to get more confidence and I started to feel
that I could make a horse do what I wanted him to do rather
than, as in the previous year, the other way round. I finished
my second season with 28 winners and being runner-up to
Tommy in the apprentices table. At last I felt that the senior
jockeys were treating me with respect, as someone who was
entitled to be where he was in a race, and no longer somebody
of no consequence who was simply getting in their way.

One of those who had taken note of the boy's ability was Christy
Roche. He was the reigning champion when Mick rode second
favourite Alcidette in a four-runner handicap at the often tricky and
now defunct Phoenix Park in July 1976. Roche, shrewd, skilful and
cunning, was on Daletta who was later to win the Irish Grand
National and the champion decided the kid was raw enough to be
made to lose this one. The outsider Imperial Fleet made the running

and when Mick began to move up two furlongs out, Roche did the
same on his outside. Mick, to his horror, found himself hemmed in
on the rails behind the tiring Imperial Fleet. Roche kept him there
until it was too late for him to get out, asked his own mount to
quicken and won the race. 'That's the way it goes, Mick,' said the
champion drily as they pulled up. Mick was mortified. He knew he
could, and should, have won.

> Christy stitched me up like a kipper. The only consolation was
> that it taught me not to get caught in a trap like that again.

Success on the racecourse was important because life in the
stables was suddenly becoming a whole lot tougher. Mick, who was
surprisingly chubby in those days, was becoming too heavy. The
only way he knew to control the weight was to stop eating – and
hunger rapidly demoralised him.

> I knew I was going to have trouble at the end of my first
> season when I got a chance ride on Ballymountain Girl in the
> Leopardstown November Handicap. After deducting my 7 lb
> claim, I should have put up 7 st 9 lb. But I was a pound
> overweight. By the time my 17th birthday came round the
> following June I was up to 7 st 13 lb. I began to go without
> breakfast because I couldn't afford to risk putting on weight.
> Liam was making me really work. I found it hard to look
> after three or four horses, ride out several times a day, go
> racing and feel hungry all the time. My morale began to sink.
> I started taking pee pills before going to the races. Laxatives
> too. Anything just to get rid of a couple of pounds. I felt
> certain I would not be able to continue as a flat race jockey
> for long but Dad said it would be very much to my advantage
> if I could go on until my five-year apprenticeship was up. I
> didn't mind the prospect of becoming a jump jockey. After all,
> I had been brought up to assume that is what I would be. But
> I knew Dad was right. If I stuck it out as long as I possibly
> could, I would go into the jumping game with the polished,
> flat race finish that looks so good on those jump jockeys who
> have had the chance to develop it.

It is surprising that Liam Browne did so little to help his
apprentices in their battles with the scales. He could have attempted

to put them on a proper diet or even sent them to a specialist dietician. But all he did was to bully them into not eating.

Tommy Carmody recalls:

> I had terrible weight problems at one stage and I felt that these, coupled with all the hard grafting, were really killing me. Some weekends I just let myself go and tucked into a good meal. The minute I came in on the Monday morning, Liam would make me get on the scales. When he saw what I weighed, he never let up.

So far as Browne was concerned, it was a case of what was good enough for him was good enough for them.

> In my day there were no facilities like saunas or sweat boxes for apprentices. Nor was there time – Paddy Prendergast sent us in the horsebox when we went racing and that meant long hours on the road. If I had to lose weight I just ate nothing and, if I was still too heavy, I would take a laxative. But when you are lean and you are trying to get weight off, there is very little you can do except not eat. Anyway when you're in digs, the landlady can't afford to give you the sort of food that might help. I knew one jockey whose diet consisted of turkey and champagne. And the boys are not going to get that in digs!
>
> Mick certainly looked like he was getting heavy and he didn't seem terribly interested in doing much about it. Most kids try to avoid wasting if they can. They don't realise that, if you don't get your weight under control when you're young, you will have a problem with it all your life. When I booked rides for the boys at a certain weight, I made sure they did it. If they didn't, I was in the soup. If any of them told me they couldn't make the weight, I would simply tell them 'You'd had fucking better.' I didn't go into any detail as to what they should or shouldn't eat. They knew the answer. Nothing.

Fortunately for Mick he heard about the diets prepared for some of the other jockeys by Dr Austin Darragh, an eminent Dublin specialist who is still possibly better known as the father of international showjumper Paul Darragh.

He put me on a special diet and on a strict exercise regime.
He started me off walking for four miles a day in addition to
all the walking I did in the course of my work. This was
steadily increased to six and seven miles. The central aspects
of the diet were grilled meat and steamed fish, six ounces and
four ounces respectively. It soon became pretty monotonous.
You knew what each meal consisted of for weeks ahead. But
it worked and after a bit I was able to ride at 7 st 13 lb once
more. Mind you, I still did a lot of running to sweat off an
extra few pounds. But the diet somehow seemed to sort out
my whole metabolism and, although I was eventually able to
dispense with it, I have stuck to the basics of it particularly
with the grilled meat and the steamed fish.

Austin Darragh did not have to spell out any warning about the
weight-increasing effects of alcohol. His latest patient did not drink.

On the occasions that I did go to a pub with the lads in the
yard, I would ask for either an orange juice or a club lemon.
Later, when I was 19, the others I was with secretly arranged
for the barman to put something into the orange. After a
couple of glasses, I remarked how good I felt. Everybody burst
out laughing. That was the end of M.J. Kinane, the teetotaller.

The then non-drinker was considerably helped by finding a new
landlady, Eilish Gorman in Kildare, who was prepared to take the
trouble to cook him the right food in the right way. But the move
to Mrs Gorman came about by accident – in more ways than one.

Liam moved Stephen and me into a little flat above the office
at Maddenstown Lodge, the famous yard that he had bought
at the end of 1976. We'd been kicked out of our previous
digs and he wanted to keep an eye on us. The head lad lived
next door and his wife was doing the cooking. But he fell out
with Liam and they were both leaving. The head lad loaded
all his belongings into a horsebox and parked it outside the
office. We went out for a few jars that night and when we
came back we could smell something burning in the
bedroom. Somehow one of the mattresses had caught fire.
One of the lads eased it out of the window. I thought nothing
more about it until the next morning when I woke up and

looked outside. There was nothing left of the horsebox except its burned out wheels Apparently the fire brigade had been called out. I'd slept through the lot. We were moved out of the flat in disgrace, and Eilish and her husband Gerry took us in.

Mick's capacity for sleep, not just heavily but seemingly at will, had already been noticed – and envied – by some of the other apprentices.

If he was riding at an evening meeting he could sleep in the afternoon,' recalls Tommy Carmody. 'If I did that I couldn't sleep at night. He could also go straight to sleep after coming home from work and not wake up until the next morning. I have always felt that this was one of his great assets. It certainly gave him a big advantage when it came to keeping his weight under control, whereas I would be unable to resist picking at bits of food all evening.

But the one time he was not allowed to sleep was when he went racing with the boss.

I would be so tired when I got into the car that all I wanted to do was fall asleep. This drove Liam mad and, if you got beaten, he would say 'How could you win? You're always asleep. You don't even show any interest going racing.' The journeys with him were a nightmare. He was a difficult man and he knew how to give you a hard time.

Browne admits that he did this deliberately:

From the moment we left the yard to the time we reached the racecourse, I never let up on them. I went through each race with them and drilled into them what they were to do and what they were not to do. So far as I am concerned there is only one way to do anything, and that is the right way. For instance I would impress upon them that they could not give away weight and a start in a race, and that therefore they must not lose ground by going wide.

I would go through it all with them again on the way home. If they had ridden a bad race they never heard the end of it.

Many of them came to hate travelling with me, and Tommy would often end up in tears, but I was simply trying to turn them into good jockeys. I only wish I could have done it with more of them but many simply didn't have the bottle for the game.

Browne soon began to notice in these homeward bound recriminations that Tommy Kinane's son was a little different from the others :

> If he rode a bad race and lost when he should have won, he took it to heart. He would also take good care not to let the same mistake happen a second time whereas a lot of the others wouldn't give a damn. They took the view that they would be riding again the next day and they could forget all about it. Not Mick. He would be furious with himself.
>
> Really, there was no need to say all that much to him but I didn't go easy on him. I was hard on them all regardless of their feelings. And I never gave him too much praise for riding a good race. I couldn't afford to put him on a pedestal. It was the same with the others. In any case they all knew I would jock them off pretty quickly if I felt like it. It didn't really matter to me which of them got the rides.

Browne also closely monitored their lives outside working hours. Those apprentices with enough money, and enough energy, to do so were banned from going round the town at night. Ex-jockeys, who had shone during their apprentice days but were now barely getting rides, were pointed out as examples of what could happen if the boys did not toe the Browne line.

His harsh treatment of them is in marked contrast to the British Racing School at Newmarket and the Racing Apprentice Centre of Education in Kildare where would-be jockeys combine stablework with lessons and lectures. Browne, not surprisingly in the light of his views, is critical of what he regards as the mollycoddling methods of such schools:

> The gentle, fatherly approach doesn't work. Apprentices need to be treated like recruits in the army, and worked hammer and tongs!

What Liam Browne regarded as breaches of discipline were firmly dealt with. On one occasion he was at the sales at Newmarket during one of the Irish festival meetings. Mick and Stephen Craine were both riding but, when he heard they had decided to stay overnight rather than return in the evening and report for work the next morning, he left word that they were to forfeit all their rides at the Curragh on the Saturday as a punishment. Tommy Kinane went to the Turf Club to complain and Browne was taken aback when he received a phone call at the sales from Cahir O'Sullivan, the Keeper of the Match Book.

'Can you make me allow them to ride?' Browne wanted to know. When he was told it was his decision whether they did or didn't, he replied: 'In that case they fucking well don't !'

There was nothing fatherly either about the way Browne dealt with those who overslept, as Mick remembers with only a hint of a smile when he relives one never-to-be forgotten morning.

> It happened in the days when I was sharing a flat with Tommy. We were both late but Tommy was up and dressed a bit before I was. And he was smart. When Liam came storming through the door to demand where the hell we were, Tommy sidestepped past him, saying 'Sorry, boss. I'm on my way.' I was left to bear the full brunt of the Browne fury. It was not easy because I was only just getting out of bed. Liam strode into the room straight towards me. As usual, I said nothing. He was so mad with me that he somehow got his foot onto the bedside table and he slammed his heel down so hard that he broke it.

On the table was the gold pen that the grateful Larry Greene had presented to Mick. It was never the same again.

3

Kauntze Calls

In the early part of the unusually hot summer of 1976 there were two events of particular significance in Mick Kinane's career. On 5 June he rode Reelin Jig in the Ballyogan Stakes at Leopardstown. He had already won on the filly at Navan and the Curragh, and Liam Browne decided he should keep the mount. It seemed a pointless decision. The Ballyogan Stakes was a Group Three race and therefore no claims were allowed. Mick still claimed 7 lb and so Reelin Jig was effectively shouldering 7 lb more than she should have been. Not surprisingly, most punters ignored her and divided their support between Willy Willy and Thrifty Trio. But Browne calculated that Reelin Jig went so well for Mick that it was worth taking the chance.

> The way I looked at it was that my apprentices were as good as the senior jockeys by the time they were claiming 5 lb and so they had a considerable advantage – nearly two lengths in sprints and more in middle distance races. Although Mick was still on the maximum claim, Reelin Jig was really only 2 lb wrong.

The race proved his point. The 6-1 chance scooted up the five furlong straight to beat Willy Willy by two lengths. It was an amazing result for such an inexperienced rider. This was only his 14th winner. To land a Group race at the age of 16 and still a 7 lb claimer is almost unheard of.

One person who had particular reason for satisfaction as she

watched from the stands was Eva Kauntze. At Limerick a week
earlier the young apprentice had ridden for her husband for the first
time on the little considered Palakan in a minor handicap. The pair
finished only sixth of nine and, when Michael Kauntze went off to
Epsom the following week to win a two-year-old race, he left it to
his wife to choose a rider for Palakan in a ten furlong handicap run
four races after the Ballyogan.

Eva felt the apprentice had done well enough at Limerick to be
given another chance. Again Palakan did not win but this time he
finished second and Eva's good report was reinforced when Michael
Kauntze read what Ireland's Sunday papers had to say about the
apprentice's Ballyogan win.

Mick kept the mount on Palakan and began to get the rides on
some of the stable's other runners. Early in September he won an
apprentice race at the Curragh on Kauntze's Myriad. The following
month Kauntze sounded out Liam Browne. He was, he explained,
planning ahead for the following season. He would like to use Mick
for quite a lot of his runners and he wanted to make an arrangement
whereby he could have first call on the Browne apprentice. It wasn't
a stable jockey's job. There wasn't even a retainer but it was a
significant step forward. Browne was quite happy to accept.

Michael Kauntze was 35 at this stage and in only his second
season. He came from Sussex where his father – an anglicised
descendant of an Austrian chancellor of the exchequer – had been a
solicitor. After leaving Downside Kauntze joined his father's firm
but, when he was halfway through his articled clerkship, Kauntze
senior suddenly died. The family's grief was accentuated when it
was discovered that the supposedly prosperous lawyer was up to his
eyes in debt. He had been fond of dabbling in property and he had
made some financially disastrous deals. His hunters and point-to-
pointers had to be sold to pay the creditors. So did his London flat
and his Sussex home. His son found himself without a penny to his
name. He also found his real self.

> The more I thought about it, the more I realised I had only
> gone into law to please my father. My real interest was racing
> and I decided to try to get into it. I applied for a job as a
> trainer's secretary with Toby Balding.

The genial Balding took on the ex-public schoolboy with the legal
training and other jobs followed including one at Newmarket with

Paddy O'Gorman. Lester Piggott rode a fair bit for O'Gorman and one day Piggott, a man of notoriously few words, hinted to Kauntze that Dermot O'Brien was giving up his job as assistant to his famous brother and the position could be vacant. Kauntze had never met the legendary trainer but he passed the interview and moved to County Tipperary in December 1968.

> I still didn't have any money but the possibility of eventually starting up on my own suddenly became much more feasible. Vincent trained for a rich international set, I got to know many of them well, and I felt that I would get horses from some of them if I stuck it out at Ballydoyle for a decent length of time. But I had no intention of settling in Ireland.

Kauntze began to think differently when he fell in love with the elder of Tom Dreaper's two daughters. Dreaper was one of the most famous jumping trainers of all time, partly because he handled Arkle – arguably the greatest chaser ever. He also trained Prince Regent on whom Tim Hyde (Tommy Kinane's one-time employer) won the 1946 Cheltenham Gold Cup. Kauntze married Eva in 1971, midway through the five years he spent with O'Brien. He started training at the beginning of 1975, mostly for owner-breeders who had failed to sell their yearlings at the recession-hit sales the previous year. He and his wife built a small prefab house at Bullstown, almost next door to the famous Greenogue yard where Tom Dreaper's son Jim was now in charge and not far from Dublin airport. Kauntze also built an American-style barn to house his string and Dick Dreaper, a brother of Tom, made 100 acres available for the construction of gallops.

The Englishman was by this time widely considered a naturalised Irishman. Despite his upper middle class upbringing and education, there was nothing of the stiff upper lip about him. Short and stocky, with prematurely grey hair that is now virtually white, he is a man of outspoken views which he seldoms refrains from expressing. He is also marvellously entertaining company and something of a bon viveur. Or at least he was until a triple heart bypass operation in 1994 forced him to dramatically reduce his intake of food and drink. He is understandably proud of the role he played in the making of the great jockey although, despite his long association with him, he still pronounces the name wrongly. He says Kin-arne.

I used Tommy Carberry quite a lot when I started training. Tommy was primarily a jump jockey but he was good on the flat too and he could ride at 8 st 10 lb. In 1977 he and Mick shared the rides but the following year Mick was the official stable jockey and he remained in that position until the end of 1982. He did not ride all the horses in 1978 because the arrangement did not include those that ran outside Ireland. By 1980, though, he was riding the lot.

I never paid him a retainer. We were both in the early stages of our respective careers and he was as pleased to be attached to a stable as I was to have a jockey of my own. But I am not the sort of trainer who requires his jockey to ride out every day and, although from 1978 on he would come over from the Curragh four mornings a week in the early part of the season, he would be over less and less as the year wore on. My main work mornings were Tuesdays and Fridays and, as Liam Browne's were Wednesdays and Saturdays, it fitted in well. The situation was also helped by my starting later than the Curragh trainers. My staff didn't come in until 8.30 a.m. so Mick was able to ride work first lot for Browne and be here in time for my first lot.

Mick was taken with his new boss:

The arrangement worked out well and I enjoyed working for him. He was a real gentleman and never in a bad mood. He gave his staff a lot of latitude and they seemed to respect him for that. He never even wanted to catch anybody doing something they shouldn't. He made sure they could hear him coming a long way off by always whistling for his dog.

In fact only six of Mick's 41 winners in 1977 were for Kauntze but they included Jade Dancer on his first ride in England. The two-year-old was sent to Chester's September meeting and Mick was in his element on the tricky, almost circular, mile course. He sent his mount to the front after two furlongs and made the rest. Kauntze recalls:

Having ridden round tight Irish courses like Bellewstown and Killarney, Chester was meat and drink to Mick. He finished up that season second in the apprentices table for the second time – on this occasion to Stephen Craine – and I had a high opinion of him right from the start. He could always read a race well beforehand and afterwards give me an accurate account of exactly what had happened. Even in those early days he always seemed to be in the right place at the right time in his races. I hate it when my runners get interfered with, or find themselves boxed in, because it's difficult to evaluate what might have happened and you don't know where to go with the horse next. The race is effectively wasted but I can never recall even one instance of this happening with Mick riding. Mind you, I often took precautions by telling him to make the running.

As a result he soon became a good judge of pace out in front. It took him a very short time to become what I would term almost the complete jockey. He was always quite strong and experience somehow seemed to bring him the rhythm. But in those days his riding was nothing like as inspired as it was to become and it was never a case of his being brilliant. You only turn into a top class jockey – assuming you have what it takes – when you are riding good horses and that did not happen to him until he joined Dermot Weld. With me, though, he was particularly good in borderline cases where the result can go either way. He won a lot more of these than he lost.

When the arrangement with Michael Kauntze firmed up into a virtual stable jockey job at the beginning of 1978, Mick bought his first car, a new Alfa Sud, out of the money held in trust for him at the Turf Club. It meant he could go over to Bullstown to ride work and that he no longer had to go racing with Liam Browne

On the opening day of the season at Phoenix Park's St Patrick's Day meeting he got off to a good start by winning the main race, the Burmah-Castrol Trophy, on Browne's Slaney Idol. But events in England two days earlier have left a somewhat understandably bigger mark in his memory.

It was Champion Hurdle day. Liam allowed us a short time off work to watch the racing on TV and I went back to my digs to see Dad win the big race on Monksfield. I was thrilled. Dad had had to battle all his life and by this stage he was late on in his career. Victory in the Champion Hurdle was a fitting reward for all the effort he had made.

Twelve months later Mick was again allowed time off to return to his digs to watch his father win the Supreme Novices on Stranfield and Dessie Hughes take his place on Monksfield in the Champion Hurdle – 'Losing the ride like that nearly broke Dad's heart and it really brought home to me just how callous this game can be.'

In April 1978 Mick won his second Group race, and his first for Kauntze, on Enid Calling in the Mulcahy Stakes at Phoenix Park. Again he was not allowed to claim his allowance – by this time reduced to 3 lb – and he had to pull out all the stops to beat reigning champion Wally Swinburn and Christy Roche by two short heads. Lester Piggott was fourth. It should have been a photo finish but, to the judge's horror, the camera failed to work and all he could do was pray that his first – and only – impression was the correct one. The angle at the finish at Phoenix Park was notoriously difficult but nobody tried to burn the stands down in protest .

The following month he won the Listed Marble Hill Stakes on Kauntze's Coalminer, and lost his claim in the process, but he was still officially apprenticed to Browne and he finally gained his revenge on Stephen Craine to become champion apprentice with 46 winners. Craine, though, was only two behind and yet another Browne apprentice, Pat Gilson, was fourth. Mick's reward was a six week working holiday in California.

> It was my first trip away from Ireland or England and I really enjoyed it. Jackie Ward-Ramos, the former wife of Liam Ward [the champion jockey who won the 1970 Irish Derby on the great Nijinsky and who was sensationally beaten on hot-pot Sir Ivor in the 1968 race], arranged the trip. Stephen was also invited and we stayed at Jackie's house. There was no race-riding. We were only allowed to ride work. The money was bad but the fun was good!

Ward had been stable jockey at Ballydoyle during Kauntze's time and his handling of Leopardstown formed part of Mick's education. Kauntze explains:

> I never tie my jockeys down to orders. I simply run through what I think would be the ideal scenario. But sprint races at Leopardstown are an exception. I'd watched how Liam rode the five furlong course, always coming from behind, and I impressed on Mick that you can wait all day and still win. He

took the point and even today you seldom see him until the
final furlong in the sprints there.

There were also other lessons from the master of Bullstown, one
of the most significant being what to do in the stewards' room.

I felt that his behaviour in an inquiry needed to be addressed
quite early on in our association. Not that he was unruly – he
was always pretty level-headed and there were never any
stories about him being about to go off the rails – but because
nobody ever really teaches jockeys how to carry on in the
stewards' room which is much the same as a court of law.
Indeed the way the evidence is presented can sometimes sway
the verdict. I impressed on him that he should call the
stewards Sir, look them straight in the eye, tell them what
actually happened without to many ums and ers, and without
unnecessarily dropping other people in the shit.

I have since been told by the stewards' secretaries that he is
the best giver of evidence of all the Irish jockeys, and I like to
think that some of the credit for this is due to me. In all the
time he rode for me we never lost a race in the stewards'
room, and we gained a few. One of these was with Public
Opinion who was a desperately hard ride and, in the nursery
at the 1979 Galway September meeting, he was beaten a
length and a half by Glenardina trained by the late Mick
Connolly. From the stands it looked as if my horse had been
nearly brought down inside the final furlong and the stewards
called an inquiry.

I always make a practice of going with my jockeys into any
inquiry and, when we went into the room, we were told that
the camera which showed the head-on picture had been
vandalised. As a result the stewards had to rely on the
jockeys' evidence much more than usual. Mick said
something definitely happened inside the final furlong and
Public Opinion almost fell. The stewards seemed impressed
and they awarded us the race. It was only after we came out
of the stewards' room that I discovered Mick had been what
is now known as economical with the truth. He told me that
he thought the something was probably that the horse had
put his foot in a hole!

Earlier that year Mick rode at Royal Ascot for the first time:

> In a way it was a bit of an eye-opener. So many people, all the
> fashions, all the men in morning suits, and the racing was
> tremendous. I felt it was a great place for a jockey to be and
> it gave me a tremendous thrill to be riding there. I had three
> mounts and, although the nearest I came was third on Back
> Bailey in the Cork and Orrery, I couldn't wait to go back
> again.

However Mick Kinane's end-of-season total was only 42, four less
than the previous year, and it put him no higher than equal sixth in
the jockeys' table. In Ireland, where the number of big name flat race
jockeys can be counted on the fingers of one hand, this was hardly a
headline-making achievement. He then went to India for the first
time but that too was a long way from being an unqualified success.

> I didn't mind the heat. In fact I loved the sun but I found the
> life in India a big shock to my system. It wasn't helped by
> falling out with the man I had gone out to ride for, Imtias Sait,
> who is now one of the country's top trainers. One morning at
> exercise I rode a filly that behaved like a lunatic so I gave her
> a few slaps. Imtias was furious with me and I lost my cool
> with him. He had me up before the stewards and I was
> suspended. Things were much better the following winter
> when I landed a job with Daddy Adenwalla who had a really
> good string.

Things were also better in Ireland in 1980 with two Kauntze-
trained Group winners among the total of 58. Only Christy Roche,
champion for the third time, did better. Off the racecourse life took
on a new and all-consuming significance.

> I was living in Moorefield Park in Newbridge by this stage
> and I was very keen on soccer. I used to train with the Kildare
> team and go to a lot of their matches. One Sunday morning
> there was one in Ballymore Eustace which is about 12 miles
> from Newbridge. I didn't have anything to do so I decided to
> drive over. I pulled into the carpark alongside a Mini. Sitting
> in it was an extremely attractive brunette. I had no idea who

she was and obviously I couldn't just go up to her and start talking. But I decided to try and find out more. Someone told me her name, Catherine Clarke, and that she would probably be going to a certain dance that evening. I made a point of going along and getting introduced. I managed to get talking to her and eventually I plucked up the courage to ask her for a date. She turned me down flat. But by this time I was so attracted to her that I wasn't going to take no for an answer, not for good anyway. I tried again a few days later, then a third time. Eventually she agreed to come out with me. The rest is history.

Not quite. Catherine, who is nearly a year younger than Mick and whose father works on a farm near Ballymore Eustace, had no connection with racing and she began to have serious doubts about whether she should the second time she went to a meeting with Mick. It was at Clonmel and Ana Carmen, his mount in the maiden, slipped up on the steep downhill run towards the straight. Mick broke his right wrist and was out of action for six weeks. Catherine went again soon after he resumed, only to look on in horror as her boyfriend took another crashing fall. This time nothing was broken but she went home convinced she was putting a jinx on Mick.

On the racecourse 1981 was a disaster. Things went badly wrong at Bullstown and Mick's total slumped to 28. Kauntze sent out only nine winners. It took him a long time to work out why. 'My horses were unable to give anything like their best,' he recalls, the agony lines on his face reliving the horror that threatened to ruin him.

I couldn't find out the reason. I had all sorts of tests done and eventually, when it was really too late to salvage much of the season, I discovered the fault was in the hay. I had bought it from a local farmer and, unknown to me, it had been kiln-dried. Not only had all the goodness been taken out of it, I was actually damaging the horses by feeding it to them. Ever since then I have made my own.

Kauntze recovered in 1982 with 25 winners and, although Mick managed only sixth in the jockeys' table – Pat Eddery was champion despite being based in England, he hit the big time. The reason was a colt Browne trained called Dara Monarch. He had cost only 5,000gns as a yearling.

I rode him work and I thought he was a fair horse. Michael Kauntze ran Sovereign Notion in the same race when Dara Monarch had his first race of the season in the McCairns Trial, a Group Three run that year at Fairyhouse, and I asked him to let me off. I don't think he liked it very much but I felt Dara Monarch was a good horse and I said so. He duly won and went on to the Two Thousand Guineas at Newmarket. I couldn't ride him there because I was required at Leopardstown where I rode two winners for Michael and one for Liam. Philip Waldron took the mount but he finished only eighth behind the French horse Zino.

He then went for the Irish 2,000 Guineas and, although he started at 20–1, I expected him to run a big race. I came up the middle on my own to lead inside the final furlong and beat Tender King by three lengths. It was a fantastic feeling.

My initial achievements, notably becoming champion apprentice, meant a lot at the time but once I became a jockey I felt I had to ride a classic winner to really establish myself and indeed to build a foundation from which I could progress. As an apprentice, I got to the stage where I felt I could ride as well as anybody. It was only when I started coming up against the top jockeys in the big races that I began to realise just how far I still had to go. Experience counts for an awful lot in race-riding, particularly in the major races.

It was also the first classic success for Browne but it came with an expensive sting in the tail. The colt was registered in the name of his wife Anne but in fact was a partnership horse. The Turf Club realised this only when the other partners were interviewed on television immediately after the race. The stewards failed to see the funny side and hit Browne with a £2,000 fine while the owners had to cough up £3,000 between them.

Next stop was the St James's Palace Stakes at Royal Ascot:

I rode a waiting race and took it up over a furlong out. At the Curragh he drifted left when he hit the front. This time he drifted right towards the rails. He had a high head carriage and, when he was in the lead, he tended to look around a bit. But he was clear and in no danger of losing the race. In fact he was a better horse that day than in the Irish 2,000.

It was a great thrill to win at the Royal meeting – and it still is today – but that one meant an awful lot. All too often Irish jockeys have been thought of as capable of riding against the best in the big races in Ireland but have then been jocked off when the horses ran in England. People seemed to think we were not as good as the English-based jockeys on English courses.

On 25 June 1982, one of the few days during the summer on which there was no racing, Mick and Catherine were married in the Church of the Immaculate Conception in Boherlahan, a village not far from Cashel. It was a double wedding with elder brother Thomas whose bride, Brigid, came from Boherlahan. There was no honeymoon for the younger brother. The Irish Derby was run the following day but the only wedding present from the racecourse was a painful taste of turf.

I had six rides and I was brought down on the second of them, on Sight Unseen in the Tyros Stakes. My back was hurting and I was a bit worried I had done some damage but I couldn't give in to it. The next was the Irish Derby, and it was only the second time I had ridden in the race. I finished last, and in the next race too, but I had to go on. I was in a desperate state that night and for the next few days. It turned out that I had crushed a vertebra. I resumed the following Tuesday but I had only just got over all the pain when I was brought down once more. It happened at Killarney 17 days after the Irish Derby. Kevin O'Brien's mount slipped up seven furlongs out, I was behind him and was brought down. I broke my right wrist again and I was out of action for over three weeks.

He and Catherine lived in Moorefield Park for the first few months of their married life but at the end of the year they bought a bungalow at Christianstown a few miles to the north of the Curragh. They were to live there for nearly six years before moving to Clunemore Lodge, a spacious bungalow little more than a furlong from the Curragh racecourse.

At the Galway September meeting, three years after the Public Opinion incident, Browne took Kauntze to one side. He wanted

Mick back, this time as his own stable jockey. Kauntze had seen it coming. He agreed on condition that he could have the latest of the rising stars at Maddenstown Lodge, David Parnell.

'I had never had a stable jockey before,' Browne recalls. 'But some of my owners, notably Paddy Conlan and Judge Frank Roe, wanted one and Mick was the obvious choice.'

The obvious choice was ready to move:

> I knew it meant going back to the stable where I had been apprenticed but, if I was to be champion or at least have a chance of becoming champion, I needed more horses at my disposal. Michael Kauntze was happy training 40 plus horses and he didn't have the ammunition I needed. Liam did. He was getting very powerful by this stage and he was training nearly 100 horses.

On the face of it, the move seemed a good one, particularly when he rode Judge Roe's Carlingford Castle to win the Group Two Gallinule Stakes and went on to partner the colt in the Epsom Derby.

> It was my first ride in the Derby and it was a major occasion for me. It had long been one of my ambitions to win the race and just to ride in it, particularly on a fancied candidate, was quite something.
>
> In the Gallinule Carlingford Castle had been up against Give Thanks who had won the Lingfield Oaks Trial and the Musidora on her two previous starts. She was odds-on at the Curragh and, when I made most of the running to beat her, I knew my horse had a right chance in the Derby.
>
> Carlingford Castle came out of the Gallinule in good shape and worked really well in the week or so before Epsom. Pat Eddery, who was first jockey to Vincent O'Brien at that time and so was in Ireland a lot, invited me to stay at his house near Aylesbury in Buckinghamshire the night before the race. I woke up to a torrential thunderstorm with lightning flashing and rain sheeting down. For me this was the best thing that could have happened because Carlingford Castle had already proved that he could go in the soft and I knew testing ground might not suit some of the others. In fact two of the horses,

Cock Robin and Northern Trial, were withdrawn while Pat
got off Lomond to switch to Salmon Leap.

When we got to the course I began to feel nervous and I was
pretty tensed up long before we were taken out to the parade
ring. The crowds were huge and the buzz of the whole place
really hit me. Then, when we got onto the course, I was struck
by all the noise. When the race started, I pushed my horse
along to get into a decent position and we went down into
Tattenham Corner well placed in about sixth. Lester Piggott
on Teenoso was only just in front of me. Once we turned for
home he set Teenoso alight and the colt quickened up well. I
tried to go after him. But Brian Rouse on Neorion was
beginning to back pedal and I ran into a pocket. It didn't hold
me up that much and I soon got running again. But I never
felt I was going to win. Even before I ran into trouble, Lester
was gone. We reduced the leeway to three lengths at the line
but we were well beaten.

Back in Ireland Mick won the Group One Heinz 57 Phoenix
Stakes for Browne on King Persian and rode a total of 54 winners.
As had been the case three years earlier, only Christy Roche rode
more. But all was not what it seemed.The fact that some of the
retainer (the first of Mick's career) was not paid was a symptom
rather than the cause of impending trouble.

I felt I wouldn't get the job again in 1984. Liam is a hard man
and it's easy to fall out with him even though I did not actually
do so. I wanted to move on. I also wanted to move to the right
place. If things did not go right for me the following season, I
could see myself sliding very quickly. But what I couldn't see
was where a job could be coming from. By the time October
came round I was beginning to get a bit anxious.

Salvation arrived in the form of a phone call. It was to transform
Mick Kinane's career.

4

Champion

Dermot Weld had thought long and hard for several weeks before making that phone call. Unusually for him, he had been having jockey problems all year. He had come to the conclusion that Mick just might be the man to solve them. But the operative word was might. All he said was, 'Could you come round and see me?'

Tall, dark-haired and eloquent, Weld was 35 at the time and he had taken over his father's Rosewell House stables – between the Curragh racecourse and the Ballymany Stud from where Shergar had been kidnapped earlier in 1983 – when he was only 23. He had promptly transformed a reasonably successful operation into a prolific winner-producing machine. In 1977 he became the first Irish-based trainer to send out 100 flat winners in a season and he was about to become Ireland's leading trainer for races won for the eighth time. He was later to stake his claim to racing greatness by becoming the first European-based trainer to win an American classic and the first to win Australia's most famous race, the Melbourne Cup.

Weld had also been brilliant in the saddle. Despite being over six feet tall, he had three times been champion amateur in Ireland and had ridden winners in America, France and South Africa as well as the amateurs' Derby at Epsom. He had the biggest string in Ireland, well over 100 superbly bred animals, and he trained them for some of the richest owners in the world. The trouble was the jockey.

> For several years Wally Swinburn [father of Walter] had been
> my stable jockey. Wally is one of the nicest people in racing

and he became a close personal friend. He lost confidence in his own ability for a time in England but I helped him to recover it and he became really good. He rode some brilliant races for me, notably in the Coronation Stakes at the 1978 Royal Ascot meeting when he partnered Sutton Place to beat Lester Piggott at his best on Ridaness by a short head.

At the beginning of 1983, when Liverpool-born Wally Swinburn was turning 46 and considering retirement, it was agreed that Darrel McHargue should move from America to take the Rosewell House job. McHargue, 28, had ridden over 2,000 winners in the United States including the 1975 Preakness Stakes on Master Derby. Those he rode for included Bert and Diana Firestone, at the time Weld's biggest owners.

> Darrel was not my choice. I had been considering Mick because I thought he was the best young rider in Ireland but the Firestones said he was too young, McHargue was a world-class rider and they had some good horses. He *was* a world-class rider but on American tracks. He moved here too late in his career to make the necessary changes and initially he didn't want to make them. He found race-riding in Ireland, the heavy going and the wet climate a dramatic change from California and in the first few weeks of the season I felt he wasn't riding all that well. He changed his style and his methods eventually but it took him a long time to accept the need to change. He became a much improved rider towards the end of the 1983 season but I wasn't happy.
>
> I still had my eye on Mick. What attracted me was his raw natural ability. I had no doubt that the talent was there but I had equally little doubt that a lot of polishing-up needed to be done. At this stage, don't forget, he was far from being a high-flyer. He had finished only sixth and seventh in the table in the two previous years.

In fact Mick had had quite a few rides for the Rosewell House maestro. Way back in May 1976, when he was still only 16, he had ridden Weld's King Eider to win a race at Down Royal. At Leopardstown six weeks later he won another for him, this time on In The Clover. In September the following year Weld used him again on Heavenly Bounty in an apprentice race at Tralee. Robert

Sangster's filly won by five lengths and at Galway four days later Mick won for Weld again.

But the trainer did not know what Kinane was like as a person. He had heard stories on the racecourse grapevine which is invariably awash with rumour and gossip, most of it derogatory. The stories did not tie in with the talent he had witnessed with his own eyes. Weld is a shrewd and careful man, almost as good at dealing with people as he is with horses. He decided he had to find out for himself. Hence the invitation to Rosewell House. Mick was shown in and asked to sit down. He was told Darrel McHargue might not be staying. Would he be interested in taking over?

> Would I? I could hardly contain myself. My insides were turning upside down with excitement. I almost asked if he would like me to start the next day. But I didn't get the chance. I found I was being interviewed. It's an interview I will never forget as long as I live. He said he'd heard rumours about me and he wanted me to explain them. He asked me if I drank much. He had also heard I was a smoker and he didn't like that. He also asked me about my temper. He didn't like that either.

The interview finished up somewhat unsatisfactorily for the man who wanted to be a star. No job offer, just a promise to be in touch. It was vague, too vague. Several weeks went by without a word. Then he heard the rumours. Steve Cauthen had been offered the job.

The Kentucky Kid had arrived from America in 1979 as a media sensation. He had broken the American earnings record for a calendar year when he was only 17. The following year he had won the 1978 Triple Crown on Affirmed. Robert Sangster had persuaded him to try England after he had struck a bad patch – 110 consecutive losers – and was beginning to have problems with his weight. Jockeys need to be lighter in America than they do in Europe but Cauthen made the transition with far less difficulty than McHargue. He promptly won the Two Thousand Guineas on Tap On Wood. He had moved to Barry Hills in Lambourn on a one year contract but he liked it so much that he decided to stay on. He was still with Hills when Dermot Weld put his proposal.

Cauthen recalls:

I gave the offer serious consideration but, after a lot of thinking, I decided to remain with Barry. I was very happy with life in England and I just didn't know if I would be as happy living full time in Ireland. I was also not sure how Ireland would work out for me. In addition, so many more of the big races are run in England. It was obviously the place to be.

While Mick was kept in suspense, Dermot Weld continued to do his homework. He was still a bit concerned about the stories. Seemingly no-one had forgotten the one about the fight with Tommy Carmody that had so infuriated Liam Browne. And temper and red hair go together. Perhaps the raw talent did not translate into riding skill. Weld decided to speak to Michael Byrne who, as the senior handicapper, would be able to measure any improvement Mick brought about in his mounts in terms of pounds. The other man he picked for an opinion was Ted Kelly, an accomplished amateur rider in his youth and at the time a stewards' secretary. The last thing Weld wanted was a jockey who was going to upset the stewards and collect repeated suspensions.

Michael Byrne confirmed my view. He said he had studied a lot of the films of races in which Mick had ridden. He had no doubt that the lad was a future star. Ted, too, had nothing but the highest praise for him, not only for his demeanour in the stewards' room but also for his riding. Indeed Ted encouraged me to take him on.

There was a full month between Mick's first visit to Rosewell House and the second invitation. If his stomach was churning at the first interview, it was nothing to how he felt as he drove over the second time. Weld quickly put him at his ease and told him that the job was his.

I was thrilled. I knew it was a great opportunity with so many good horses in the stable and such a good trainer. Later I realised just how astute he had been at the original interview. He wasn't just trying to find out whether what he'd heard was true, he was sounding out my weak points to see how I reacted. Thank God Steve Cauthen said no. If he had taken the job, my life could have turned out very differently.

Cauthen was to say no three times more in Mick's life. On each occasion the effect would be dramatic.

Dermot Weld was used to his stable jockeys not arriving back from India until the end of February – Wally Swinburn had spent most winters out there – but in 1984 Mick left soon after the Indian Derby to begin his new job. There was an enormous number of horses to be ridden and to get to know.

> I was riding out six mornings a week, sometimes seven. On work mornings, usually Tuesdays and Fridays, I would ride out all three lots and ride work on between 17 and 20 horses. Sometimes more. On cantering mornings I would ride out just two lots. These days I don't do as much of the home work but on a busy Tuesday or Friday I often ride gallops on 18 horses.

But the gossip mongers had not given up on Kinane. Weld remembers:

> One Curragh trainer told me that he would not last three weeks once the season started because, so this trainer maintained, he was temperamental and difficult. Most of all, he said, Mick was not a team player and an awful lot of my success is based on team work. Others said he had an attitude problem although I never found this to be the case. Mind you, I went out of my way to make sure it didn't get a chance to develop. I'd also heard that for a time he wouldn't speak to some of the press.

At Navan on 1 May 1984 those same pressmen had a field day. Mick had ridden seven winners for his new boss by this stage, including a double at the Curragh the previous Saturday, and the stable was just beginning to click into gear. He partnered Mountain Brook in a mile and three-quarter handicap and sent the 7-4 favourite to the front over two furlongs out. Navan has a gruelling uphill climb to the finish and, really, this was too far out to go on. But, instead of kicking clear, Mick allowed second favourite Bold Prelate to draw up almost alongside him. From that moment on he was content to sit with a tight rein, watching Tommy Manning working away like a demon, desperately trying to peg back Mick's

neck advantage. Close home, though, Manning's persistence very
nearly paid off and he went under by only a short head.

> It was hardly one of my best performances. My fellow was
> hacking up but, just as he neared the line, he pricked his ears
> and stalled. It was too late for me to do anything by that stage
> and luckily he held on by a whisker. Dermot didn't say a
> word. He realised that I knew I'd made a stupid mistake and
> that I was unlikely to make a blunder like that ever again.

But the press said plenty. There were reports of unnecessary
cockiness and scarcely veiled hints of riding for trouble. Weld's
answer was to step up his tuition – 'What Mick needed was
somebody to help him express his talent and encourage him in his
confidence – although not over-confidence. I wrote off the Navan
incident to youthful enthusiasm. He may have been cocky but that
was just a phase he went through and he was riding winners. So
long as he kept winning I didn't mind.'

The Weld tactics were drilled into the new stable jockey – 'On
Sunday mornings I would bring him in to the house to watch the re-
runs of the races he had ridden. We would go through the videos
and I would point out what he had done wrong – and we went on
doing that Sunday after Sunday until he fucking got it right.'

Weld seldom swears. The fact that he did so when recalling these
lessons is an indication of all the frustration he went through:

> He had the ability to get it right so I felt justified in giving out
> to him. Fortunately he also had the ability to listen whereas
> so many jockeys don't. He began to realise that I knew an
> awful lot about tactics from the days when I was riding in
> races. I won on average one out of three in bumpers and often
> the only way I could win was through tactics. I was studying
> in a veterinary college all week and I just wasn't as fit as many
> of my rivals.

To be hauled in Sunday after Sunday and be lectured on his
mistakes was a considerable indignity for a man at the head of the
jockeys' table and Mick remembers the room in which these
schooling sessions were conducted as 'the torture chamber'. But it
was the making of him. He also realised the value of these lessons.
For years after they stopped, he would religiously buy the films of

each day's racing from the closed circuit television people and spend every spare moment studying them to work out if he could have done better and, if so, how. Even today he often records the racing when it is televised and critically plays back his own performances.

> I realised that Dermot was training me to ride the way he wanted. He likes his horses to be waited with but not too far off the pace, to be brought with one run to win with, if possible, the minimum of fuss. He hates them getting there too soon and then having to fight off challengers. He also does not like them being unnecessarily abused. It took me quite a long time to build up the necessary confidence to ride like this. When you are young and trying to impress, this particular style of race-riding does not come all that naturally. In the first few months I had a lot of difficulty in getting it right.
>
> Dermot can be a hard taskmaster and he was particularly tough on me in my first few years with him. Often we did not see eye to eye. I would tend to speak my mind and I would sometimes lose my cool. I might have a calm exterior but I have a bad temper underneath it and, when I am pushed, it's apt to burst out. But whenever things flared up and we had a fight, we would be back to normal within half-an-hour. We both seemed to feel we could put it behind us and forget about it once we had got matters out into the open and cleared the air.

Weld's demands could also be testing. When he was with Michael Kauntze, Mick would stay in County Kerry during the festival meetings at Killarney, Tralee and Listowel. But at Rosewell House the stable jockey was expected to be on hand whenever there were gallops to be ridden. Mick had to drive the 150 miles home after riding in the 8.00 p.m. race and be on the gallops at 8.00 a.m. The minute he finished on the Curragh, he was back to Kerry: 'It was tiring but I didn't mind. I was young and I was keen. All I really wanted was to ride winners.'

He wanted to ride more than he was doing but his agreement excluded him from those horses that ran outside Ireland. It was the old story of the Irish jockey being good enough for the horses in Ireland but not good enough for the runners abroad. And Mick didn't like this one bit.

Brent Thomson, who had an agreement with Robert Sangster, took over on Committed when she won the Cork and Orrery at Royal Ascot and, although I was back on her when she landed the Hardwicke Cup at Phoenix Park, Brent promptly took over to ride her to victory in the William Hill Sprint Championship at York. Then, in the Prix de l'Abbaye at Longchamp on the day of the Arc de Triomphe, Steve Cauthen won on her. Lester Piggott took some of the rides too. I found all this hard to take even though it was provided for in the agreement. I'd hoped that I had got myself into the picture to such an extent that I would be able to keep the rides when the horses went overseas. Obviously not.

He finished up his first year with Weld as champion for the first time with 88 winners in Ireland. It was quite an achievement. Only once before had this total been bettered, by Wally Swinburn when he rode into the record books with 101 in 1977. 'It was a great thrill despite some adverse comment in the press, notably in the *Guide to Irish Racing.*' This well produced but sadly now defunct publication had this to say about Ireland's new star:

> The plum job on the domestic scene as principal jockey to Dermot Weld's powerful team allowed Michael Kinane full scope to take his first championship. A strong finisher, if not universally popular, he soon overcame an unnerving tendency towards needless showmanship to have the crown in safe keeping long before the end of the season. Kinane will be difficult to unseat too as his fairly light weight allows him almost unlimited opportunities between the Weld runners and outside mounts. It's arguable though whether he will rival Roche and Declan Gillespie, who continues to impress with his quiet determined approach, where the big name races are concerned.

Mick Kinane's expression turns grim as he remembers these words: 'They don't hurt now but they certainly did then!'

The critics were made to eat their words the following season but 1985 contained some serious setbacks too. One of these came in Rome in April when he won the Italian 2,000 Guineas, the

Premio Parioli, on Again Tomorrow only to be suspended for ten days. Mick was most unhappy about the outcome and Weld was furious.

> Mick was riding like a true champion and with tremendous confidence. He really rose to the occasion in Rome and rode a great race. There was a lot of tight-riding in the last two furlongs and, when the inquiry was announced, I assumed that it concerned the second horse who appeared to have leant on the third. There was absolute mayhem in the stewards room with everybody shouting but, when I watched the head-on, I was astounded that my jockey should have been suspended.

The suspension was to prove rather more costly than just ten days on the sidelines. When Weld had some fancied runners at the Curragh at the end of April, he brought over Lester Piggott to ride them. Piggott won on three including Theatrical. Mick was back for the horse's next run, the Derrinstown Derby Trial at Leopardstown, and partnered the colt to an emphatic four length win. He was just on the point of booking his plane ticket for Epsom when Piggott spoke to Bert Firestone, Theatrical's owner, and said he would like to ride the colt in the Derby. The agreement came into play yet again and Mick was jocked off.

In the Irish Derby three and a half weeks later, though, he was back on board and for a few glorious moments he felt he was going to win.

> Theatrical ran disappointingly at Epsom – the ground was not fast enough for him – but when I let him loose early in the straight at the Curragh he quickened so well I didn't think he could be caught. But Pat Eddery on Law Society collared me 100 yards out and beat me half a length. Lester was third on Damister but my immediate reaction was one of dreadful disappointment. However things started to click for me around this time and I soon began to ride most of the horses when they ran outside Ireland. I even got the ride on Committed. Brent Thomson rode her at Royal Ascot but I was second on her in both the July Cup at Newmarket and in the Prix Maurice de Gheest at Deauville. After winning two races on her at Phoenix Park she went for a second Prix

de l'Abbaye. Again I kept the ride and we beat Freddie Head on Vilikaia by a short head. It was my first Group One winner in France.

It was the first of the magic weekends. At Phoenix Park the previous day he beat Wally Swinburn's eight-year-old record when winning the C.L. Weld Park Stakes (sponsored by Weld in memory of his father) on Gaily Gaily.

> I can remember feeling pretty good that day but it was basically a question of my own satisfaction at setting a new record rather than of being aware of people talking and writing about me becoming a bit special. In fact I wasn't really conscious of that at all. I was just happy that my career was going so well and that I was heading in the right direction.

There were still six weeks of the season to go and, with Weld's horses firing on all cylinders, Swinburn's total seemed set to fade into oblivion. But racing's cruel fates decided that Kinane had done enough. They struck at Gowran Park little more than a week later when his total had reached 105.

> I was riding a horse called Halifax in the second division of the two-year-old maiden and, as we were coming down off the hill towards the final turn, the field was closely bunched and I was tracking Christy Roche on Tite Street. Something caused Christy to snatch up and my horse clipped his mount's hind heels. We fell and the horses behind galloped all over me. I was kicked in the face and my jaw was broken in three places. I also had a big gash on the inside of my leg. It was a horrific fall but, funnily enough, what I remember most vividly are two separate incidents that were really nothing to do with me. The first was in the ambulance that took me to Kilkenny Hospital. Making the journey with me was a racegoer. He'd had a heart attack on the course and he died before he reached Kilkenny. Then, when I was in one of the hospital corridors waiting to be attended to, a woman and child were brought in. They were both badly hurt. They had been out collecting for charity and had been hit by a car. My injuries looked pretty minor in comparison.

When the doctors studied the preliminary X-rays, they told me I had also damaged my back and fractured a vertebra. I was transferred to St. James's Hospital in Dublin where they X-rayed me again. The vertebra that looked bad on the original X-ray was simply the one that I had crushed in that fall at the Curragh on the day after I got married. But my jaw was in a bad way and they had to elevate the cheekbone to put it together. What worried me most, though, was that the clock was ticking away. I was due to ride in the Breeders' Cup at Aqueduct in New York on 2 November, only 19 days after the Gowran Park fall. I was desperate to get right for it. At this stage, remember, I had never even ridden in America and the Breeders' Cup meeting is racing's equivalent of the World Cup. Dermot had a big raiding party lined up for Aqueduct – Field Dancer in a Grade One on the day before the Breeders' Cup, Committed in the Sprint and Theatrical in the Turf. The folowing day Easy to Copy was to run in a Grade Two and two days after that Kamakura was in a Grade Three. If I was to make the trip, I knew I had somehow to be back in action for Leopardstown on 26 October. That was only 12 days after the fall. The doctors thought I was pushing it a bit but I was determined.

I had to prove to Dermot I would be fit. On 24 October I got up on a horse for the first time since Gowran Park. The following day was Friday, a work morning. Dermot really put me through it. He gave me a lot of horses to ride gallops on but I couldn't do the lot.That gash on the inside of my leg split open and I had to stop. But I still went to Leopardstown on the following day. I had to.

I was beaten three-quarters of a length in the opener and a short head in the next, and I knew I was in trouble. Each time I got back to the weighing room my heard started to feel fuzzy. I'd picked up a bad cold too and that simply made things worse. My body couldn't cope with it all and, as I slumped back on the bench in the jockeys' room, I realised I was beaten – for that day anyway. I had pushed myself to the limit, possibly beyond it, and my system simply couldn't take it. I had to give up my other rides. I gave myself a rest on the Sunday – General Knowledge was running in the French St Leger at Longchamp but obviously I couldn't make it – but I felt, if I could get through the Leopardstown meeting on the

Monday, I would be OK for Aqueduct. I would have a few days to help me get better before flying to New York.

But because I'd had to stop on Saturday, I had to pass the racecourse doctor before being allowed to ride on Monday. To my horror, not only did he refuse to pass me, he stood me down for a fortnight. Pat Eddery took my place on Field Dancer and he very nearly won. Steve Cauthen was unplaced on Committed and Lester was down the field on Theatrical. Jean Cruguet rode the other two. He was third on Easy to Copy and fourth on Kamakura. The fact that none of the five actually won did little to minimise my feelings of bitter disappointment.

His one consolation came when he learnt that Robert Sangster wanted him to ride Celestial Bounty in the Hollywood Derby. The horse failed to win but at least he had that all-important first ride in the States. Then it was back to India where he won both the 2,000 Guineas and the Derby on Sir Bruce, a horse whose aura of invincibility was regarded as a challenge by certain unscrupulous locals.

Sir Bruce's next run was in a valuable invitation race over a mile and a half in Madras and I was asked to stop him. I'd had a few similar approaches in India before and I turned them all down. But this time the money was huge. I can't recall exactly how much except it was a hell of a lot. The people concerned knew somebody I knew and the approach came through him. I said no. The horse started hot favourite but he had been proving difficult to train and, even though he had won the Derby, he didn't really get the trip. I hate to think what went through the minds of those who had tried to bribe me when they watched the race. I was beaten a neck!

5

Classic Progress

Back in Europe the Italian trips were starting to prove costly. Mick
went again early in April 1986 and he was suspended for a second
time – he had only had a total of five rides in the country at this
stage. On this occasion the stewards took the view that he had
crossed over too quickly after the start. He also had trouble keeping
straight on Flash of Steel in the Irish 2,000 Guineas and had to
endure not only an inquiry but also an extraordinarily optimistic
appeal by the owner of the runner-up.

Heavy rain made the ground at the Curragh exceptionally testing
and, although Mick drove Bert Firestone's Flash of Steel to the front
a furlong out, Martin Browne (Liam's younger son) on Mr John was
between the Weld colt and the rails. Flash of Steel began to drift in
and Mick had to put his whip down 60 yards from home to stop the
two colliding. At the inquiry he was given a caution by the stewards
who said 'he had a responsibility to make a greater effort to keep a
straight course.' They maintained that he should have pulled his
whip through to his right hand and used it to keep his mount away
from Mr John.

> I was clear when I put my whip down and I could tell Flash
> of Steel was not going to drift in much more. But two days
> later John Michael, the owner of Mr John, lodged an appeal
> against the stewards' decision. I still felt I was in no great
> danger of losing the race but it meant going right through the
> inquiry all over again, this time in front of the senior stewards
> with lawyers doing much of the questioning. We had a

solicitor and a barrister, and so did John Michael. The hearing lasted nearly four and a half hours and in the middle of it there was a bomb scare. The garda were called in and had to check all the cars in the car park. Fortunately it turned out to be a hoax. Equally fortunately, the senior stewards turned down Mr Michael!

Mick was by now an established star and, although Lester Piggott was still king, the crowds were beginning to shout for Kinane. At Phoenix Park on 7 June he had rides for Weld in all six races. He won on the first five and he would have gone through the card if the Dermot Hogan partnered-John Oxx trained Hungry Giant had not proved half a length too good in the last.

However despite all the winners – there were many other successful days – Dermot Weld continued to prove a hard taskmaster. He could be difficult to please as he showed in no uncertain manner when Innsbruck was backed from 6-4 to 4-6 for a six furlong race at Naas in July. One of the 33-1 chances in the race was In The Dock who had been off the racecourse for nearly three seasons and was trained by Mark Roper who had not had a winner for five years. The English-educated Roper was little known in those days but in 1995 he was to buy Maddenstown Lodge from Browne. Innsbruck was ridden by Salvador Martinez, a Spaniard brought up in Bordeaux and back in Ireland for only three weeks after having spent the previous two and a half years in America. Martinez sent his mount straight to the front and, although Mick made desperate efforts to catch him in the last two furlongs – 'the trip was too short for my filly and she was never on the bridle' – the post came just too soon and he was beaten a short head.

Weld was livid. At the first available opportunity he took his stable jockey into the narrow but secluded corridor that leads to the stewards room and gave him a lecture.

> I felt he had miscued it in no uncertain fashion. I told him that, if we couldn't outmanoeuvre people who hardly ever had a winner and started getting beaten by horses who had been off for years, we should give the fucking game up and go in for something harmless like gardening .

The following month disaster struck again, this time at Laytown. Ireland's once a year beach meeting – the racing takes place on the sand when the tide has gone out – is often a dangerous affair and this was no exception.

> In the second race I rode Donny Brae, the favourite. In those days you raced down the course, negotiated a bend at the far end and then came back up again. But as we turned the corner Donal Manning on Moutalina fell in front of my mount and brought him down. Stephen Craine was just behind me on a horse called Dejeunesse and they came down on top of me, breaking my left wrist and my right thumb. Both wrists had to be put in plaster and I was out of action for a month. As a result I again missed out on an important American trip. I was to have gone over to partner Theatrical in the Arlington Million.

Mick took care never to ride at Laytown again and so he missed the horrific carnage at the 1994 meeting when three horses were killed and seven jockeys injured. After that, the bend was eliminated and the fixture was moved to earlier in the year when the crowd was less of a problem.

But he was lucky not to be injured again at the Curragh at the beginning of November when he was involved in another three horse pile-up. Jimmy Coogan broke three ribs and a collar bone and, while Tommy Manning was left to nurse two broken ribs and a collar bone, Mick emerged more or less unscathed and was able to ride his 80th winner of the season that same afternoon. He was champion for the third successive year. He again spent the winter in Bombay – his eighth consecutive stint there – and, although he won the Indian 1,000 Guineas, an event of far more significance was his first visit to Hong Kong.

> Because I was champion jockey in Ireland, I was entitled to a temporary licence. I was there for only two meetings and I had just nine rides. But I rode a winner and it was more than enough to give me a taste for the place. I made up my mind to go again the following winter if I possibly could.

The jockey who grabbed most of the headlines in Ireland in 1987 was not Mick but Cash Asmussen, and mostly for the wrong reasons. The dark-haired Cash, a tall wafer-thin Texan, was as

Five on a donkey: Katheryn, Thomas,
Mick (aged seven), Jayo and Susanne. On
the right is Tommy Kinane.

Taking part in a fancy dress parade at the age of ten.
Mick went as Lester Piggott.

On Crohane after winning a showjumping competition at the Dublin Horse Show at the age of 14.
(Bobby Studio)

James Kinane, the founder of a racing dynasty, with nephew Michael Keane.

Stephen Craine (left) joins in the celebrations at the jockeys' dance in Newbridge's Keadeen Hotel on the night Mick was crowned apprentice champion in 1978.

Post-race analysis with Dermot Weld. (Pat Healy)

After winning on Chaqall at Sha Tin in January 1996. David Oughton is on the right.

Jane and David Oughton with Frances and Tommy Kinane at the Oughton's Sha Tin flat in February, 1996. Also in the picture is Paul Kan Man Lok, owner of the 1996 Hong Kong Derby winner Che Sara Sara.

handsome as he was eloquent. Vincent O'Brien brought him over from France, where he had achieved the not inconsiderable feat of beating all the French jockeys to become champion, but Cash's ultra-stylish low crouch and his habit of bringing his mounts late and without much evident use of the stick, did not go down well with Irish punters – especially when he lost races they thought he should have won. He was frequently accused, usually unfairly, of leaving it too late. Phoenix Park, in particular, tended to erupt into a barrage of jeers and catcalls. 'Go home Yank' and 'Texas, here we come' were two of the printable ones.

Mick's relentless pursuit of winners and his fourth championship tended to pass unnoticed amongst all the controversy surrounding the American who seemed to revel in his celebrity status. Even when the crowds were having a go at him, he would give them a cheerful wave.

So far as the public and the papers were concerned, Asmussen was one of the more colourful chapters in the celebrated Ballydoyle saga and what they were all expecting was another champion to follow in the hoofprints of Sir Ivor, Nijinsky and the others O'Brien turned into racing history. The successes – or more often the failures – of the latest of Vincent's big names tended to hog the limelight along with the new stable jockey.

At Leopardstown on 9 May, for example, all the attention was centred on Seattle Dancer whose defeat of stable companion Ancient Times was greeted with just about every emotion from relief to scepticism. He was one of the most expensive horses ever bought – he had cost an incredible $13.1 million as a yearling but he tended to commit one of the worst crimes in the racing book. He swished his tail and, even though Asmussen dismissed it as being of no significance – 'If you had never been hit in your life before, you would swish your tail ' – it was widely regarded as a sure sign of ungenuineness in a colt. Doubts were cast as freely as coins into a fountain. It was just about the sole subject of discussion that day. But for Dermot Weld and his jockey there was a far more pressing concern.

Mick won the second race on the card, the six furlong Killiney Handicap, on Steel Commander getting the gelding home by a hard-fought head. But he ran into a lot of trouble on the way. After two furlongs he was bumped and knocked several places sideways. When he regained his position, his mount leaned on one of the other horses who was nearly brought down. The stewards blamed Mick and, as Weld recalls, it really affected him.

For a time during his early years with me, I felt that Mick did not always ride Leopardstown that well and I was thrilled he had shown so much courage in driving Steel Commander through such a narrow gap to get up and win. It was a legitimate gap in my opinion, and in Mick's, but the stewards thought otherwise. They said he was guilty of gross carelessness and suspended him for four days. He was absolutely livid and I knew I was in trouble for the rest of the afternoon.

In those days Mick tended to let it get to him if things went against him. I had five more runners and four of them were strongly fancied. When he came up to me in the parade ring for the next race, I had to really work on him to remove his troubles from his mind and persuade him that what he had to concentrate on was the next race. But it didn't work. He was beaten on all five, three were second and he should have won on those. Happy to say, he has since learned to master his feelings. If the same thing happened today, he would be able to overcome it.

The following month Mick Kinane rode his second Royal Ascot winner – five years after his first – on Weld's Big Shuffle in the Cork and Orrery Stakes and there were some significant two-year-old successes for Rosewell House in the latter part of the season, notably Flutter Away in the Group One Moyglare Stud Stakes and the C L Weld Park Stakes on Trusted Partner.

This filly was owned by Walter Haefner's Moyglare Stud Farm. Haefner, born in Zurich and the son of a missionary in Tibet, is one of Switzerland's major car importers and his worldwide financial interests include computer software. He was the champion European amateur in 1963 and the previous year he had bought land at Moyglare in County Kildare in order to develop it into one of the world's top studs. Haefner's financial advisers thought he was mad to pour so much money into a stud – he spent a fortune on buying the best mares – but he was determined to prove that he could make it, not just a success, but a profitable one too. In 1974 Moyglare went into the black for the first time and in 1980, after several years of sustained profits, he decided that operating a commercial stud was too easy. He elected not to sell yearlings any more but instead he would race them all in the Moyglare name – and in the stud's red, white and black colours. He continued to keep out of the limelight – personal publicity embarrasses him – and, although he has found it far more costly to race his own horses, he revels in their successes. By the end of 1987 Weld was training virtually all the Moyglare horses and Haefner was beginning to take over from the Firestones as the stable's most important patron.

Haefner and his horses were to play an important role in Mick's success story but he had little idea just how important when he left Ireland in November 1987 as champion for the fourth time with 86 winners. He was far more preoccupied with his first ride in Tokyo's Japan Cup (Cockney Lass who ran disappointingly) and his second trip to Hong Kong.

Most of the winter, though, was as usual spent in India where the sunshine and the less demanding racing schedule had long made the country a popular venue for English and Irish jockeys. Christmas was invariably celebrated in style and one in particular stands out:

> There had been a problem with the drainage at the stables in Bombay – and the sewerage overflowed all over the place – so the Poona season was extended and several of the visiting jockeys and our families decided we would have Christmas lunch together in the Poona Club. Kevin Darley, Richard Fox, John Lowe and Ernie Johnson were in the party. A huge frozen turkey was brought up from Bombay the previous day and we gave it to the bearers to prepare. On Christmas morning they laid places for us all at a big table and, while we were all sitting back enjoying a few pre-lunch drinks, they brought in several bottles of wine, opened them and put them on the table. They asked us if we were ready to eat and, when we were, they brought in the vegetables piping hot. We were all getting hungry by this stage and they carried in this big turkey on a huge plate. We told the bearers to start carving. They seemed to have a lot of difficulty with this – or at least they were taking a long time over it – and someone got up from the table to see what they were doing. Most of the turkey was still frozen solid. None of us had thought to tell the bearers it had to be defrosted before it was cooked!

The 1988 season began with a bang on Weld's Gay Burslem in the Italian 2,000 Guineas – no suspensions this time – and in the Irish 1,000 Guineas on 21 May Mick teamed up again with Trusted Partner. She had not raced since the Park Stakes over seven months earlier and few thought she had much chance without a run under her belt. She started at 10-1.

> There was quite a big field, 16 runners, and I rode a waiting race on Trusted Partner. I deliberately dropped her in about ninth or tenth and stayed there until halfway. I then started to make up a bit of ground and I could soon see that I was in control of those around me. I asked her to quicken in earnest, she responded in good style to hit the front just over a furlong out and she did it nicely, staying on well to beat John Reid on Dancing Goddess by two lengths.

Haefner was thrilled and his decorative wife France led in the filly, who was by Affirmed, the horse Steve Cauthen had ridden to victory in the American Triple Crown. But most of the plaudits went to Weld. There used to be a saying in racing that it's the jockey first, the trainer second, the horse third and the owner nowhere. In the last 25 years there has been a subtle reversal in the positions of the jockey and trainer so far as their media importance is concerned. Now the trainer is the one everybody wants to interview.

Weld has made the most of this. Right from the start of his brilliant career, he impressed the press corps by turning to them in the winner's enclosure and, instead of waiting for the questions to be asked, launching into an impressive spiel about what he thought of the horse and what the future plans were. He spoke the language of the newspapers. All the pressmen had to do was write it down and relay it. Weld could even reel off impressive statistics about how many winners he had trained and the number of times he had won that particular race. He also seemed to know what the questions, when eventually anybody had a chance to ask them, would be. Plans for the more newsworthy of his horses would also be rattled off, again often without having to be asked. Weld rapidly became a media man's dream and, as he realised only too well, a trainer who could talk like this was going to get a lot more coverage than those modest rivals who could seldom be persuaded to say more than a few words. But on this occasion the Rosewell House maestro, as he was fast becoming, deserved every line of praise. To win a classic with a horse who had been off the course for so long was a remarkable achievement.

But the racing stage is a small one, and few of the players are magnanimous in defeat. Envy, jealousy, resentment and backbiting tend to override all else. Brutus would have been in his element on the racecourse! As Mick did better and better, accusations of unfair tactics began to be levelled by some of the Weld stable's rivals. Mick was, at various stages, accused by the gossips and rumour-mongers of riding off his opponents with his elbows and of persuading his mounts to hamper other fancied horses by leaning on them.

But much more serious were the accusations publicly levelled by French trainer Maurice Zilber and his jockey after Silver Lane was beaten into third behind Sheikh Mohammed's dead-heaters Diminuendo (ridden by Steve Cauthen for Henry Cecil) and Melodist – trained by Michael Stoute and ridden by Walter Swinburn – in the Irish Oaks at the Curragh in July. Tony Cruz, a Hong Kong jockey at that time based in France, did not get a clear run on Silver Lane and Zilber reckoned Mick – fourth on Paul Kelleway's Miss Boniface – was partly to blame. So did Cruz who complained 'Mick hit my filly across the nose and head with his whip. Silver Lane then completely lost her balance.'

Cruz and Zilber asked the officials to show them the patrol film and afterwards the trainer, by this time almost purple with rage, came storming out of the stewards room, fuming 'There should have been an inquiry. My filly was interfered with.'

The following May Vincent O'Brien spoke to both the stewards and the press after his Puissance, ridden by John Reid, overcame a fair bit of bumping to beat Mick on Big Shuffle by three-quarters of a length in the Greenlands Stakes. The Ballydoyle boss lodged an official complaint with the stewards about Mick's riding and the stewards appeared to substantiate O'Brien's viewpoint by cautioning Mick for moving off a straight line although, to be fair, he did so only to avoid clipping the heels of another horse.

However a few days later O'Brien was quoted in a press agency report as saying that Puissance had developed a chip fracture in his knee, would be forced to miss Royal Ascot as a result and the 'injury appears to be as a result of the rough passage he had in the Greenlands'.

This was too much for Dermot Weld who was incensed that any trainer, even the great Vincent O'Brien, should single out his stable jockey in this way – 'If the chip fracture happened in the Greenlands, how come the stable didn't know earlier than they did?' he asked pointedly. 'If a horse injures himself in a race, you will know when he cools down. You will certainly know by the next day. Puissance could have suffered that injury at any time, even in his box at home. It's unfair to blame Kinane.'

By mid 1988 it was widely believed that a doping gang had been in operation in Ireland for the previous nine months. Several short-priced horses ran unaccountably badly and, although all the dope tests came up negative, the Turf Club had been sufficiently concerned the previous December to issue a warning to trainers to be on their guard. Suspicion was later to centre on a man who had already been warned off but the Turf Club was never able to prove anything against him. Nor could its officials pin down what the doper was using, although it was suggested that the substance may have been insulin. This would not show up in the tests but too much of it takes the glucogen out of the system, leaving the victim feeling temporarily weak. However nobody could pinpoint when the man and his aids were interfering with the horses.

Mick Kinane believes he knows: 'I am sure whoever was doing the doping was somehow getting at them in the stable yards. I am equally sure that a few of Dermot Weld's were got at. I rode horses that were hardly able to walk, let alone gallop. Maybe that's an exaggeration but it's how it felt when you were on them.

In the autumn of that year there started what was to prove the beginning of a long-running saga when a report in *The Star*, written by Colin Fleetwood Jones under an exclusive tag, said that Mick Kinane was on the shortlist to succeed Walter Swinburn as stable jockey to Michael Stoute's ultra-powerful yard at Newmarket. According to Fleetwood Jones, Mick was rumoured to have been approached already.

Such stories were to reappear, in various guises, for the next few years. This one had an unsettling effect on Swinburn who was going through a sticky patch with Stoute. A month before *The Star* report, Swinburn – known as the choirboy because of his angelic features – won the Group One Heinz 57 Phoenix Stakes on Superpower trained at Newmarket, not by his boss, but by Bill O'Gorman. Afterwards, when he was speaking to the press about the win, he said "Make it look good for when Michael Stoute reads it." His words were accompanied by a smile but he meant it.

Most people are annoyed when they read these sorts of reports in the papers. Not Mick:

> It was good publicity for me. It also kept Dermot Weld on his toes and helped me when I was negotiating a new agreement with him. We did that at the end of each season and for many years the major objective of the negotiations, so far as I was concerned, was more money. In fact Michael Stoute never made any sort of job offer to me.

He had plenty of ammunition when he sat round the Rosewell House negotiating table in November that year because he had left behind him his 1985 record of 105, beating it by eight.

> It was obviously very satisfying to set a new record like that but I still felt I could achieve a better total in the future if everything went right. But I'd learnt by this time not to go out chasing records. If you start doing that, you somehow find them incredibly difficult to achieve. You just have to accept that if a new record comes, that's great. If it doesn't, it's not the end of the world. By this stage it was only when a record was getting close that I would dare say to myself 'OK, now you can go for it'.

6

Feeling Lucky

In July 1989 the legendary Willie Shoemaker rode at Phoenix Park for the first and last time. The diminutive Willie the Shoe – so called, apart from the obvious reference to his surname, because he was so small as a baby that his mother put him in a shoe box rather than a cot – was on a whistle-stop tour of Europe as he finished up his celebrated riding career in his late fifties with over 8,800 winners to his name. He had no success at the Park but he did make friends with Ireland's champion jockey. Less than a year later Shoemaker's friendship was to prove valuable.

But what was on Mick's mind that weekend was a call he had received from Henry Cecil. Steve Cauthen had just said no a second time and the master of Warren Place wanted to know if Mick would be free to partner Alydaress in the following Saturday's Kildangan Stud Irish Oaks. Cauthen recalls:

> My brother Doug was getting married back home in the States that weekend and I felt it was important for me to be there. I wanted to give him my support and show my happiness for him. I went to Henry and explained the situation. If he had said he wanted me to ride Alydaress at the Curragh, then I would have gone to Ireland. But Henry was very understanding. He gave me the option and I said I would go home. It was nice for me and Mick's good fortune that he was able to take advantage.
>
> By this stage I had known Mick for some time. The first occasion I really noticed him was at Royal Ascot seven years

earlier when he won the St. James's Palace Stakes on Dara
Monarch. I was immediately struck by what a good young
rider he was. He had both style and strength. From then on
we would always have a chat whenever we saw each other
and I followed his progress. I also got to know his elder
brother, Thomas, and his parents.

Aliysa was obviously going to be hard to beat in the Irish
Oaks. She was trained by Michael Stoute for the Aga Khan
and she had won the Gold Seal Oaks at Epsom in good style
beating Snow Bride, who I rode, by a convincing three lengths
but I liked Alydaress too. I rode her to win the Ribblesdale at
Royal Ascot and she was starting to come good.

Eleven days before the Irish Oaks, Aliysa suddenly became the
centre of a controversy that was to reach far beyond the racing
pages and have devastating consequences, particularly in
Newmarket. It was revealed that she was the first classic winner
since Relko 26 years earlier to react positively to a dope test. A
derivative of the prohibited substance camphor had been detected
in the urine sample taken after her win at Epsom. Normally any
trace of a prohibited substance results in disqualification but the
Jockey Club seemed afraid to take action. The stewards kept
putting off the evil day and in December the Aga Khan resigned his
honorary membership of the Jockey Club as he voiced his
opposition to its drug-testing procedures. But it was not until the
following year that Aliysa was disqualified and the classic awarded
to the Henry Cecil-trained, Steve Cauthen-ridden Snow Bride. The
Aga Khan then withdrew his 80-strong team – shared between
Stoute and Luca Cumani – and vowed that he would have no more
runners in Britain until significant improvements were made in the
testing procedures. It was another four years before he declared
himself satisfied.

Mick Kinane was more concerned with Alydaress's prospects at
the Curragh and in making the most of the windfall ride. Cecil was
also running Snow Bride in the Irish Oaks and had booked John
Reid, but he shared Cauthen's faith in Alydaress and he showed it
by agreeing with Sheikh Mohammmed that the filly should be
supplemented at a cost of £20,000. The Sheikh, a leading member
of Dubai's oil-rich royal family, also owned the Kildangan Stud that
was sponsoring the race – and he wanted to win it.

I'd only ridden for Henry Cecil once before and, so far as I can remember, only once for the Sheikh. I rather thought, wrongly as it turned out, that Steve had decided to go to his brother's wedding partly because he didn't think Alydaress could beat Aliysa. On the Wednesday before the Irish Oaks I was riding at Dundalk. That evening I flew to Newmarket because I was riding Big Shuffle in the July Cup the following day. I hardly knew Henry at the time – I had met him on occasion at the races but really only to say hello – but we agreed that I should ride work on Alydaress that Thursday morning. I was very taken with her and I could tell immediately that she was pretty good. I began to feel the American wedding just might prove a good opportunity, particularly when Henry started talking to me about her. He said she was peaking at just the right time and he made it clear that he was really wrapped up in her.

Cecil ('Alydaress was very well in herself and, although I didn't necessarily think she would beat Aliysa, I felt she had a fair chance of doing so') missed the race – the big yearling sales at Keeneland were starting two days later and he decided he should be there to give himself enough time to look at the horses before the sales started – and he was represented by his then wife Julie, daughter of Sir Noel Murless who had trained at Warren Place before Henry and established himself as one of the great trainers of the twentieth century. Julie, after contacting Henry from the Curragh, decided to withdraw Snow Bride and the stewards hit her husband with a £1,000 fine. The betting suggested that only two of the five runners mattered. Aliysa, ridden by Walter Swinburn, started at 7-4 on and Alydaress the same price against. The next best was a 14-1 chance. The other two were 50-1 and 100-1.

When we turned for home, Walter went to the front and I followed him. I was going so well that I felt pretty confident I could pick up my mount and beat the favourite, always assuming Walter did not have more up his sleeve than he appeared to. I got down to work on Alydaress, I challenged two furlongs out and gained the advantage inside the final furlong to win by three-quarters of a length. It was my fourth Irish classic win and also the fourth for Henry.

The fact that Cecil, eight times champion trainer at this stage, had chosen to use the Irish champion instead of bringing over a jockey from England did not go unnoticed among his Newmarket rivals. Nor did the fact that Mick had succeeded in turning over the favourite.

Ireland's biggest race meeting takes place at Galway in the height of the summer. The six-day festival is an orgy of gambling – those with sufficient reserves, physical as well as financial, also sit up most of the night playing cards – and Dermot Weld makes a point of turning the meeting into a personal benefit. One of the races he most likes to win is the two-year-old race on the opening evening and in 1989 the horse he laid out for this was one of Moyglare's called Go And Go. He had run just once before, he started even money favourite and Mick swept him clear turning for home without having even an inkling of the heights the colt was to scale the following June.

At Galway the next evening Mick won the feature race, the McDonogh Handicap, on another Weld trained horse, Popular Glen, owned by Michael Smurfit who had been in Los Angeles on business 24 hours earlier. He had flown to Galway via Belfast so he could fit in a few hours work before going to the races!

Smurfit was the son of a tailor in St. Helens who had changed his religion when he became engaged to a Catholic girl from Belfast. The priest who performed the wedding ceremony revealed at the reception that he owned part of a cardboard box factory in Dublin. Smurfit senior promptly bought the priest's shares and set about converting the factory into a business empire. When he handed over the reins to his sons, Michael Smurfit was little more than 30. Working a minimum of 14 hours a day, Michael turned it into one of the biggest companies in the world. He then switched some of his attention to racing. At the time of Popular Glen's win he was chairman of the Racing Board – despite being officially resident in Monte Carlo, primarily for tax reasons – and was becoming an increasingly significant patron of Dermot Weld's stable.

A month later Mick Kinane received a call from Michael Jarvis. He had never spoken to the Newmarket trainer before but he knew all about him, and a fair bit about the horse that Jarvis wanted him to ride in the £200,000 Group One Phoenix Champion Stakes. Weld had no runner and so he was free to accept the ride.

Jarvis, then 51, had worked his way up from the bottom. The son of a jump jockey, he rode a few winners after leaving school but only a few and when he was 20 he joined Towser Gosden (father of John, the celebrated Newmarket trainer) at Lewes in Sussex as a stable lad. He was soon made head lad and when Gosden, suffering from poor health, sold out to Gordon Smyth, Jarvis was inherited by the yard's new boss. So was Charlottown who won the 1966 Epsom Derby. The following year Gosden was asked to come out of his enforced retirement to train for David Robinson, a TV rentals millionaire who was the biggest owner in England. When Gosden explained he was not well enough, he recommended Jarvis for the job. But in the mid 1970s Robinson decided to virtually close down his huge racing empire and Jarvis became a public trainer. In 1989 he had over 70 horses at his Kremlin House stables on Newmarket's Fordham Road, and Carroll House was very much the star. Jarvis recalls:

> The ten furlongs of the Phoenix Park race was Carroll House's absolute minimum and I was seriously toying with the idea of giving the big Irish race a miss to go for the following day's Grosser Preis Von Baden, a valuable Group One over a mile and a half at Baden-Baden. Then I received a fax from Jonathan Irwin, who was running Phoenix Park, to say they'd had rain and it looked like being decent ground. I had to find a jockey. At this stage Carroll House was Walter Swinburn's ride. He had won the Princess of Wales's Stakes on him at the Newmarket July meeting and finished fifth in the King George VI and Queen Elizabeth Diamond Stakes at Ascot. But on the day of the Phoenix Champion he was claimed by Michael Stoute for Kerrera in the Ladbroke Sprint Cup. I made inquiries before ringing Mick and found that he looked like being free. He was obviously the best available and I had long admired his riding. But I was still worried that the trip would be too short and I told Mick to have him fairly handy. Carroll House had a good burst of speed but there were only nine runners.

The jockey found the orders hard to carry out and for much of the race he was far from happy:

> Carroll House proved to be an extremely difficult ride. He had lost a big race in Germany the previous season by

hanging left and he did the same much of the way up the
straight, possibly because the ground was a bit fast for him.
He was continually hanging in behind those in front and I had
to fight with him for the best part of three furlongs as I tried
desperately to pull him out to challenge. I never really thought
I was going to win until inside the final furlong when I finally
managed to extract him. I led about 100 yards out and I beat
Steve Cauthen on Henry Cecil's Citidancer by three-quarters
of a length.

Jarvis immediately announced that Carroll House would go for
France's richest race, the Prix de l'Arc de Triomphe, the following
month but he said that riding arrangements would depend on
whether Swinburn was again required by Stoute. The horse
Stoute eventually decided to run proved to be none other than
Aliysa. Jarvis rang Mick Kinane again.

But in the meantime life continued at the same frenetic pace,
punctuated by yet more press stories – this time emphatically
denied – that he was on the verge of signing up for a major
English stable for the following season, and at Listowel on 22
September he achieved his Irish century for the third time in his
career.

Winning the championship and setting new records meant a
lot to me. I felt then that I had a good chance of beating the
previous year's 113. I wanted to reach a total that would
stand for a long time and I decided to go for it. But it didn't
work out and I failed to beat the 1988 figure by one.

It didn't really matter. The first weekend in October put all
domestic records firmly in the shade. The big race at Phoenix Park
on the Saturday was the Cartier Million which, as its name
suggested, carried a prize fund of £1,000,000. Jonathan Irwin, also
the boss of the Goffs sales company in those days, borrowed the
idea from Australia and, with showmanship typical of the Old
Etonian with a theatrical background, he turned it into a major
attraction. The race was funded by those who sold their yearlings
at Goffs and those who bought them. The huge prize guaranteed
an enormous field. Sadly, Irwin was to leave Goffs less than two
months later following a boardroom row – partly over calls for
Cartier to contribute more to the sponsorship – and the new

management team eventually decided to abandon the race.

Mick rode The Caretaker for Dermot Weld and on the way to the races he eventually broke off from his normal silent and intense concentration on how he was going to ride each race to declare to Catherine, who was driving, 'I feel so lucky.'

> I still don't know quite why I said that. It's not the sort of remark I normally make but the press siezed on it in a big way when they interviewed me the following week. Seemingly, few of them have ever forgotten it. But the race went amazingly well. I'd planned to give The Caretaker a breather two and a half furlongs out but instead she took hold of the bridle. I thought this is it and decided to go for it. There were 20 runners so there wasn't much room but I managed to find a gap and, although it was fast closing on us, The Caretaker went all out for it and we just got through. After that it was easy. She went right away to win by three lengths from Cullinan ridden by Frankie Dettori and Steve Cauthen's mount Anshan. Winning such a valuable race was unreal and my family were overjoyed. My parents were there and with Catherine was her sister and her parents. They all seemed to be in tears.
>
> I had a big day on the Sunday so I was keen to get home but I felt that I couldn't just drive off so I agreed to have a glass of champagne with Tim Mahony, one of the owners of The Caretaker. That night I had much the usual dinner, just the one course – steak, fresh vegetables and a boiled potato. I was in bed by 11.30 p.m.
>
> I was up at seven the next morning. Breakfast was no more than a mouthful of coffee and at 8.15 a.m. I left for Dublin Airport with Christy Roche who was riding a filly of Jim Bolger's in the Prix Marcel Boussac. We took the 10.00 a.m. flight to Paris and Christy told me something Yves Saint-Martin had once said to him about riding in the Arc – get into the position you want before you reach the little straight, and then sit. If you attempt to improve at this point, you are as good as in the graveyard. It sounded good advice. I stored it in my mind along with the videos of previous Arcs that I had been studying at home.
>
> When we arrived we picked up a chauffeur-driven car from Avis and reached Longchamp in plenty of time. Christy

promptly went for a sweat while I walked the course. I had ridden in mile and a half races there before but this was my first Arc. I then tried to relax. Or at least I did until I was told I was not riding Chummy's Favourite in the Prix de l'Abbaye, the big sprint run immediately before the Arc. Frankie Dettori had been declared but he was to switch to Statoblest. The stewards said no, he couldn't. It was after declaration time and so too late to make any changes. It was a bitter blow. I had counted on that ride to get me warmed up for the big one.

I then sat down alongside Michael Roberts while he and several of the other jockeys ran through the Arc runners. They discounted one horse after another until they had boiled it down to five. Carroll House was one of them. I could feel my palms beginning to sweat.

The jocks came in after the first race saying the ground was riding good, and after the second they said it was softer. Christy was one of them and he told me it was sure to suit Carroll House. This made me more nervous but I wondered if perhaps Christy had got that impression because his filly hadn't run that well. It always seems softer when your horse is not travelling.

I still wasn't warmed up so I locked myself into the gents, flexed my muscles and really got the circulation going before walking out into the parade ring in front of the huge crowds to meet Michael Jarvis and owner Antonio Balzarini, and get my instructions.

No-one was happier about the softening ground than Carroll House's trainer:

The more rain we got the more the horse's chance increased. There had been a fair bit the previous night too. I didn't give Mick too much in the way of detailed instructions because he knew the horse well enough by this stage. But I did tell him that Carroll House was in extremely good form. He was bucking and kicking so much that it took three of us to get the saddle on him!

Some of the best middle distance horses in Europe were missing from the line-up from what was widely considered a sub-standard

Arc but few gave the Italian-owned, English-trained, Irish-ridden four-year-old much chance and he started at 19-1 on the Pari-Mutuel, the French Tote. But Jarvis had faith and Mick's was increased as the parade came to an end and the horse's lad released his hold.

Carroll House felt really great going down to the start. Clearly Michael was right. The horse was in top form and, when we reached the start, he showed it by letting out a kick. I was drawn 16, four from the outside, which I felt was ideal. He had been a bit slow in the early stages of the Phoenix Champion Stakes and an inside draw could have landed me in trouble very early on. And I knew he didn't have enough pace to make up a lot of ground from behind.

I also knew that Young Mother, the Prix Vermeille winner, would be prominent in the early stages and I had planned to use her as a lead. Coming out of the back straight, I was able to move in a bit. As I did so, there was a lot of shouting and roaring behind.

Carroll House was moving sweetly, though, and as we went down the hill into the little straight I remembered the advice Christy had passed on. But three furlongs out I just couldn't believe how well I was going. I made my move at the same time as Alain Lequeux made his on Behera but my fellow quickened past him. I hit my horse left-handed as he'd previously hung left. But, for some reason, he changed his legs and rolled to the right. Quick as a flash, I pulled my stick through and corrected him. Fortunately there was no contact between him and Behera – and no shouts from Lequeux. So there couldn't have been any real interference. But, as we swept past the post in front, I began to feel there might be a problem. The French interference rules can be interpreted very strictly.

I was also having other problems. A crowd of people were beginning to surge round me and, although I gave a thumbs-up sign when I heard an Irish voice shout out 'Give us a wave, Mick', I was starting to worry about the inquiry which I knew by this time was bound to be coming. But the nearer we got to the winner's enclosure, the bigger the crowd became round the horse. Carroll House didn't like it one bit. He put his ears back and prepared to lash out. I shouted at the people to keep clear but those closest to us were being pushed in by all those behind. As I dismounted, he swung round and I could feel his quarters touching my back. I knew he was going to let fly. There were even more people round us and, almost in panic, I barged my way through them.

Michael Jarvis was also finding the going tough:

The whole thing was pretty scary. When I was trying to make my way through the tunnel to meet the horse as he was being led in, I was stopped by some strong-arm heavyweights. I told them I was the trainer and eventually I was allowed through. But, when I got to the horse, I found myself wishing they had made a better job of stopping me People were slapping him on the backside and he was starting to let fly left, right and centre. How nobody was killed, or even seriously injured, I will never know. He sent some of the rails flying, yet they still kept crowding in on him.

It was even worse in the winner's enclosure. To this day I still don't know who all the people were. They were certainly unknown to me, to Antonio Balzarini and to his friends. The following year the Longchamp authorities tightened up the security.

With all the excitement I wasn't too worried about the objection lodged by Lequeux but then Brough Scott interviewed me. As he was talking to me, I saw the replay. I could tell there might be problems and I began to get a bit anxious.

Mick felt the same, only worse:

My French was not up to much and, as I didn't want to run the risk of the stewards misunderstanding me, I asked them if Cash Asmussen could go with me into the inquiry to act as an interpreter. When they showed the side-on film I was worried but the head-on seemed to show things much more in my favour. I could see that the French jockey had never stopped riding. It was only after I had gone clear that he moved off a straight line. But, as we were shown out of the room, the stewards seemed pretty uncertain. The next few minutes were grim. I don't know exactly how long it all took but it seemed like an eternity.

Eventually an official came up to me. He asked me to go with him to collect my prize. It was only then that I realised I was in the clear. The relief absolutely flooded through me. I felt on top of the world. I went through endless photo sessions and interviews. But I didn't mind. I would happily have gone on all night. Even so, I missed my 6.35 p.m. flight and I had to get somebody to change my ticket. Luckily I'd had the foresight to make a reservation on the 9.00 p.m. plane. When I got on it, the aeroplane was filled with racegoers. Aer Lingus congratulated me over the public address and opened the bar.

When I finally reached Dublin Airport, Catherine and her parents were waiting to meet me. They were in tears again!

7

The Belmont

A fortnight after the Arc Dermot Weld ran Go and Go in the Laurel Futurity at Laurel Park in Maryland. The Grade Two race was an important event in the American calendar and carried a first prize of £100,000 but the transatlantic trip looked a long shot in more ways than one – Go and Go had managed only seventh of ten in the National Stakes, his second start since Galway – and the general view was that the Irish colt did not have a hope in hell. Mick had little hesitation in electing to stay at home to ride at the Curragh meeting on the same day.

Craig Perret, an American jockey, took his place on Go And Go and fate intervened in a most unexpected way. It rained so heavily that the turf course became flooded and the race had to be switched to the dirt track. This was of little concern to most of the other runners – dirt racing in America is the norm – but it seemed the final nail in Go And Go's coffin. He had neither raced nor worked on such a surface. Yet he won the race. Few realised it at the time but, despite his breeding (by Be My Guest out of Irish Edition – both bred by Moyglare), he was a much better horse on dirt than he was on grass.

One who grasped this immediately was the famous Angel Cordero who promptly did his best to book himself for the ride in the Breeders' Cup Juvenile – first prize £250,000 – at Gulfstream Park in Florida a fortnight later. But Weld and Walter Haefner were determined to stay loyal to their stable jockey despite his lack of American race-riding experience. So Mick finally rode in the Breeders' Cup. But there was no happy ending. All the travelling, and the stifling heat in the barn where the overseas horses were stabled, took their toll on the colt. Second was as close as he could get and that was on the far turn with quite a bit of the race still to be run. He faded, and suffered interference, to finish with only four behind him. All those who thought the Laurel win was a fluke now had no doubts.

Dermot Weld, however, had long hankered to have a runner in an American classic. He knew that the Laurel running, not that of Gulfstream, was the real Go And Go and he looked again at the horse's pedigree. The sire of Be My Guest was the great Northern Dancer who did his racing on dirt. So did Grenzen, the dam of Irish Edition. To be strictly accurate, she also raced on turf but she was second in the Kentucky Oaks and proved a high class performer in California.

No horse trained in Europe had ever won a leg of the American Triple Crown but hardly any had attempted it. The domestic classic programme has always been considered more important for the best horses but Weld knew it was possible, not least because Clive Brittain had gone close in the 1986 Kentucky Derby with Bold Arrangement, the first British-trained horse to even run in the race.

Weld persuaded Walter Haefner to go for the Belmont Stakes but only after a fair bit of soul searching. The problem was the horse. Although he won on his reappearance at Phoenix Park, he scored by only half a length and in the Derrinstown Derby Trial at Leopardstown ten days later he managed only fourth. If he had won, incidentally, Weld would have given the American trip a miss and run the horse in the Epsom Derby. But, not only was Go And Go clearly some way behind the best of his generation, he was not doing well enough on the Curragh gallops to make a third American trip worthwhile. Weld decided to work him in a visor. This meant that he no longer galloped with a clear view of the wide-open green expanses of the Curragh plain. His vision was restricted to the gallop in front of him and his concentration was centred on the horse working alongside him. The visor had the desired effect and the colt's work reports immediately went from uninspiring to sparkling. His plane was booked and so was Mick's.

On the Wednesday before the race the horse left with Ray Carroll, at the time Weld's second jockey and an extremely capable rider who won the 1980 Irish St Leger for Vincent O'Brien on Gonzales but who had since faded out of the limelight. Mick did not fly out until the day before the race. With him on the flight to New York was Stan Cosgrove, the manager of the Moyglare Stud Farm.

The bespectacled Cosgrove had long been one of Ireland's most successful horse vets and indeed he was Shergar's vet when the Aga Khan's dual Derby winner was kidnapped from the Ballymany Stud in February 1983. He was also a breeder and a shareholder in the stallion. His investment was to cause him years of problems and battles with the Norwich Union Insurance Company. It was also to cause him considerable financial loss.

In the month following the kidnapping he received a phone call from a detective who said he had been contacted by a County Clare horse dealer who had seen Shergar. The kidnappers wanted their reward before revealing where the stallion was. A complicated arrangement was set up whereby Cosgrove would produce £80,000 in cash which would be placed in the boot of the detective's car, the dealer would be taken to Shergar and the dealer's girlfriend would be held by the kidnappers as a temporary hostage to ensure that nobody tried to shortchange the men holding the stallion. One of the men would then be taken by the girlfriend to the detective who would hand over the cash while the dealer would drive off with the stallion. It proved to be a costly hoax. The boot was broken into and the money was stolen. But this was only a fraction of what the unfortunate Cosgrove lost.

He and his brother-in-law had borrowed £155,000 for the downpayments on one of the 40 £250,000 shares in Shergar. It looked a cast iron investment. The stud fee was £75,000 so investors stood to get most of their money back in three years, and the income was tax free in Ireland. Like the other shareholders, Cosgrove and his brother-in-law insured their shares. But, unlike most of the others who invested in the famous horse, there was a mix-up in the drafting of their policy. Cosgrove assumed that all risks were covered but, for some reason, loss by proven theft was not. The Norwich Union, the company with which the policy was placed, insisted that it required firm evidence that Shergar had died within the year of the policy and refused to pay up. Cosgrove took legal action against both the company and the firm of brokers who acted for him, but to no avail. His search for evidence eventually went as far as the Maghaberry Prison near Lisburn in County Antrim where Sean O'Callaghan, a former member of the IRA who turned supergrass, was held. On 18 February 1993 O'Callaghan signed the following statement:

I was a senior IRA volunteer from 1970 to 1985, as well as a
Garda Siochana informant from 1979 to 1985. Acting on
Garda requests as well as my own initiative, I investigated the
Shergar kidnapping in 1983. The clear and consistent
statements of those directly involved were that the horse was
shot in February 1983. I informed the Gardai accordingly at
that time. Since the kidnappers were never convicted of that
offence, they are unlikely to offer sworn evidence for a civil
action.

But still the Norwich Union refused to pay. Cosgrove, though,
was able to forget about his Shergar losses as he and the jockey flew
across the Atlantic. He is a formidable raconteur and for years used
to have his audience in fits of laughter as he told his stories at the
Moyglare Dinner in Dublin each December. Eventually he gave this
up, saying that he could not remember which ones he had told
before and which he hadn't. But it really didn't matter. He tended to
change the stories as he went along. Even those who had heard them
before never failed to be amused at both the new twists and the way
they were expressed. It was a classic case of 'the way he tells them'.
If he had not become a vet, he would have had no trouble earning
his living as a comic.

However he took Go And Go's Belmont bid seriously. So did the
Americans. Only three of the nine runners were preferred in the
betting to the Irish colt – Craig Perret's mount Unbridled who had
won the Kentucky Derby and was second in the Preakness but was
now unable to run on lasix (a drug that, among other things, helps
to prevent burst blood vessels), the Wood Memorial winner Thirty
Six Red and Yonder who had won the Jersey Derby. But there was a
suspicion that the Irish horse's jockey did not think he had all that
much chance. It's a suspicion which Mick denies but both Dermot
Weld and Stan Cosgrove detected a slightly less intense approach than
normal. For once he didn't study the videos of previous races and,
amazingly, nor did he walk the track. Indeed by the time the second
race was run he had still not arrived at the course. Weld and Cosgrove
were beginning to worry. Weld decided to ring the Garden City Hotel
where Mick was staying. He was astonished to find that, not only was
he still there, he was lying on his bed watching television.

The World Cup was on and it was the Romania – Russia
match. I'd had a tiring flight and I reckoned I was far better

off relaxing in the hotel bedroom than sitting in the weighing room getting edgy. I hate hanging about in the jockeys' room with nothing to do and the Belmont was the eighth race. If I had gone down there early, I would simply have used up nervous energy and got myself uptight. I wouldn't have been much use to anyone if that had happened. But what I didn't know was that I had to have a medical before I could ride. That was mainly why Dermot was panicking. He said 'Where the hell are you? You'd better get down here right away.'

The hotel was only about 20 minutes from the course. But I didn't walk it when I got there. I didn't see much point. It was a typical American track – big, sweeping and wide. I had a good look at it and I also met up with Willie Shoemaker. He told me where I should be at the various stages in the race if things went right for me. It proved valuable advice. It also decided me to make a point of keeping low in the saddle like the American jocks so that all the dirt flying up didn't hit me in the face.

But otherwise I didn't make any changes to my style and I kept my leathers level. The Americans ride what is known as 'acy-deucy' which is with one stirrup leather shorter than the other. It helps them to balance because they are on the turn almost all the time. I felt the whole thing was basically a question of whether or not the horse was good enough and whether or not he was going to travel well enough in the race. If he was, then I shouldn't have any worries. And if he wasn't, he wasn't going to win.

Cosgrove's doubts about his rider's commitment were reinforced, though, when he caught Mick's eye as he was being led round on Go And Go before going down to the start. 'As he passed me, he rolled his eyes up to heaven as if to say "What in the name of God are we doing here?" I spoke to him about it afterwards and he said he hadn't meant that at all!'

Thirty Six Red, ridden by Mike Smith who the following year was to win the Irish 2,000 Guineas on the American trained Fourstars Allstar, was drawn on the inside next to Go And Go – and he went straight to the front while Mick settled his mount on the rails in mid-division.

They went a good, hard pace and I was about sixth for much of the way. I was still in the same position in the back straight but I then began to move up a bit and he was travelling nicely. As we made the last part of the long turn from the back straight to the straight, I had to move out to get into a slot and Go And Go was racing a bit too laid back. I clicked my tongue and shook the reins at him. I shouted at him to go on, and the response was immediate. I said to myself 'Ooh. I'm going to win this.' In the same moment, he leapt forward onto the bit and I could see that just about everything else including Unbridled was flat to the boards. From that point on it was simply a matter of getting into the home stretch and switching out to get a clear run. Frankly, I was amazed at how easy it turned out to be. We won by over eight lengths. We came in to a fantastic reception and a huge garland of white flowers was draped over Go And Go's neck.

It proved to be a fabulous day but I didn't stay on. I had booked myself on the early evening flight out of New York but for once I didn't get that much sleep. By the time dinner had been served – and I ate it all! – quite a bit of the journey time was gone. With the five hour time difference, I was back in Dublin at 7.00 a.m.

Earlier the previous month Mick had ridden his first English classic winner, and been christened 'the super-sub' by the papers in the process, on Tirol in the General Accident Two Thousand Guineas.

The colt was the third winner of the Newmarket classic trained by Richard Hannon who was then 44. The son of a jump jockey, Hannon had been more concerned with pop music than racing as a teenager and he was the drummer for two successful groups in the swinging '60s. One was The Troggs and the other went under the curious name – at the time Hannon and the other members of the group thought they were particularly with it – of Dave Dee, Dozy, Beaky, Mick and Titch.

However Hannon decided to leave the pop world to join his father's stable just before the two groups hit the big time. On occasion he must have wondered at the wisdom of this decision – Harry Hannon had only 14 horses at his Wiltshire stables in 1969. But the following year Hannon senior retired and handed over to his son and in 1973 Hannon jnr won the Two Thousand for the first time with Mon Fils, a 50-1 shot he had backed at 200-1.

By 1990 he had expanded his once struggling stable into an establishment that numbered well over 100 inmates including Tirol who won the Craven Stakes, one of the most informative of the Guineas trials, on his reappearance at Newmarket in April.

> Pat Eddery, who rode Tirol to win the Horris Hill on his last start as a two-year-old, again had the mount in the Craven,' recalls the gruff, sometimes outspoken Hannon. 'He got into a bit of a pocket but the colt showed what a fine turn of foot he had by accelerating out of trouble to catch Sure Sharp in the last stride. That race was over the Guineas mile, so I knew he would get the trip and I had every reason to think he could win when he went back to Newmarket 16 days later.
>
> As I saw it, there were not many who could possibly beat him with the exception of the French colt Machiavellian who was to start hot favourite and was the talking horse of the race. Pat was claimed by Prince Khalid Abdullah for Guy Harwood's Now Listen and so I went for the best jockey I could find. That, of course, was Mick Kinane who had ridden for me quite a bit over the years and who had come over to ride three for me at Kempton on Easter Monday that year. We agreed that he should partner Tirol in a getting-to-know you exercise on Newbury racecourse so he flew over, stayed the night at my place, and rode him a nice piece of work the following morning. The Newbury executive is very helpful. Ground permitting, they let me work on the course when I have runners going for Group One races and Mick rode Tirol in a spin up the back straight.

The more Mick went into the chances of the horse, the better he was convinced they were:

> Tirol worked extremely well that day at Newbury and I then spoke to Pat Eddery. He said that he liked the horse a lot and much preferred him to his own mount. He also told Richard that he felt Tirol had the best chance of all the English-trained horses. In the race we were always going well on the stands side and I began to make progress over three furlongs out. I drove him to the front over a furlong from home and kept him going to beat Freddie Head on Machiavellian by two lengths.

Head, who rides with exceptionally short stirrups, is a good jockey in his native France but comes in for plenty of flak on his overseas trips. This race was no exception. He somehow managed to get boxed in on the rails and then bumped Willie Carson's mount, Elmaamul.

Mick went home that evening – he was riding at Gowran Park the next day – but for Tirol's enthusiastic owners the big win was an excuse for a good party. John Horgan, in whose colours Tirol raced, was the eldest of 12 and all but three were at Newmarket. Most of them flew back to County Cork to pour into the Briar Rose pub at Douglas. When they had won their previous Two Thousand Guineas three years earlier with Don't Forget Me, also trained by Hannon, the party laid on by the wealthy cattle dealers went on for a week. Since then, though, John Horgan had undergone a heart bypass operation, given up smoking and taken up walking several miles a day. He pulled out of the Tirol party at 11.00 p.m. – it was only just getting going at that stage – but he made up for it by holding another at his house that lasted throughout the next day.

A fortnight later Tirol paved the way for another Briar Rose binge by landing the Irish 2,000 Guineas with Pat Eddery back on board. Mick was a close third on Lotus Pool, a short head in front of Machiavellian on whom Freddie Head again managed to get boxed in!

Just before he went off to New York to ride Go And Go in the Belmont, Mick had his third ride in the Derby. What was significant about this one, though, was that the colt was owned by Sheikh Mohammed and trained by Henry Cecil. The Sheikh and Cecil also had Razeen in the race. He was ridden by Steve Cauthen and started favourite and River God, a 28-1 chance, was very much the second string. Not that this mattered all that much, as it turned out, because Razeen trailed in 14th of the 18 runners and River God was two places behind him.

8

Flying the Cecil Flag

On the evening of Thursday 26 July 1990 Mick Kinane was riding at Tipperary and, when he returned home for his one real meal of the day, the phone rang. It was Henry Cecil. He had decided to run Belmez as well as Old Vic in the King George VI and Queen Elizabeth Diamond Stakes at Ascot on the Saturday. Steve Cauthen normally rode Belmez but he had decided to partner Cecil's other runner. Could Mick come over to ride Belmez? The jockey explained that, although he would dearly love to do so, Dermot Weld had several runners at Leopardstown that day and was expecting his stable jockey to ride them. Mick would have to ring him and see if he would let him off.

Mick was, naturally enough, keen to ride at Ascot. The King George is one of the most valuable, and sought-after, races in Europe:

> Henry was bullish about Belmez. He said that he had the horse right for the first time since he won the Chester Vase in May and he had beaten the subsequent Epsom Derby winner Quest For Fame that day. Belmez's only subsequent run had been in the Irish Derby when he was third to Salsabil. I'd had a good view of him because I was fourth on Blue Stag. I was even more encouraged when Henry said that the colt had been a bit rusty at the Curragh and was capable of better. I was optimistic that Dermot would let me off because my arrangement with him was by now slightly different. We had spoken earlier in the year about big race

rides coming up and he said he would not stand in my way
if I was offered mounts on good horses and the races in
question were not clashing with important ones in Ireland.

Henry Richard Amherst Cecil, at that time 47, had been training
at Newmarket for 21 years. A tall, dark-haired man, slim with a
swarthy skin and a deceptively laid back approach to life, Cecil had
long since become one of Newmarket's best-known personalities.
He has a fondness for designer clothes, Gucci footwear and flashy
ties, and he owns more pairs of trousers than most women have
shoes. Such was his fondness for clothing products that at one time
he actually owned a shop in Newmarket – he was able to browse to
his heart's content. He also has a passion for rose-gardening but his
seemingly casual outlook belies a deep commitment to his highly
successful stable.

He will often amuse, and confuse, members of the racing press by
turning their questions back on them. 'What do you think?' he will
casually reply when he is asked how good a horse is. The racing
community, which takes its business so seriously, was taken aback
one day to read Cecil quoted as saying 'I don't think God really
cares who wins the 2.30.'

Although he is one of the wealthiest trainers, he has not always
had it easy. The silver spoon he inherited was tarnished at birth. He
and his twin brother David – who had no luck as a trainer and now
runs a pub in Lambourn – never met their father who was killed in
action with the Parachute Regiment in North Africa a fortnight
before they were born. His mother, by all acounts a singularly
beautiful woman, later married Captain Cecil Boyd-Rochfort, the
Queen's trainer and a man who presented a forbidding figure in a
grey homburg and with a walking stick normally in his hand. In fact
the Captain had a soft side to his nature but this did not always
show itself to the two boys. Henry, not much good at his lessons,
failed to get into Eton and was sent to Canford in Dorset where a
system of black marks operated. Three black marks meant the cane
and, somewhat understandably, Cecil grew to resent both the
beatings and the unfairness of them.

He also found it tough when he took over on his stepfather's
retirement at the beginning of 1969. He had over 30 runners before
he trained his first winner and he had to bear hurtful accusations
such as 'not being able to train ivy up a wall'. Sir Noel Murless, his
famous father-in-law, put him on the right road by telling him to

make sure his horses worked when they galloped – 'Instead of going about like a lot of old gentlemen' – and he had hardly looked back since, although at the time of the 1990 King George he had split with Murless's daughter Julie after falling for Natalie Payne, an attractive lawyer's daughter who had been born in Nigeria. The fact that she was young enough to be Cecil's daughter shocked Newmarket almost as much as the trainer's decision to ditch Julie.

Cecil recalls:

> I had wanted to run Belmez all along but the actual decision was taken quite late. With the ground being fast, I felt I could not rely on Old Vic who was having only his second race of the season. Belmez was really fit by this stage, as well as being very well in himself, and I thought he had to take his chance. Mick Kinane had won the previous year's Irish Oaks for me and I had watched him win the Arc on Carroll House. He was the obvious choice for Belmez and, after speaking to him on the phone that Thursday night, I rang Dermot Weld. He kindly agreed to let him off his commitments in Ireland.

But there was an important proviso, one which could have meant Mick sitting out the big race in the jockeys' room feeling foolish and frustrated:

> Because of the ground there was a continuing doubt about Old Vic running and the arrangement was that, if he was pulled out, Steve would switch to Belmez. I flew to Heathrow on the Saturday morning not knowing if I had the ride or not. I didn't know even when I arrived at Ascot. Henry had still to walk the course.

Old Vic was finally given the okay but Belmez only carried Sheikh Mohammed's third colours. In addition to Old Vic, the Sheikh also had In The Wings in the race and the Andre Fabre-trained Coronation Cup winner (ridden by Cash Asmussen) started favourite in preference to Old Vic. Belmez was a 15-2 chance.

Steve Cauthen maintains:

> The ground was drying out fast and Old Vic needed give in it. He had been jarred up for most of the spring because the weather was so dry at Newmarket that year. But we had a

piece of decent ground to work him on and he was ready to run. The problem at Ascot, though, was the speed with which the course was drying. If the race had been run 24 hours earlier, I have no doubt that Old Vic would have beaten Belmez. I felt I was going to win until halfway up the straight when we reached the stage where I had to really let him down. As I did so, I could sense he was beginning to feel the ground. Belmez and Mick were challenging me strongly. Old Vic picked up as I put the question to him and he started to fight. But so did Belmez.

By this stage his opponent was scenting victory:

Although I hadn't seen it, Cash Amussen was hampered over three furlongs out and in the straight I drove Belmez up to old Vic. From then on it was a battle all the way to the line. When I drew up alongside I felt I could win if only I could control him and keep him straight. Belmez was going marginally the better but he was proving difficult to ride. He hung a bit to the right, and then a bit to the left, whereas Old Vic seemed to be staying on strongly and as straight as a die. It was nip and tuck all the way to the post where I was a neck in front.

Anthony Stroud, the Sheikh's racing manager, came up to me as I dismounted and said 'Well done, a great ride' and Henry said much the same. Afterwards I was introduced to the Queen. I'd never met her before and I was struck by how interested she is in racing, and by how much she knows about it. She presented me with a special key ring and said 'It looked a great race. Was it as thrilling to ride in as it looked from the stands?'

Henry seemed happy enough about the outcome but I couldn't help sensing that he was a bit disappointed that it was Belmez, not Old Vic, that had won it for him. But there was no disappointment on my part, and I wasn't too worried about Old Vic either!

Cecil, though, confirms that Mick's impression was correct: 'Although I was thrilled to have both first and second, I would love to have seen them finish the other way round. I was a bit sad that Old Vic hadn't won. He was rather special to me, having won both the French Derby and the Irish Derby the previous year.'

This was Cecil's second King George and the first for Sheikh Mohammed who showed his appreciation by sending the jockey a handsome cheque. It was also the first time that a trainer had sent out both the first and second in this race. Cecil, in a manner more reminiscent of a warring monarch in the Middle Ages than of a modern-day racehorse trainer, invariably orders his family flag to be raised when he has a Group One winner. Belmez's victory proved no exception and the flag stayed aloft for a week.

Two days afterwards it might well have had to be lowered to half mast because Belmez's headline-making jockey was involved in a helicopter scare which, if the fates had been a little less kind, could have seen the end of M. J. Kinane.

> It was the first day of the Galway festival and, because the traffic can be appalling, I travelled backwards and forwards most days with Dermot Weld by helicopter. On that Monday evening Mick O'Toole flew back to the Curragh with us and the chopper was piloted by Ciaran Haughey, son of the then Taoiseach, Charlie Haughey. The first sign that something was wrong came ten minutes after take-off when we noticed some smoke coming from the engine. But it soon cleared and we thought there was no need to worry until some time later when Ciaran said it was leaking oil. We were well over halfway at this stage but Ciaran insisted it was much too risky to try to carry on. He said he was going to make an emergency landing but there was nowhere suitable. We were all getting a bit windy by then and Ciaran set us down in the middle of a bog. We could see where the nearest road was. We made our way across the bog to it and started thumbing. We managed to get a lift into the nearest town – Portarlington – and we then rang for a car to pick us up. It was quite an experience.

But the King George win, particularly as it was for Sheikh Mohammed, fuelled speculation that Mick would move to England. It seemed only a question of when and the newspapers were determined not to be caught flat-footed. Some actually succeeded in jumping the gun. Even three weeks before the King George, one paper carried a report that he was on the verge of accepting an offer to ride for John Gosden the following season.

It wasn't true. I received no approach from John Gosden and, at that stage, none from anybody else either. I told the papers that too but it didn't stop the stories continuing.

Indeed it didn't and in mid-October, when the speculation was reaching fever-pitch, I put the phone down after speaking to Mick convinced that something would be fixed up by the weekend. My impression was that he would stay in Ireland, with Weld still having first claim, but there would be greater freedom to take big race mounts for Sheikh Mohammed who would pay him a retainer. When my story appeared in *The Sporting Life* the following day Anthony Stroud, whose patience was fast wearing thin with the authors of such reports and the papers who printed them, wasted little time in ringing with an angry denial accompanied by an aggrieved 'Why don't you check these things with me before you write them?'

In fact, as Stroud reveals, the agreement was little more than an understanding: 'It was simply that, whenever there was an opportunity for Mick to ride for us, he would do so. But there was no question of a retainer.'

The Arc went by without the super-sub but in the Cartier Million, run a week later that year, he was on the fourth favourite and the most expensive horse in the race. Cost seldom proves to be a decisive element in a racehorse but Rinka Das, an American bred colt by Nureyev and trained by Dermot Weld, landed the £515,000 first prize in style.

The crowd was the biggest the Park had seen since Lester Piggott won the Phoenix Champion Stakes on Commanche Run just over five years earlier, and I was coasting all the way. I tracked Michael Kauntze's strongly fancied Stark South to begin with but, despite all the money for him, he was not travelling all that well and so I moved up to track Michael Roberts on Too Conspicuous. Rinka Das was not much bigger than a pony but he had a lot of speed. Even three furlongs out – the race was over seven – I knew none of those in front could beat me. I started riding over a furlong later. I hit the front just inside the last and we came away to beat Kooyonga – Michael Kauntze's other runner – by a length and a half. The sponsors presented me with a gold watch and at Dundalk two days later I rode my 1,000th Irish winner.

Muscari, the horse who started it all. This picture was taken after he won a sprint at Bellewstown in 1980 ten days after Mick Kinane's 21st birthday. Note how chubby he was. (Liam Healy)

(left to right) Thomas, Tommy, Mick and Jayo. This was taken at Thurles nine days before Mick's 20th birthday. (Liam Healy)

Being led in after winning the 1986 Indian Derby on Sir Bruce, the horse Kinane was offered a small fortune to stop later in the season. (R.S. Gupta)

Royal Ascot 1994. The press praised this ride to the heights as Mick's determination got Grand Lodge (near side) home in the closing stages of the St James's Palace Stakes. But the stewards banned him for the use of his whip. A storm in a tea cup, though, compared with what happened 48 hours later when a drunken spectator ducked under the rails and brought down both Mick and his mount. (Ed Byrne)

'Will you win on this one, Daddy?' Sinead goes through the form with her father while Catherine and Aisling look on. (Pat Healy)

Classic Cliche is led in after winning the 1996 Ascot Gold Cup. (Gerry Cranham)

Cartier Million day marked the end of racing at Phoenix Park after 88 years. It had come near to closing back in 1930 when the previous year's Wall Street crash had a disastrous impact with the depression setting in and attendances slumping. In 1979, though, the major shareholders – the Arnott family – indicated they wanted out and two years later they sold to a consortium that included Robert Sangster, the millionaire whose fortunes were based on Vernons Pools and who used his money to turn horses into fortune-earning stallions.

> 'I was at a coursing fixture at Thurles,' says Sangster, 'when I was summoned to a meeting with Patrick Gallagher of the Gallagher Group, a Dublin-based building firm which sponsored some of the Park's best races. Patrick wanted Vincent O'Brien, John Magnier and me to take 25 per cent each while he would also buy a quarter share. I pointed out that owning racecourses was not my scene. What I wanted was to be able to race my horses on them and so I said I was only prepared to buy five per cent. We eventually agreed that Vincent and John would also take five per cent. So would Danny Schwartz and Stavros Niarchos, while Gallagher would own 75 per cent. We also agreed that the place had to be brought up to date and rebuilt. However, when the builders were three-quarters of the way through their work, Gallagher went bust and the rest of us were landed with the whole course. I was a most reluctant purchaser and I found myself with almost 42 per cent of the shares.

When the Phoenix rose from the ashes, or to be more accurate from the builders' rubble, in 1983 a massive sponsorship campaign saw a backer for every race. It seemed the course could not go wrong. But it did. While Ireland's high society were encouraged to bring their money and their friends to the Park, the ordinary racegoer found himself being treated as just that. He was less than amused by the sight of a noisy, privileged few knocking back champagne by the crate in sacrosanct areas fenced off from the common hordes by white-painted railings. Joe Soap was, quite literally, beyond the pale. He began to stay away, despite all the hard work put into the promotion of the course by Jonathan Irwin who somehow found the time to run Phoenix Park as well as

Goffs. The course's early losses continued and they started to hurt for reasons totally unconnected with attendance figures.

When the course was reopened under the backing of Sangster and his racing partners, a well bred yearling could – in two years – be transformed into a stallion that was worth more than his weight in gold. Of course this didn't happen to them all but it could be made to happen to enough if you had sufficient Group races to aim at and you were sufficiently skilful. It was Vincent O'Brien who had the Midas touch with selecting and training the horses while his son-in-law was able to exploit the stallion opportunities.

But it didn't last. The bloodstock market went into decline, those Phoenix Park Group races no longer boosted a horse's value sky-high and, as O'Brien, Magnier and Sangster cut costs at the Coolmore Stud they owned between them, so the racecourse losses came under scrutiny. Eventually the shareholders decided to call it a day.

When they did so, the course was owned two per cent by Michael Smurfit and 98 per cent by a company called Lymond Investments. Robert Sangster and Vincent O'Brien each owned 42 per cent of the shares in this company and John Magnier held the other 16 per cent. To the horror of just about everybody else in Irish racing, they submitted an application to build nearly 600 houses and flats on the 100-acre course plus a hotel. Eventually the planning authorities said no but the owners refused to countenance a return to racing. Indeed the course had already closed when the planning application was turned down.

Most of the Group races were transferred to the Curragh, Leopardstown and Tipperary but the loss of Phoenix Park was a bitter blow to Irish racing, not least to Mick and his boss who had enjoyed so many great moments there.

Mick also lost his championship in 1990. Jim Bolger set a new record for races won and the bulk of his 125 flat winners were ridden by Christy Roche. The jockey who had stitched up Mick 'like a kipper' at the Park 14 years earlier scored a runaway title win to end Mick's six-year reign and equal his 113-winner record. The outgoing champion finished 33 behind. Had it not been for all the big race victories it might even have been depressing.

Roche put it all in perspective by saying, 'My aim all that season had been to ride 100 winners because that was something I had never done. Equalling Mick's record was a bonus but taking the title off him meant a lot to me simply because he was riding so well.'

In many ways 1991 was an anti-climax. Mick did not even have a ride in either the Derby or the King George and nor, surprisingly, did he have one in the Irish Derby. There was no winner at Royal Ascot either and, although he and Dermot Weld had another crack at the Belmont, Smooth Performance failed to live up to his name in the American classic and finished with only two behind him.

In the Arc he was booked by American trainer Billy Wright for El Senor, a seven-year-old who had won 12 of his 40 starts in the States plus nearly $1.8 million. But he proved no match for the top European horses and managed only ninth behind the Cash Asmussen-ridden Sauve Dancer. Even the jockeys' title was not all it might have been. True, he regained it but his 111-winner total was two short of the record which was now only half his.

His only real achievement that year was in causing the Irish rule book to be rewritten – and he regarded that as an achievement he could have done without. At Tipperary in August he rode the Weld-trained Desert Thunder in a five furlong nursery. The gelding started hot favourite but, as he left the stalls, he brushed the blinkers he was wearing against the metal framework and they were knocked out of position. Instead of restricting the horse's vision to what was in front of him, the blinkers were almost blinding him. It was a frightening moment for both horse and rider. Mick leaned right forward and managed to pull them off. Then, carrying the blinkers in his non-whip hand, he drove the horse to the line to snatch a neck verdict. He duly weighed in, still carrying the blinkers. Neither the spectators nor the stewards had seen what had happened. It was only when the photo finish print was pinned up outside the weighing room that somebody noticed the horse was not wearing blinkers when he passed the post. By the time this reached the notice of the stewards and they decided to hold an inquiry, Mick was on his way home.

The rules stated that, if a horse was declared to run in blinkers, he must wear them on the way to the start and during the race. If he did not, he was to be disqualified. The rule did not specifically state that the blinkers had to be worn during the whole race but that was the implication.

The stewards resumed their inquiry at Tralee six days later and amazingly they ruled that Desert Thunder should keep the race but they put all the all the blame on the trainer and jockey. Dermot Weld was given a severe caution for failing to ensure the blinkers were properly fitted and Mick was hammered with a £500 fine. Quite how Weld was meant to make sure that the blinkers remained in their original position after striking into the stalls was something the stewards failed to explain. Mick was ruled to be 'grossly negligent' in failing to report the incident to the stewards yet the reporting rule (which stipulates that anything that may have affected a horse's running must be reported to the stewards) applies only to the trainer and the owner, not to the jockey.

> The fine cost me more than if the stewards had taken the race off me. I considered lodging an appeal against the decision but I eventually came to the conclusion there was little to be gained. I still felt I was harshly treated, though, and I believe the stewards had decided to make an example of me.

It was not much consolation when the relevant rule was later changed to state that a horse should not be disqualified when it failed to wear the blinkers with with which it was declared.

The 1992 season began badly. Mick made his worst ever start and the campaign was five weeks old before he got off the mark on Supportive at Leopardstown on 18 April. Two races earlier he had been beaten a neck by Lester Piggott on the Vincent O'Brien-trained Portico in the 2,000 Guineas Trial. The horse he was riding was Brief Truce, one of Moyglare's American breds, on whom high hopes were pinned. The colt returned to Leopardstown three weeks later to win a Listed race in fine style but in the Irish 2,000 Guineas he managed only third to Robert Sangster's Rodrigo de Triano on whom Piggott, at the ripe old age of 56, was winning his 16th Irish classic.

Brief Truce had been the first of the six runners to come under pressure and it looked ominously as if he was not going to be quite up to the required standard. This impression was confirmed when he won the ten furlong Gallinule Stakes the following month. He raced lazily and only scored by a length, and then only after Mick had had to drive him along. Weld and Moyglare decided they could not justify the £75,000 supplementary entry fee for the Irish Derby – in any case the colt was not bred to get the trip – and they elected to drop him back to a mile in the St James's Palace Stakes at Royal Ascot.

However even that looked a shot in the dark. Rodrigo de Triano was again among the opposition and, even more to the point, so was the supposed wonder horse Arazi trained in France by Francois Boutin. This colt had swept all before him as a two-year-old and had produced the most amazing turn of foot to win the Breeders' Cup Juvenile at Churchill Downs in Kentucky. He had surprisingly flopped when sent back there for the Kentucky Derby but he was expected to make amends in the Royal Ascot race and Steve Cauthen's mount started odds-on. Brief Truce was ignored at 25-1.

But Lester Piggott this time failed to shine on Rodrigo de Triano and Mick got up in the last stride to beat Richard Hills on Zaahi who had tried to lead throughout. Arazi flopped again while Mick went on to complete his first Royal Ascot double on Richard Hannon's Beyton in the King Edward VII Stakes just over an hour later.

Kinane and the brave Brief Truce then went close in both the Prix du Moulin at Longchamp and the Queen Elizabeth II Stakes at Ascot. Next stop was the Breeders' Cup Mile, worth an incredible £267,380 to the winner, at Gulfstream Park in Florida. The race was run on turf and so was expected to suit the European-trained horses. Arazi, who had gone some way towards redeeming his reputation by winning at Longchamp on Arc day, again started favourite but Mick fancied his chances. At least he did until things went disastrously wrong at the start.

> There were 13 other runners – nine from America, Ian Balding's Selkirk and three from France. In America they have teams of handlers to hold the horses' heads when they are in the stalls. This helps to keep them steady and standing square but Brief Truce was not used to this and so we made a special request that no handler should be with him once he was loaded. They were almost all in when one of the team saw Brief Truce with no handler. He leapt up onto the framework to grab the horse. He thought he was helping.
>
> I shouted at him 'No. We don't want a handler. Leave him go. Leave him go.' Brief Truce, who was a particularly intelligent horse, turned his head round to see what was going on. As he did so, the starter pressed the button and the gates opened. Brief Truce totally missed the break and he lost an impossible amount of ground as well as all chance of getting into a decent position. In America the

courses are on the turn most of the way and so it's hard to improve your position without going wide and losing even more ground. Brief Truce ran on really strongly in the closing stages but he could only manage third. I'm not saying I would definitely have won if that handler had not intervened. Lure, who made all, won very easily and he proved just how good he was by winning the race again the following year. But Brief Truce was the only horse that day to come from stone last to make the frame and I am convinced we would have given Lure a real run for his money.

The Breeders' Cup Meeting was held at the very end of October and I flew there from Hong Kong. I'd left Ireland nearly three weeks earlier because this was the first winter I was to spend six months in Hong Kong. When I left, Christy Roche was 16 winners behind me but he was going great guns so I decided to stop off in Ireland on my way back. I had time to take in just one meeting, the Wednesday one at the Curragh, and I won on Sinissipi for John Oxx. It was my 100th Irish winner of the season and, since Christy drew a blank, it meant I was champion for the eighth time. But the long flight back that night was just about the only chance I had to reflect on it because I was riding work at Sha Tin at 5.00 the next morning!

Brief Truce was not his only big race ride of significance that year. At the end of May he won the Italian Derby for the first time on In A Tiff. Henry Cecil again called him up for a ride in the Derby and he finished fifth in the Sheikh Mohammed colours on Twist And Turn. He also donned the now famous maroon with white sleeves to win one of Germany's best races, the Aral Pokal, on Tel Quel who was trained at Chantilly by the brilliant Andre Fabre.

However in Ireland he was out of luck on Market Booster in the two fillies classics. He rode this game Moyglare-owned filly to win both the Pretty Polly and the Meld Stakes, but in the Irish 1,000 Guineas he was beaten a length by Walter Swinburn on Marling and in the Irish Oaks he failed by only a neck to floor the odds laid on User Friendly.

If Mick felt sick at this narrow defeat – he has never found getting beaten exactly easy to take – it was nothing to what his old

rival Christy Roche went through. Roche finished last on Ivyanna
– on whom he had won the Italian Oaks – but he was about to lose
a far bigger battle. At Naas in June the patrol film suggested that
he had hit an apprentice with his whip and the stewards gave him
a 15-day ban for improper riding. It meant that he would miss the
ride in the Irish Derby on St Jovite.

Roche lodged an appeal and the hearing was fixed for the Friday
before the big race. The jockey's legal team maintained that this was
not suitable and they unsuccessfully applied to the High Court for
an injunction to stop the hearing going ahead. The stewards, having
won the opening skirmishes, then climbed down and adjourned the
hearing. They were widely condemned for giving in and Roche
stormed to a 12-length victory on St Jovite in Ireland's most
important race.

But this proved to be a long way from the end of the matter.
When the appeal was eventually heard, Roche lost and was told he
had to pay £5,000 towards the costs. On the eve of the Irish Oaks
his lawyers sought an injunction again and this time they were
successful. But the injunction was only an interim one, the
stewards decided to fight it and two days before Roche was due to
ride St Jovite in the King George VI and Queen Elizabeth Diamond
Stakes the High Court ruled that he could not have any further
injunctions. His suspension started immediately, Stephen Craine
won the King George on Jim Bolger's brilliant colt and Roche was
left with legal bills that made the £5,000 levied by the stewards
seem like peanuts.

Mick was also involved with the stewards at this time and he
too was hit with a suspension that threatened to stop him riding
in the Irish Oaks. He also brought in lawyers to help him.

> At Bellewstown in the week after the Irish Derby I won a
> race on Cliveden Gail who was later to become a much
> improved horse, winning the Irish Cesarewitch and running
> in the Melbourne Cup. Warren O'Connor, who finished
> third on Marilyn, tried to hold me in when I went for a gap.
> The two horses made contact and the local stewards said I
> was to blame. They suspended me for three days, starting
> on the day of the Irish Oaks. I don't normally lodge appeals
> – there doesn't usually prove to be much point – but I was
> harshly treated and I felt that this was one I could win. The
> hearing took place in the stewards room on the Curragh

racecourse and I won my case. But there were no hard feelings with Warren. He made a point of shaking hands with me as we came out of the hearing.

9

Delhi Difficulties

On Wednesday, 13 January 1993 the phone rang in the Kinanes' luxury flat overlooking Hong Kong harbour. It was Anthony Stroud and the call heralded one of the most turbulent fortnights in the jockey's life.

Steve Cauthen, said Stroud, had decided not to renew his contract as first jockey to Sheikh Mohammed and would not be returning to England for the 1993 season. Stroud was offering the job to Mick. It would be a one year contract and he would need to be based in England, probably at Newmarket. Stroud wanted to know if he would be interested.

It was, although Stroud did not say so, the best job any jockey in Europe could wish for. Sheikh Mohammed bin Rashid Al Maktoum – to give him his full title – is by far the world's biggest racehorse owner, with some 600 horses, and they are bred to be the best. The third eldest of the four Maktoum brothers (Maktoum Al Maktoum, Hamdan and Ahmed are the others), he is the Crown Prince of Dubai and the Minister for Defence of the United Arab Emirates. A slight man with a black beard and a serious expression seemingly permanently on his face, he is quiet and reserved. He studied at Cambridge and at the Mons Officer Cadet School in Aldershot. He is a qualified airline pilot and his many property investments include a huge estate in the Scottish Highlands as well as a significant part of the best stud land in County Kildare. He is best known for his passion for racing and for the millions he spends on it each year. These millions come from the oil wells of Dubai on the Arabian Gulf. Dubai, although small geographically, is immensely wealthy and this wealth is concentrated in the hands of the Maktoums.

Sheikh Mohammed and his brothers are generous employers and to be given the chance of riding as first jockey to the most famous of them would have had most of his colleagues jumping for joy. But Kinane is a reserved character and, as those who have had occasion to telephone him will testify, a man who gives away as little as possible over the phone.

When Stroud asked if he would be interested in taking the job, the caller was greeted with a guarded 'I might be.' Mick asked for more details of exactly what was involved. Stroud said he would put them on paper and fax them to him within a few days. Mick discussed the call with Catherine and what would be involved if he said yes.

> To be Sheikh Mohammed's first jockey is the ultimate and I felt it was a great honour even to be asked. I also felt that I had worked for much of my life for the chance to be offered such a job. On the other hand taking it would have meant a big disruption in the lives of Catherine and our two daughters, Sinead and Aisling. The two girls had just begun one big change in their lives, spending half the school year in Hong Kong with a different educational system and different friends. They would have had to change all over again. I wasn't at all sure that I had any right to ask this of them. But Catherine said I should give it a go. I think, though, that she was worried I might say no for the sake of her and the girls. By saying go ahead, she thought she was making it easier for me.

The fact that Steve Cauthen had decided to turn his back on the job was a shock. He had long since put his early Kentucky Kid nickname and image behind him. He had become one of the most important, most successful and most respected figures on the English turf. He was also the best paid with a huge retainer – said by some press reports to be £750,000 a year. But both he and Anthony Stroud are adamant that this was a figment of somebody's imagination.

'That figure was simply not correct,' says Cauthen while Stroud adds, 'Although I never discuss such sums, I am prepared to state that £750,000 was a gross over-estimate.'

It has also been reported that Cauthen had been informed his retainer was to be halved in 1993. This was nearer the mark.

> The facts of the matter were that I was being offered a cut in pay and I was not at all happy about it. I didn't feel it was right and that's why I chose not to renew my retainer. Indeed I have not ridden professionally since. Instead I run my stud farm in Kentucky and I work for my local track, Turfway Park. I do PR for them as well as their radio and television commercials. I have also done a bit of commentating for ABC and ESPN, and I play a lot of golf.

Cauthen was only 32 when he bowed out of race-riding. It was a terrible waste of an outstanding talent. Even though he constantly had to battle with his weight, he could have continued at the top for another ten years. Mick decided to ring him in Kentucky.

> Steve was most helpful. We talked at length about what was involved in the job and the complexities of it. As a result I had a much greater understanding of the whole thing.

On Monday, 18 January Anthony Stroud's detailed offer arrived and just after 6.00 p.m. that evening he sent a short fax to the Press Association stating that Steve Cauthen's contract would not be renewed. There was no mention of who would replace him but the racing journalists were in little doubt. It would be either Mick Kinane or Michael Roberts, who had been champion jockey the previous season. Those same journalists started ringing Hong Kong. Some already had Mick's number. The rest soon found it.

> There seemed to be massive press interest and the never-ending telephone calls nearly drove me round the bend. I have found that the attentions of the press soon become the hardest part of anything like this and the tension the calls bring makes life very difficult. Over the next two days I often took the phone off the hook but I couldn't do it all the time. I had my life to lead and, as I was negotiating with Anthony Stroud and his people, I had to be both in contact and contactable.

One of the first things Mick did when he received the offer was to ring Dermot Weld. The Rosewell House boss trained the odd horse for Sheikh Mohammed but that was all. Moyglare and Michael Smurfit were his main patrons.

I felt I should put Dermot in the picture. Our long association deserved that, at the very least. I was a bit concerned that he might have already left for America but fortunately he was still in Ireland. He was very good about the whole thing and he did not put any pressure on me to turn down the offer. Indeed he said it was an honour for me to be asked. We had already agreed terms for 1993. There was no signed contract, there never has been, just a verbal agreement, but I knew he would not have stood in my way if I had decided to take the Sheikh Mohammed job.

The following morning Mick sounded out David Oughton at Sha Tin:

He and I had become good friends by this time. Initially he seemed to think I should take the job even though it would have meant leaving him, or at least substantially reducing our six month arrangement because I would have been committed to England from March to November. We discussed it over and over again. We then got down to the nitty gritty of the actual contract and the pros and cons of accepting it. I began to realise there was quite a lot against it.

By this stage Anthony Stroud had confirmed to the press that an offer had been made to the Irish champion. Mick's phone hardly stopped. Those who got through were told he could not comment. But more and more it was taken off the hook. Sometimes, when he did answer it, he picked up the receiver and remained silent. He waited for the caller to announce himself. If it was a journalist, he stayed silent until the caller hung up. On other occasions Catherine answered and informed the bemused reporter that he was speaking to a Chinese laundry!

But the constant phone calls were incidental to Mick's most pressing problem, the contract. This was not sufficiently specific, the money wasn't as much as he had expected and the implications of making the wrong decision were building up like a black storm cloud darkening the horizon. He wasn't feeling well either.

I rang Anthony Stroud a few times about various points but I didn't really feel I was getting anywhere. I came to the conclusion that the only way to negotiate the thing properly was to meet and talk it over face to face – that way you can assess exactly what the other person's feelings are on any particular point – and so I told Anthony that I wanted to fly to London to meet him. He was happy enough about this and I booked myself onto the British Airways flight that left Hong Kong late on Wednesday night. I planned to meet Anthony for lunch on Thursday and fly back that night. Hong Kong is eight hours ahead so I would be back on Friday afternoon in plenty of time to ride at Sha Tin that weekend.

Mick then realised why he wasn't feeling well. He had 'flu and was running a temperature. Most people would have gone to bed and postponed the trip until they felt better. Not Mick Kinane. He went ahead as determinedly as if the most valuable winning post in the world was in sight, and in a way it was.

I felt it was important to go ahead and get things sorted out without any further delay. I thought that, with a bit of luck, the worst of the 'flu might be over by the time I reached Heathrow. Certainly it should have been by the time I got back, and I was travelling first-class so I knew I would be reasonably comfortable. The fare cost me quite a bit, nearly £4,000, but it was worth it. Apart from the 'flu and getting over it, I wanted to arrive in the right frame of mind for the discussions.

Sheikh Mohammed's racing manager said he would book him into the Maktoum owned Carlton Tower Hotel in Knightsbridge. Mick then made another call, to Michael Surdival in Dublin. The chartered accountant handles Mick's tax affairs and is a close friend. He agreed to fly to London for the discussions.

Despite the 'flu, Mick rode at Happy Valley on the Wednesday evening and then went straight to the airport. The problems of the previous week and all those telephone calls were nothing compared with the flight.

It was the worst I have ever experienced. When the plane touched down for the scheduled stop in New Delhi I was still feeling dreadful and the stop seemed to go on a long time. We were told that the plane had developed hydraulic problems and, some two to three hours after we landed, there was another announcement. British Airways had to get a part flown out from London. The plane was going to be delayed between 22 and 24 hours. This was no good to me. It meant I wouldn't have enough time to travel on to London and be back in time for Sha Tin. I thought of cancelling the whole thing and heading back to Hong Kong. But I found that plane had already left. I was snookered. I was also feeling more and more ill. I still had a temperature and it seemed to be getting worse. It was like a nightmare, only more so.

Eventually I found out that there was an Air India flight going to Frankfurt. I felt that, if I could get as far as Germany, I should be able to pick up a London plane without being delayed all that much more. But I promptly ran into more hassle. There was some sort of dispute with the ground staff and I was told that I could not board the Air India plane. This was ridiculous. I had no luggage, only hand baggage, I told them. All I had to do was walk up the steps. I wasn't involving the ground staff. Still they said no. They then said that the dispute meant they could not even change my ticket. I tried again, and again, and again. It was almost impossible to believe that I could be in such a pickle. I would have given anything to get out of it. It was not until I had been in the airport for eight hours that somebody eventually relented and let me travel on an Air India flight to London. I finally reached Heathrow in late morning.

Anthony Stroud, alerted to the problems in India, decided there was no point in rushing back from Ireland where he was staying. He went hunting instead. The meeting was put back until the evening when the discussions would take place over dinner. Sheikh Mohammed's racing manager had already made plans to take with him Simon Crisford and Justin Wadham. The latter was a lawyer, then attached to the Sheikh's Darley Stud Management team on a consultancy basis and subsequently appointed its managing director. Crisford was also to go on to higher things. He had been assistant trainer to Sir Mark Prescott and then the *Racing Post*'s Newmarket correspondent before becoming Stroud's assistant. He was later promoted to racing manager when the Sheikh set up his own highly successful Godolphin operation.

Anthony Stroud, though, was very much the man in charge and he hosted the dinner. He is a Kinane fan and Mick, although he didn't realise just how much at the time, owed a lot to him. He was also to owe a whole lot more to him before the year was out.

Stroud, tall and fair-haired, has the sort of upright bearing that a generation ago might have suggested a Guards officer. He is typical of the sort of public school-educated men the Maktoums have picked to help them run their breeding and racing empires. He projects an image of a person confident in himself but wary of what others are going to say to him, as if he is about to face a question that might dig deeper than he is prepared to go. Possibly this comes from all his dealings with the press who normally want to probe what lies behind all the various decisions made by his boss. Sheikh Mohammed, like many people in his position, usually prefers to keep himself and his thought processes a dignified distance apart.

The son of a reasonably well-off farmer, Anthony Stroud was born on New Year's Day 1956 and brought up in Downpatrick in Northern Ireland. He was sent to prep school at Mourne Grange and, when he was 13, to public school at Rydal in Wales. He was mad on riding and did a lot of showjumping, hunting and three-day eventing. When he left school, he decided he wanted to go into racing. He began by helping to prepare yearlings for the sales at the McGrath family's Brownstown Stud on the Curragh. From there he went to the National Stud at Newmarket and then to the British Bloodstock Agency.

He moved to America and got a job with the legendary trainer Charlie Whittingham. By this stage he wanted to become a trainer. He spent a season with Fred Winter but it was only when John Dunlop offered him a job as his assistant that he realised he did not have the necessary capital. His career then took off in a new direction, thanks to a curious combination of circumstances. His parents had asked their racing-mad son to buy them a cheap racehorse. Anthony found one for £500. Called Quarry Stone, the gelding was trained near Dundalk by Bunny Cox and he proved useful. Bunny's wife, Sally, is the daughter of Aubrey Brabazon who was then a director of the Curragh Bloodstock Agency. The CBA was on the lookout for a suitable young man with the necessary experience. Aubrey, formerly a brilliant jockey both on the flat and over jumps, told his fellow directors about Quarry Stone and the man who had bought him. Stroud was offered the job.

One of the trainers the CBA's new man began buying horses for was Vincent O'Brien's elder son, David, whose brilliance attracted the patronage of Sheikh Mohammed. In 1985, some five years after Stroud joined the CBA, the Sheikh's stud manager Robert Acton –

another in the same slightly reserved, public school mould – informed him that his boss was looking for a racing manager. Acton wanted to know whom Stroud would recommend. The bloodstock agent put forward half a dozen names, all of people a lot older and more experienced than himself. The Sheikh studied the list and decided he preferred the man who had drawn it up. Stroud was asked to fly to Dubai for an interview. He returned with one of the most influential jobs in racing.

'It was me who picked Michael Kinane to ride Alydaress in the 1989 Irish Oaks,' Stroud recalls. He seldom refers to Kinane as Mick, seemingly prefering the more formal Michael. 'I considered him to be an extremely able rider, he was strong and he knew the Curragh really well. I recommended him to Henry Cecil and he did an admirable job. By the time it came to River God in the following year's Derby, it had been established that Kinane was a really talented jockey of international standing, and one that we'd had luck with.'

When Steve Cauthen said no to the reduced retainer, Stroud asked the four trainers who had the bulk of the Sheikh Mohammed horses who he should go for. Andre Fabre said that Michael Roberts was the man and so did Michael Stoute ('I was on holiday in Barbados when Anthony rang with the news. I pointed out that Kinane was based in Ireland and had his life sorted out over there, whereas Roberts was based in Newmarket and was the reigning champion jockey'). But Henry Cecil and John Gosden both wanted the Irishman.

'So did I,' says Anthony Stroud, 'and I used my casting vote. But, perhaps significantly so far as the future was concerned, I remember saying to Simon Crisford that the bold step would be to sign up Frankie Dettori instead.'

When Sheikh Mohammed's racing manager was on his way from Ireland to the Carlton Tower Hotel, the phone rang in Mick's room. It was Stan Cosgrove. Moyglare wanted Mick to stay with Dermot Weld and, if he did, the stud was prepared to increase his retainer. And that wasn't the only incentive. The Aga Khan, through his intermediaries, also got in touch. If Mick stayed in Ireland, the Aga would like to take out a second retainer on him to ride the horses he had with John Oxx.

Mick lay back on his bed contemplating the options and for the first time in 48 hours he was able to forget his bout of 'flu. Everybody likes to be wanted and the Moyglare offer, while not substantial, showed just how much he was needed. The Aga Khan call was considerably more than the icing on the cake. The Aga had some superb bloodstock, almost all of his own breeding, and John Oxx trained more than 80 horses for him. With two of the three most powerful stables in Ireland (Jim Bolger's was the third) at his disposal, he would be saying goodbye to an awful lot if he moved to Newmarket. On the other hand, how could he turn down the best job in racing?

Anthony Stroud was also marshalling his thoughts as he headed towards Knightsbridge, and weighing up his chances of success. Kinane was the man he had chosen, he was convinced he was the right person for the job but the reservations the jockey had expressed in his calls from Hong Kong suggested he might well say no. He had, though, taken the trouble to fly a third of the way across the world to discuss the matter. Surely, that meant he was not far off accepting?

When they met Mick introduced Michael Surdival, shook hands with Simon Crisford and was introduced to Justin Wadham. This is Anthony Stroud's version of what happened in the Carlton Tower Hotel that Thursday night:

> We talked all through dinner. The financial aspect was obviously a major consideration. Michael was not happy with the money and he made it clear that the retainer we were offering was less than what he was already getting. With his Hong Kong arrangement and his backing from Moyglare, he was obviously in a strong negotiating position whereas Sheikh Mohammed had told me that there was only a certain amount that we could pay him. I suspected, although I obviously didn't know for sure, that increased offers had been made to encourage him to stay put. Clearly he loved Ireland and, equally clearly, he had strong reservations about moving his family to England. At the end of the meal my feeling was that, although I myself had certain fears about him turning down the job, he still had an open mind about it.

But Stroud read the final signals wrongly – as Mick relates:

> I left the table thinking I would end up saying no. The money was a significant factor because it wasn't as much as I wanted. I don't think it would be right to say how much the offer was

– as they haven't said, I feel I shouldn't either – but it wasn't enough. Also Anthony and his team didn't seem quite sure exactly what their structure was going to be so far as, for example, riding all the French-trained horses was concerned. I felt it could well prove to be the most difficult year of all to hold down such a job. There was also some doubt in my mind as to whether it was too big a job for one jockey with all those horses spread among so many different trainers. Also the initial contract was for only one year. But the principal drawback was that I would be exchanging for all these uncertainties everything I had – my contracts with Dermot Weld and David Oughton, and now with the Aga Khan too, and a way of life that I loved.

When Mick returned to Hong Kong, one of the first things he did was to see the top officials in the Jockey Club in a bid to find out where he stood as regards the future. He didn't want to find that, after kissing Sheikh Mohammed's job goodbye, his Hong Kong contract would be taken away from him.The Hong Kong Jockey Club likes a rapid turnover of expatriate jockeys because it fears they could become victims of corruption if they keep going back every year. Mick informed the officials that a six month contract was no good to him if its renewal was going to be subject to an annual question mark. The final nail was hammered in the coffin of the job offer when the officials told him he would be welcome to go out every year for as long as they had the power to say yes or no.

On Tuesday, 26 January 1993 – just 13 days after that first call from Anthony Stroud – Mick rang him back to say that he was sorry but he could not accept the job. Stroud was surprised.

I understood his reasons, particularly those involving his family and his loyalty to Dermot Weld, but I couldn't understand him turning down the chance to ride the best horses in the world and to gain access to trainers of the calibre of Andre Fabre and Henry Cecil. If I had been him, and been champion jockey in Ireland eight times already, I would have jumped at the opportunity of having a crack at the British title. After all Pat Eddery did it, albeit the other way round. He was champion in Britain before linking up with Vincent O'Brien and winning the Irish title. I would have thought the lure of the championship would have been an ultra-powerful incentive for a man at the top of his profession.

Anthony Stroud was right in what he said. The British championship would have added a real crown to Mick Kinane's many achievements. Also the top job in European racing would have been a natural progression for him and the chance to ride the best horses is something most jockeys can only dream about. But Mick is different from most jockeys. Who else would have spent 13 days researching the whole thing before stunning the world's media by choosing to look the golden gift horse in the mouth? However neither Stroud nor his first choice jockey had a crystal ball and, as things turned out, that British championship would almost certainly have proved no more than an agonisingly painful illusion and Mick Kinane's career would have suffered an almost irreversible blow. He would have gone down in racing history as the Irish champion who failed to bridge the gap between his native country and the more exacting demands imposed by racing in Britain. He would have been driven back to Ireland with his tail between his legs. Instead he was to establish his claim to the title of big race king with an across-the-world double never before achieved in the same year.

10

The Jam Stick

Soon after that 26 January telephone call, Anthony Stroud signed up Michael Roberts as the Sheikh Mohammed stable jockey. His was also a one year contract, although by this time the decision had been taken to exclude those horses trained in France by Andre Fabre. Roberts was the obvious second choice. The previous season he had ridden an amazing 206 winners. At the time only one other jockey – Pat Eddery in 1990 – had succeeded in reaching the 200-mark in Britain since Gordon Richards did it seven years on the trot between 1946 and 1952.

Roberts, a South African, was born in Cape Town in May 1954 and was a racing sensation when still a teenager. He later became the first in his native country to ride 200 winners in a season and was champion 11 times. Despite meeting with only modest success – 25 winners in six months – when he first tried England in 1978, he moved to Newmarket in 1986. By the end of his third year he had comfortably topped the 100-winner mark and he had done so in every subsequent season.

Small and a natural lightweight – he can do 8 st without much trouble – he is a friendly, likeable man and appeared to have everything going for him. Certainly he seemed well up to the challenge of the Sheikh Mohammed job and he was confident he would make a success of it. Yet the man whom the Sheikh would rather have had was to haunt the South African all season. However there was little thought of this in either man's mind when Mick Kinane eventually returned to Ireland on 20 April. Mick, in fact, was concerned that his big race opportunities were going to be severely limited.

Having said no, I was apprehensive about how many – or rather how few – calls I would get from the Sheikh's people. I felt that, no matter how lucky I'd been for them in the past, my rejection of their offer was bound to have left its mark on our relationship.

In fact his first ride in Ireland in 1993 was in the Sheikh's colours, Advocat in the three-year-old maiden at a muddy Gowran Park, and the gelding ran out a convincing winner. The press made much of the coincidence. In fact it was not coincidence because John Oxx, who trained Advocat, had the bulk of Sheikh Mohammed's Irish string as well as all the Aga Khan's huge Irish-based team. Oxx needed a jockey because he had split with the immensely talented Johnny Murtagh (who had worked his way up from stable apprentice to stable jockey) the previous July when the young rider's terrible weight problems seemed on the point of destroying his career. Murtagh was later to stage an amazing fight-back, regain his job with Oxx and become champion. But this was all very much in the future and so the master of Currabeg turned to the jockey who was already retained to ride the Aga Khan's horses. He made a verbal agreement with Mick that he would ride for him whenever he was not required by Dermot Weld.

Oxx had taken over the stable from his father, also John, at the beginning of 1979 when he was 28. Balding and bespectacled, he looks more like a university professor than a racehorse trainer. But he has considerable ability and he has become one of the most successful trainers in Ireland. He is also a considerable talker – not blarney but a man who speaks sense and plenty of it, and he has a good sense of humour. His winner's enclosure press conferences tend to be as entertaining as they are informative.

Neither Oxx nor Weld had anything good enough for either the Two Thousand or the One Thousand Guineas but one who did was Richard Hannon. He didn't have a Tirol this time but he told Mick he could have the choice of Right Win and Revelation in the Newmarket colts' classic and the mount on Lyric Fantasy in the One Thousand two days earlier. Mick said no to the two colts. He felt they did not have much chance – the pair were to finish with only one behind them – and, even more important, he had his new obligations to the Aga Khan to consider.

But Lyric Fantasy was a different proposition. The pocket rocket had won five of her six races as a two-year-old, including the Queen Mary at Royal Ascot. There was a doubt about her getting the stiff mile and this was her first race of the season, but she had class. Her stamina, though, gave out in the final furlong and she weakened into sixth behind Sayyedati, ridden by Walter Swinburn.

Ten minutes before the Two Thousand Guineas started, with the mighty Zafonic looking unbeatable, Idris was considered even more of a certainty in the Broadfield Race at Naas. The world and his wife knew that this was the horse for which Mick Kinane had turned down a mount in a classic, and they backed him accordingly. The Aga Khan's colt started at an incredible 3-1 on.

> Unfortunately things didn't go according to plan. Idris jumped awkwardly leaving the stalls. Paul Carberry on Colour Party was able to steal a big lead. I managed to make up most of the leeway to challenge inside the final furlong but the leader kept galloping and my horse could get no closer. We were beaten a neck.

The Naas punters, their fingers burnt, gave the favourite's rider a frosty reception. Not until the next day, when they read their newspapers, did they find out that Idris had been suffering from a respiratory infection, had been on antibiotics and off his food. Mick watched on television as the French-trained Zafonic powered home under Pat Eddery in the Khalid Abdullah colours in the Two Thousand Guineas. Chasing him home was Barathea, ridden by Michael Roberts. Less than two hours earlier, Eddery (born in Ireland but tutored in race-riding in England by the legendary Frenchie Nicholson) had partnered Commander In Chief, also owned by Abdullah, to an easy win in a minor conditions race. Mick missed it. He was riding in a two-year-old race and finished down the field.

A fortnight later the Irish 2,000 Guineas was run at the Curragh. Mick trailed in last on Dermot Weld's Unusual Heat, and Roberts had his first big pay day for Sheikh Mohammed. Not only did he win the classic on Barathea, he came in for the mount on the Sheikh's George Augustus in the Tattersalls Gold Cup even though the horse was trained by Oxx. The South African won that race too. Mick, bitterly disappointed, was left wondering what might have been.

It was galling to see two big ones that could have been mine rolling in for somebody else and the thought did run through my mind that I'd got it all wrong with the decision I'd made back in January. However one of the things I have learnt in life is that, once you have made a decision, you have to live with it. You can't keep saying to yourself I should have done this or I should have done that. I still had certain reservations about having said no. But only deep down. Whenever I went through it in my mind, I came to the same conclusion – that I'd done the right thing.

The outcome of the Irish 2,000 Guineas turned the spotlight on the Epsom Derby just two and a half weeks later. Roberts was to ride Barathea, despite doubts about the colt's stamina. There seemed to be nothing for Mick except possibly Hannon's Geisway who had won the Predominate Stakes at Goodwood but had little else to recommend him. In truth, nothing seemed to have much to recommend them with the exception of Tenby, owned by Khalid Abdullah and trained by Henry Cecil. This Caerleon colt had never been beaten and as a two-year-old had swamped the French on their home ground in the Grand Criterium.

On his reappearance at Newmarket on the eve of the Two Thousand, Tenby won a Listed race and then ran in York's Dante Stakes – widely recognised as the most important of the Derby trials. The four who had the temerity to take him on were galloped into the ground. So few of the bookmakers could envisage Tenby's defeat at Epsom that a week before the big race the horse was quoted at an astonishing 5-2 on.

Cecil and Abdullah were in the fortunate position of having two other high class three-year-old colts – Armiger, brilliant the previous season and who had put up a good trial for the Derby in the Chester Vase, and Commander In Chief who was so backward at two that he did not even race. Pat Eddery rode the Dancing Brave colt to win on his debut at Newmarket when Mick was still in Hong Kong and, after winning again at the same course on the day of the Two Thousand, he went to York for the Glasgow Conditions Stakes, a relatively humble £5,425 affair which attracted only four runners. Commander In Chief started at 9-2 on but the Roberts-ridden Needle Gun made him fight to the line and the favourite got home by only a neck.

Eddery was convinced that it was a pointless exercise to run the horse against Tenby in the Derby – 'Commander In Chief just didn't have the experience. He needed time to mature. I suggested he should wait for the King Edward VII Stakes at Royal Ascot.'

Armiger, it had already been agreed, was to go for the French Derby – the Prix du Jockey-Club. In fact, he was pulled out three days before the race with a sore shin. Cecil, Abdullah, and Grant Pritchard-Gordon, the Saudi prince's racing manager, debated long and hard as to whether or not Commander In Chief should join Tenby in the Derby line-up.

When Mick returned home one lunchtime, after spending the morning riding work for Dermot Weld, Catherine had a message for him. Henry Cecil had telephoned. He wanted Mick to ring him back. The master of Warren Place explained that Commander In Chief was pleasing him in his work since York. If they decided to run him in the Derby, would Mick ride him?

> Naturally, I said I would. Although I had not been impressed when I'd watched that York win on TV – Commander In Chief had only scrambled home – I knew enough about the way Henry operated by this stage to realise that he must have come on a fair bit if he was considering the Derby. And, if he was, Commander In Chief would have a chance.

The next call from Cecil was to ask Mick to go over to Newmarket to ride a piece of work on the colt. That was just a week before the big race. Mick flew to Stansted on the Tuesday evening when Cecil gave up two hours of his valuable time to meet him off the plane and drive the Irish champion back to Warren Place. Early the following morning the colt did a fine gallop and Mick was impressed.

> I found him a nice horse to ride. He was well balanced and did not take a particularly strong hold. I though he would handle the course. I also felt he had a better chance of winning the Derby than any of my four previous rides in the race.

So did Cecil:

> By this stage I had persuaded Prince Khalid that Commander In Chief should run in the Derby. Although we had all been considering the matter, it was my decision – nobody else's –

and I felt the colt had a good chance of winning. Mick told me after he had ridden him that he thought the horse would give him a very good ride. I thought he could well do more than that because he was an improving horse. I impressed on Mick that, although I also had Tenby who was hot favourite, he was not to think he was on the second string but on a horse that had a really good chance.

The statistics, though, were distinctly unfavourable. Only two horses since World War II had won the Epsom Derby without having run as a two-year-old, Phil Drake in 1955 and Morston 18 year later. Furthermore, Commander In Chief was the youngest horse in the field.

'Tenby first – forget the rest,' was the widespread advice of the newspaper tipsters. But confidence in the Commander and his jockey quietly increased and the pair started second favourite at 15-2. Tenby was 5-4 on.

Derby day for Mick began with a 7.30 a.m. cup of tea at his Curragh home. There was no breakfast, not even a piece of toast. But he took with him a new saddle and a new whip.

Over the years I've found that new things are lucky for me. It's a superstition that can prove expensive But I felt lucky that morning, although I didn't say so as Catherine drove me to the airport. My thoughts were full of the busy day ahead. When I kissed her goodbye, I told her not to forget to pick me up when the helicopter landed at the Curragh that evening. I had some important mounts for Dermot Weld, including Goodnight Kiss who had finished second in the Irish 1,000 Guineas.

On the Aer Lingus plane was Charles O'Brien, younger son of the famous Vincent O'Brien, Charles's wife and her father. Vincent, who had won the great race six times, was running Fatherland ridden by Lester Piggott who was bidding for his tenth Derby win. Breakfast was served, but the jockey said no, even though he had eaten nothing since lunch the previous day. He was to ride Cecil's Queenbird in the first. She had only 8 st 9 lb and Mick was worried that he would be half a pound over. Instead, he had a cup of coffee and spent the journey studying *The Sporting Life* and the *Racing Post*. He memorised the colours in the big race, where the horses were drawn and every factor about each horse that could conceivably be relevant.

Catherine had ordered him a chauffeur-driven car and John Reid, who was riding Planetary Aspect – twice second to Tenby, had given Mick instructions for a back route to Epsom that avoided the worst of the traffic. There were already a lot of people at the racecourse when the chauffeur dropped him off at 12.40 p.m.

After a quick interview with Irish radio Mick went to the trial scales and found, to his considerable relief, that he was a pound lighter than he had thought. But that still did not allow for any lunch. He sat down in the jockeys' room and watched the replays of past runnings of the Derby on the closed circuit television.

> I was beginning to feel edgy and my adrenalin was pumping. I'm sure the other jockeys were in much the same state. Nobody admits to it, of course, but we all suffer from nerves on Derby day. I reckoned I was lucky to have that ride in the first. As I have already explained, I find few things more trying than hanging about with nothing to do on the day of a big race. Henry told me Queenbird was smart and sure to go close but I was drawn wide and I missed the kick. I was beaten a length and a half.

It was hardly a good omen. Mick went back into the jockeys' room and to the television. He watched more of the build-up as he changed into Khalid Abdullah's second colours, the ones with the distinguishing white cap. He waited until immediately after the second race – won by Frankie Dettori on the Queen's Enharmonic – before weighing out and handing his saddle to Cecil.

At 3.15 p.m., fully 30 minutes before the Derby was due off, the jockeys were called out and ushered into a minibus. Sitting almost next to Mick was Pat Eddery, seemingly ice cool despite Tenby's short price. Eddery had already won the Derby three times, but he would hardly have forgotten the one that got away. In 1984 he rode the seemingly unbeatable El Gran Senor. So easily was he travelling two furlongs out that he was able to sit motionless, looking across at Christy Roche on Secreto. To the amazement of the millions watching on television, Eddery kept looking at his fellow Irishman. But when he eventually pushed the button he found, to his horror, that there was nothing there.

In the paddock Mick was introduced to Khalid Abdullah. He had never met the oil-rich Saudi prince before. Abdullah, unlike Sheikh Mohammed and the other Maktoum brothers from Dubai, only rarely went to watch his horses run. But this day was different. Tenby was supposed to be a certainty.

> I remember well what Henry said to me: 'We've had a chat already. You're probably sick of listening to me by this stage. Anyway, I keep repeating myself. It must be the first sign of insanity!'
> I laughed at the joke, but the Prince was deadly serious. 'No,' he insisted. 'It's very important to have your plans worked out and everything in order.' We had agreed on tactics when I was at Warren Place the previous week. I might well force the pace. My horse was guaranteed to get every yard so I was determined to make it a true test, and not give the speed horses any advantage.

When the signal came to mount, Cecil went off with Eddery and it was left to the travelling head lad to swing Mick into the plate. Dave Goodwin, Commander In Chief's lad, was excited. 'The horse is in great nick. I've never seen him as well as he is now. He's really ready for this.'

Unfortunately, though, Commander In Chief was excited too. It was the last thing his rider had expected. When they got out onto the course for the parade, Commander In Chief really began to sweat. But Mick's lucky star was shining. Traditionally the runners for the Derby were walked across the Downs to the start along a railed path and through the crowd. This invariably killed off the last remaining hopes of the nervous ones. In 1993, though, for the first time, it was decided that the horses should canter the reverse way round to the start. By the time Commander In Chief got there, he was dry and relaxed. If he had been forced to take that walk through the crowds, he would have been in a muck sweat.

Back at the Curragh, though, it was Catherine who was sweating. To calm her nerves, she took a bottle of pink champagne out of the fridge.

As Mick was loaded into the stalls, Lester Piggott on Vincent O'Brien's Fatherland was on one side of him and Alan Munro on Canaska Star on the other.

I broke nicely and settled in just behind the leaders. I started to tack over to the right for the first bend but, as soon as I rounded it, everybody began to charge. Pat Eddery had taken Tenby right up to the leaders and everyone else wanted to get close behind him. I saw John Reid on Planetary Aspect trying to move out to get a bit nearer, but Christy Roche on Desert Team was keeping him in. There was a fair bit of jostling. Somebody shouted. Somebody else yelled. Then somebody swore. I eased back. The last thing I wanted was to start fighting on an inexperienced horse. As a result, I found myself a fair bit farther back than I had planned.

When we came to the top of the hill, I found I had nine in front of me. Too many. The only good thing was that the pace was still strong and Commander In Chief was travelling easily on a loose rein. As we went down the hill towards Tattenham Corner, I began to poke him along. I looked across to see how the others were going. Michael Roberts on Barathea seemed to be travelling the best of all and, as we turned for home, he was on my inner. I could see he wanted to get out. He was half a length up on me and, since I didn't want to get jostled, I let him go. Barathea swept forward and, as he did so, I saw Pat Eddery suddenly go for everything. I knew he was beaten. Hallelujah!

I changed my grip on the reins. I wanted to get my horse balanced before I asked him. When I did, he really surged forward. I suddenly realised this was it. My dreams of winning the Derby were about to come true. I will never forget that feeling as long as I live.

He was really motoring, but I was determined to take no chances. I picked up my stick and gave him a couple as we swept past Blues Traveller and into the lead. There was still two furlongs to go. I hit him again, and then twice more. He began to drift in towards the rails but I knew I was well clear so I let him.

Amazingly the place suddenly went quiet. In most races the roar of the crowd hits you somewhere in the straight, but in the Derby you hear the noise all the way. I was about to give him another one. Instead, I looked round to see what had happened. It was an amazing sight. They were all strung out with the washing way behind me. I switched my whip to the carry position and all I did was give him a tap back-handed. But the winning post was taking an awfully long time to come. I just hoped to hell nothing would go wrong. I looked back again as the jam stick came near. They were strung out like a long line of brown cows.

The emotions that ran through me at that moment are almost impossible to describe. Ever since those early days at Farney Castle, when I used to run up to the gallops to get a ride back, it had been my ambition to win the Epsom Derby. Now I'd done it. It was fantastic.

Bruce Raymond shouted 'Well done' and added, with a note of disbelief in his voice, 'I finished second.' He seemed almost as pleased as if he had won. Then Willie Carson congratulated me and there was a shout from behind of 'Gimme five.' It was Frankie Dettori. He laughed like hell as I slammed my hand down on his five. Christy Roche reached out to shake my hand. So did Dave Goodwin when he came running up. Peter Chapple-Hyam, the trainer of Planetary Aspect, did so too and two mounted policeman came up on either side of me.

But, as we went into the winner's enclosure and the Prince congratulated me, they announced a stewards' inquiry. Normally I would be worried, but I couldn't see how it could possibly have involved me. Not until I reached the weighing room, though, was there a second announcement – 'The inquiry does not involve the winner.' Thank God.

Henry Cecil was equally thrilled:

I was very pleased, even though Tenby was well beaten. You see, Commander In Chief was by Dancing Brave with whom Prince Khalid very nearly won the 1986 Derby and to succeed with a colt sired by him was sweet compensation. Also Commander In Chief was from a family that the Prince adores – that of Warning – so it was all rather appropriate.

Mick ordered two crates of champagne for the other jockeys, as was the custom. A TV interview with Brough Scott and a presentation followed. Lord Carnarvon invited him to meet the

Queen. After another interview, this time with Tony O'Hehir of Irish radio, and a press conference, Mick put his suit on over his riding clothes and went up to the Royal Box.

'Well done. That was a fantastic performance,' said the Queen.

11

Mohammed's Man

Less than ten minutes after his necessarily brief visit to the Royal Box, Mick was running for the helicopter to take him to Heathrow.

> As it soared up into the sky, I looked down at the course, the stands and the packed enclosures. I suddenly felt empty. It was one of the best moments of my life and there I was rushing off and leaving it all. I knew I should have stayed on to savour all the glory and the enjoyment.

For some reason the helicopter had to land at Terminal Four, quite some way from the Aer Lingus departure gate in Terminal One. Mick climbed into a minibus. Charles O'Brien and his family were already in it. There had been no celebrations for them. Fatherland had only managed ninth. The Irish contingent were all made to go through the normal check-in procedures despite their desperate hurry. Mick had made reservations on the 4.35, 4.45 and 5.45 flights. This was the last of them.

Once on the plane, the smell of food proved overpowering. Mick tucked into lamb and vegetables, his first meal for 29 hours. The stewardess gave him two bottles of champagne to take away with him.

At Dublin airport there was another minibus, another helicopter, and 20 minutes later he was on the Curragh. After giving her husband a kiss and a big hug, Catherine drove him to the jockeys' room and told him that she had already laid on a party at the house. She had the champagne on ice and had arranged for the Chinese restaurant in Kildare to bring over the food. Among those waiting to congratulate the hero of the day was Mick's father. Tommy Kinane was overcome with emotion and for once in his life was stuck for words.

Mick had made it in time for only one ride, the appropriately named Goodnight Kiss and she started at 4-1 on to round off the champion's incredible day. Mick made his move just under two furlongs out and was convinced that he had the race in the bag. Suddenly a horse that had never run before and that he had not even considered – the Oxx-trained Lock's Heath – rocketed past. The horse was carrying the Sheikh Mohammed colours.

Mick returned to the scales and grimly informed the unusually large number of people in the weighing room 'This is a great game. Just when you think you have got it licked, it puts you straight back on your arse.'

The following day Michael Roberts, only fifth on Barathea in the Derby, had some compensation when he won the Coronation Cup on Opera House and two days later his Sheikh Mohammed star seemed firmly in the ascendant when he rode a fine race to land the Oaks on Intrepidity. But it didn't burn brightly for long and he went through the four days of Royal Ascot without a winner. The South African was given an ominous portent of things to come when he rode the Sheikh's Inner City in the opening Queen Anne Stakes. The 6-4 favourite looked sure to win when Roberts sent him past Mick on the Clive Brittain-trained Alflora a furlong out but Mick came again to spring a 20-1 shock that was as unwelcome for Roberts as it was for the punters. But it was nothing to what was to befall him in the Eclipse on the first Saturday in July.

The Sheikh ran two, and to be fair, Roberts had a desperately difficult choice to make. Both Opera House and Barathea had carried him to important victories and, partly because this race was two furlongs shorter than the Coronation Cup, he opted for Barathea who had clearly not got the trip at Epsom. Anthony Stroud stepped into the Mick Kinane picture once more.

> I was convinced that Opera House, not Barathea, would win the race. I knew that Michael Kinane was due to ride at Naas on the day of the Eclipse, so I got on the phone to Dermot

Weld and I pleaded with him to release his stable jockey from
his commitments. I also rang Michael and told him 'You have
got to ride this bloody horse. He is going to win.'

Mick recalls:

Anthony also said that Michael Stoute was really happy with
Opera House and, unlike the Belmez-Old Vic-Steve Cauthen
situation in the King George of three years earlier, I agreed
with Anthony that Michael Roberts could not get back on
Opera House should anything happen to Barathea. Nothing
did. Barathea started favourite in preference to Tenby, who
was again in the field, but Opera House was next in the
betting.

Sandown is a tough course and it can be a trappy one too.
The uphill finish is particularly stiff and a lot can happen in
the last furlong and a half. It can sometimes be difficult to get
a run along the rails and it can also be easy to find yourself
blocked in. Ideally you should come up more towards the
middle. I tracked the leaders for much of the race, started to
move coming to the two furlong marker and led a furlong and
a half down. Opera House had quickened well when I asked
him but, once he was in front, he started to idle. Frankie
Dettori came at me on the Italian horse Misil but I was
acutely conscious of the whip regulations and I didn't dare
ask my horse for everything he had. As a result Opera House
idled almost too much but, when I asked him again, he picked
up once more and we held on by a short head.

It was a very important ride so far as my relations with
Sheikh Mohammed and his advisers were concerned. Their
reaction to the victory seemed to suggest that, if there had
been any hard feelings about my turning down the job earlier
in the year, these were now forgotten. I felt they now knew I
was more than happy to ride for them in the big races
whenever I could. Certainly the win seemed to put them at
their ease with me.

But the one person not put at ease was poor Michael Roberts. He
had been forced to watch a victory that could have been his from a
bitterly disappointing vantage point nearly five lengths behind. It is
always sickening for a jockey to have picked the wrong one but for

Roberts the outcome could hardly have been worse. Not only had he got it wrong but the man his boss had preferred had taken the spoils. To add insult to injury, the press weighed in with a mass of speculation that there could be a second approach to Ireland's big race king, pushing Roberts out into the cold.

The *Racing Post* even ran a caption competition. The paper's readers were shown a photograph of Mick unsaddling Opera House in the Sandown winner's enclosure. He was grinning broadly, seemingly at a remark made to him by Anthony Stroud who was at his shoulder. Readers were asked to come up with suggestions as to what Stroud was saying. Malcolm Blackett of High Wycombe in Buckinghamshire won with his 'How about an oil well, 2,000 camels and as much Guinness as you can drink?'

Needless to say Roberts was not amused. For him Mick Kinane was fast becoming bad news. And so were his troubles with the stewards. When he had won the Irish 2,000 Guineas back in May ,Roberts was suspended for three days for failing to do enough to keep Barathea straight and he picked up two further suspensions before being hit with a ten-day ban for his riding of the subsequently disqualified Sabrehill at Newbury on 17 July. Such suspensions do little for a jockey's confidence and, when one follows another – and another in Roberts's case – they can have a demoralising effect. They also destroyed any chance he might have had of retaining his championship. The little South African must have wondered what he had done for the fates to be so continually unkind to him.

They relented a little a week later when he rode Opera House to a fine win in the King George VI and Queen Elizabeth Diamond Stakes. But, much as the ghost of Banquo did to Macbeth, the dreaded spectre of M.J. Kinane continued to haunt Roberts. Mick rode five winners at Leopardstown that afternoon and, while the Irish champion did not exactly steal the South African's glory, he certainly took the gloss of it.

Even worse was to come in the Aral Pokal at Gelsenkirchen in Germany in mid August. The Sheikh's representative in this valuable Group One race was the John Oxx-trained George Augustus. Roberts succeeded in getting him home in front but his mount hung left under pressure and slightly impeded second-placed Monsun. The stewards showed the Sheikh's rider no mercy. They took the race off him, awarded the prize to Monsun and slammed yet another suspension on the unfortunate jockey. What made the pill even more difficult to swallow was that Monsun was ridden by none other than Mick Kinane.

Yet again the press made comparisons between the Sheikh's first choice and the man who got the job. In fact some of them had been intermittently attacking Roberts since early in the season when he picked the wrong Sheikh Mohammed runner in a number of important races. Soon after the Aral Pokal reporters, quoting unspecified sources close to the Maktoum camp, began writing about how certain of the Sheikh's trainers – again without specifying which ones – were unhappy with the South African's riding and wanted a change.

The most widely believed of the reports from the various sources – I was just one of several journalists who were tipped off by people with Maktoum contacts – was that John Gosden, in particular, did not want Roberts. He wanted Frankie Dettori who was already riding quite a bit for him. Gosden – tall, eloquent and prematurely bald – had been assistant to Sir Noel Murless before taking a similar post with Vincent O'Brien. He started training in California in 1979 and rapidly made a name for himself. In 1988, though, he was persuaded to return to England to train at the famous Stanley House stables in Newmarket's Bury Road. In September 1993 he was 42 and trained over 170 horses, the majority owned by Sheikh Mohammed and his brothers. He was an important and influential figure in the Maktoum empire.

While all this speculation continued to unsettle Roberts, events on the racecourse made his life even worse. In the Guinness Irish Champion Stakes at Leopardstown on 11 September he was beaten on Opera House, who started hot favourite and was having his final race before the Prix de l'Arc de Triomphe. Possibly because it was an Arc warm-up, he did not ride the horse as hard as he might otherwise have done or as hard, in the view of many observers, as he should have done.

'It was a half-hearted effort by Roberts,' insisted Ted Walsh, the outspoken Irish television commentator. 'He never got serious with Opera House. This was a Group One race and he should have done so.'

It looked as if salt was being rubbed into the Roberts wounds when Mick rode a treble on the same card to beat his own record for the fastest century in Irish racing by no less than 11 days. At the Curragh the following day Roberts was given yet another suspension, this time for making too much use of his whip. This did nothing to stop the speculation. What did was a statement issued by Darley Stud Management, Sheikh Mohammed's racing office, nine days later.

This stated that Roberts' contract would not be renewed 'as part of a policy decision not to retain one specific jockey for all our horses and trainers'. It was also announced that Gosden's wish had been granted. Frankie Dettori would be his stable jockey.

Mick was at Listowel when the news broke. All sorts of people were asked for their opinions on the Roberts situation. Journalists even rang Steve Cauthen in Kentucky (his verdict: 'The job was too big for any one jockey. It was just not possible to please so many different trainers and to always pick the right one from so many different horses') but only one asked Mick what he thought. The journalist received simply a grin and a quip – 'I don't know. I haven't tried it'. But his mind was working furiously.

> There was obviously some restructuring going on and, despite it appearing that the jockeys already attached to the various stables would ride the Sheikh's horses in those stables, I felt deep down that I just might have a chance of figuring in the new set-up somehow or other. But I was afraid to think about it too much. I didn't want to build up my hopes.

The six-day Listowel festival finished on the Saturday, three days after the papers had carried the stories of Roberts losing the most coveted job in racing. Mick, having won eight of the 16 flat races, decided to have a lie-in on Sunday morning. But his plans for a late start to the day were interrupted by the telephone.

'Good morning.' It was Anthony Stroud, as hearty as if he had been up for hours. 'I've got an offer for you. Would you like to hear it now or do you want to wait until later in the week?'

Stroud had spoken to Sheikh Mohammed after the Roberts announcement and after he had mulled over the situation once more. The Sunday morning telephone call was the end result.

> The year of Michael Roberts taught us a great deal, including that we needed to have a jockey in France who could work closely with Andre Fabre, and Thierry Jarnet had been doing just that. We also realised that John Gosden was better off having his own stable jockey with whom he could communicate on a daily basis rather than having to rely on

one who was going here, there and everywhere. In short, the job was too big for one man.

Michael Roberts was hard working and diligent, as well as an extremely nice man, but it just wasn't working. Sheikh Mohammed wanted to stay loyal to the contract which expired at the end of the year and I had nothing in mind so far as Michael Kinane was concerned when we announced that the contract would not be renewed. However, after thinking things over, I began to put together an idea. It had become a proposition that had Sheikh Mohammed's blessing by the time I rang that Sunday. In fact my first call that morning had been to Dermot Weld. I felt the honourable way to go about things was to speak to Michael's employer before speaking to him. Indeed I was also in touch with Dermot very early on in the January negotiations.

Michael Kinane has all the qualities you need in a top jockey. He is strong and aggressive, tactically brilliant, he has good balance and good hands, he has a nice style and sits low on a horse. And, although he is a man of few words, he talks a lot of sense when he comes in after a race. Naturally I wanted to come to an agreement with him if I could, and if it could be fitted into his existing arrangements with Dermot Weld. We ended up by agreeing that, in the event of a top rider not being available, we would have first call on him in Group races whenever Dermot Weld was prepared to release him. What it meant was that, if we had a runner in a big race and Khalid Abdullah, for example, approached him, he would check with us first.

It has proved to be a much better arrangement than hiring him full-time.

It suits us and it suits him. He likes going to England to ride at the big meetings and he is mentally stimulated by the big occasion. At the same time he is still living and riding in Ireland. The only real drawback is that he is not able to ride as much work at Newmarket as I would like. If an English-based jockey rides a two-year-old in four or five pieces of work, it can be very difficult for us to replace him with Kinane when that horse runs at one of the big meetings.

Mick was, somewhat understandably, delighted by the new set-up:

It meant that I really did have the best of both worlds. I had a retainer to ride for Sheikh Mohammed in many of the top races, I was still riding most of Dermot Weld's horses and I could still spend my winters in Hong Kong. My arrangement with John Oxx and the Aga Khan had to come to an end which was a pity in a way but it would have been impossible to include that job as well.

The Sheikh Mohammed retainer was tied up within a fortnight of that Sunday morning call but no details were released to the press and it was a well kept secret when Mick flew out to Hong Kong on 10 October with a new 115-winner record to his name. But later that week rumours began to circulate on Irish racecourses and on the Saturday *The Irish Field* carried a brief piece. In *The Sporting Life* the following Monday Anthony Stroud was quoted in detail on the full extent of the new arrangement. However what surprised many was that he had not made an announcement earlier. He had come in for a lot of stick in the press for taking so long to confirm that Michael Roberts' contract was not to be renewed, and he seemed to be making the same mistake again. But he now admits that he would have preferred to wait for several more weeks. *The Irish Field* story, though, forced his hand:

> We'd wanted a bit of time before we announced anything. We didn't want it to look as if on the one hand we were saying we hadn't sacked Michael Roberts – just not renewed his contract – and on the other we were signing up somebody else. But I wasn't a bit surprised that the news got out. In racing everything leaks – except Shergar!

12

Sure I'd Killed Him

Mick Kinane hoped to celebrate his new contract with Sheikh
Mohammed by winning the 1994 Two Thousand Guineas on King's
Theatre in the maroon and white colours. He had won the Craven
on him and the Henry Cecil-trained colt started favourite for the
Newmarket classic. But King's Theatre was most disappointing and,
although he ran rather better in the Dante at York, he still only
managed fourth behind Erhaab. But he had an attack of ringworm
after the Guineas and he showed signs of it when he ran at York.
Cecil expected him to do better in the Epsom Derby in which Foyer
also represented the Sheikh.

> There were a lot of runners – 25 in all – and it turned into a
> rough race. They went hard from the start and, whenever that
> happens in the Derby, you are going to get horses who give
> way under the pressure of the pace by the time you get to the
> top of the hill. Sure enough, a grey horse came back out of the
> pack towards the rest of us like a missile. It was The Flying
> Phantom ridden by Philip Robinson. Obviously I couldn't
> afford to let King's Theatre run into the back of him and I
> checked. Willie Ryan, who was on my inner on Foyer, was
> not so lucky. His horse clipped the rail and came down.
> I had a good run after that and, when I hit the front over a
> furlong out still going strongly, I felt the Derby was mine for
> the second year running. I'd come from a fair bit back and,
> although I didn't look round, I was travelling so well that I
> didn't think it possible for anything to come from behind and

beat me. However I'd reckoned without Erhaab. I hadn't seen him at all in the race but he and Willie Carson finished like a train to flash past me. They were moving so fast that they were more than a length clear at the post.

King's Theatre started hot favourite for the Irish Derby later the same month but I never felt I was going to win. Frankie Dettori on Balanchine took it up five furlongs from home and the filly had me in big trouble even turning into the straight.

Next came the King George VI and Queen Elizabeth Diamond Stakes. By this time most punters had given up on King's Theatre and he started at 12-1. Erhaab was the favourite but the whole complexion of the race changed when Ezzoud unshipped Walter Swinburn soon after the start and proceeded to cause as much trouble as a riderless horse in the Grand National.

Ezzoud's antics bothered me a fair bit. He was in front of me and I had to keep trying to avoid him. I went left to do so in the straight. Then he went left and I had to switch King's Theatre to the right. When I moved right, though, I squeezed White Muzzle as he was coming through. That stopped him in his run and he was beaten a length and a quarter, so in the end Ezzoud helped me almost as much as he hindered me. Once again I met the Queen and this time she presented me with a belt that had a lovely buckle on it studded with diamonds. As she did so, she said: 'There were a lot of incidents, weren't there? What was it like?'.

That was the last time I won on King's Theatre. I led three furlongs out on him in the Juddmonte International at York but Ezzoud beat us into third. In the Arc he ran a bit flat. He'd had quite a few hard races by this time and they were beginning to tell. I knew the speed was going to come from behind and my only chance was to try and get ahead of it, so I sent him on two furlongs from home. But I was already struggling and he soon faded out of contention.

At Royal Ascot in 1993 Sheikh Mohammed had just one winner – in a handicap – and no less than eight seconds, six of them ridden by Michael Roberts. At the 1994 meeting he won two Group races on the first day and Mick Kinane, successful on both of them, also landed the St James's Palace Stakes on Grand Lodge to force the bookmakers to suspend betting on the Ritz Club Trophy which goes to the jockey riding the most winners at the four-day meeting. The press erupted into collective fury when the Irish champion was suspended for his use of the whip on Grand Lodge and he again made headlines for the wrong reason on the third day when a racegoer suicidally ran out into his path.

James Florey, a 21-year-old student who lived with his mother only a few miles from Ascot at Bracknell, had spent much of the afternoon drinking with his friends in the enclosure on the inside of the course. For a dare, he climbed over the five foot high wire mesh fence, ducked under the rails and ran across the course in the closing stages of the Ribblesdale Stakes. All but two of the runners – Papago, ridden by Mick Kinane, and Frankie Dettori's mount, Little Sister – had just gone past. The former was still doing over 30 mph when she hit him. The force of the blow was enough to knock Florey unconscious and bring Papago crashing to the ground.

> I caught a glimpse of him out of the corner of my eye as he was climbing over the fence. When he got under the rails and onto the course, he looked in the direction of the horses that had just passed him. I'm convinced he didn't realise there were more to come. It was all over in a second but, before it was, Frankie and I yelled at him. However he didn't hear us and in the next instant I hit him with an almighty thump. I was sure I had killed him.
>
> Frankie's mount just missed him but Papago fell and came down on top of me. The weight of her body, and the force of it, winded me but a far bigger problem was that I was pinned underneath her hind legs and my foot was trapped in the stirrup iron. I thought she was badly hurt and I was afraid she was going to start kicking. I had to get her off me before she did. Somehow I managed to pull my foot out just as she moved. It was all a hell of a shock. Papago got to her feet after a few minutes but the man remained on the ground. He was face down and he never moved. I thought he was dead. They took him to hospital in Slough and he was believed to be suffering from severe internal injuries. In fact he had done amazingly little damage. What saved him, I'm convinced, is that he didn't see my horse coming. As a result he didn't tense up and was totally relaxed when Papago hit him. The Jockey Club later warned him off for five years.

One of the two Sheikh Mohammed Group winners on the opening day of the meeting was Foyer who was trained by Michael Stoute, with whom Kinane's name had first been linked back in 1988.

Stoute, a thickset, pleasant character, would today have Julian Wilson's job on BBC if he had not lost out in a trial early in his career. That trial, or rather his failure in it, persuaded Stoute that he should stick to his original plan to become a trainer. The son of a Commissioner of Police in Barbados, he moved to England in 1965 when he was 19 and joined Pat Rohan, then training at Malton in Yorkshire. From there he moved to Newmarket to work firstly for Doug Smith and then for Tom Jones. He started training in 1972 and nine years later won the Derby, Irish Derby and King George VI and Queen Elizabeth Diamond Stakes with the ill-fated Shergar.

In 1994 – by which time he was training at Freemason Lodge (where Sir Cecil Boyd-Rochfort used to rule the roost) and was living with Coral Pritchard-Gordon, ex-wife of former Newmarket trainer Gavin Pritchard-Gordon – his two best five-year-olds were Ezzoud and Cezanne. Ezzoud, not least because of his exploits in the King George, was the better known but Cezanne was improving with every race and filling Stoute with ever-growing enthusiasm.

> I also trained Cezanne the previous year and at the end of the season he went out to Dubai for the winter. He won all his five starts and was rated the Dubai champion. Hilal Ibrahim had him for his first two runs in England in 1994 and then he returned to me. Gary Hind had been riding him in Dubai so it was natural for him to keep the mount and he won a Group Three on him at Baden-Baden at the end of August. Cezanne won that race pretty easily and so I decided to supplement him for the Guinness Champion Stakes at Leopardstown on 10 September. This was the day of the St Leger at Doncaster and, with Walter Swinburn riding Sacrament for me in that, I decided to get Mick Kinane for Cezanne.
>
> There was no better man for the job, particularly round Leopardstown which he knows like the back of his hand. He has loads of ability, tremendous power in the saddle and he is very quick to grasp what is required. Two sentences and he's got it. I told him about the horse and how he should be ridden – 'Lie handy just behind the leaders and pick them up in good

time.' Mick Kinane showed a fair bit of opportunism that day. Frankie Dettori tried to dictate it on Del Deya but Kinane always had Cezanne in a position to strike and he took it up well inside the final furlong to beat Del Deya by a neck with Grand Lodge and Muhtarram only just behind.

Mick followed up his four Royal Ascot victories – out of just 24 races – with another four the following year to take his second Ritz Club trophy and Alastair Down, then racing journalist of the year, wrote this in *The Sporting Life* :

> The abiding memory of the four days has to be M. J. Kinane. He stole the show last year on Grand Lodge and hasn't become a lesser jockey in the interim. He was good in defeat on Alzianah but simply awesome on the stayers Stelvio (Queen's Vase) and Harlestone Brook (Ascot Handicap). Both horses had a bit to do on the home turn but there was an inexorable air of inevitability about them winning as soon as Kinane really got down to work. Of all the jockeys riding today, he is the one who must gladden the punters' hearts most when he is in overdrive and on their side.

Mick was thrilled:

> Earlier on in my career I never gave a thought to winning things like Ritz trophies. But, when I got the job riding for Sheikh Mohammed, I wanted to become the leading jockey at the top meetings, particularly at Royal Ascot. To win the Ritz two years on the trot meant a lot. I also won the one at the York Ebor meeting in August.

Earlier in the season there were Group One wins on Red Bishop in the Queen Elizabeth II Cup in Hong Kong and on Luso in the Italian Derby in Rome but the one that got away was the Irish Derby at the Curragh.

> I rode Definite Article for Dermot Weld and Moyglare. He had been impressive on his reappearance over ten furlongs at the Curragh the previous month but he was not bred to get the trip and there was a big doubt about him doing so, despite

a searching gallop he had done over 12 furlongs eight days before the race. He started joint second favourite with Sheikh Mohammed's Winged Love who was trained in France by Andre Fabre and ridden by Olivier Peslier. Celtic Swing was the hot favourite and also well fancied was Annus Mirabilis on whom I had finished second in both the Dante and the Prix Jean Prat. But my knowledge of this horse was to prove my undoing.

He was ridden this time by Walter Swinburn, and he and Celtic Swing were going really well when I pulled out behind them as we turned into the straight. I knew Annus Mirabilis probably wouldn't stay and I felt I had to get him off the bridle to beat him. As a result I went a bit sooner than I wanted. Just inside the final furlong I was clear and I thought I had it. In the last 75 yards, though, Definite Article ran out of gas. His suspect stamina was shown up for what it was – suspect. Winged Love, who had been brought with a dream run up the inner by the French jockey, beat me a short head.

Kinane came in for criticism from some of the riders in the stands. If only he had waited a bit longer, they said. And he should have done – he was on a horse that couldn't possibly get the trip on breeding. But none of them criticised the jockey more than the man who had just been beaten. He promptly ran his own mental video through his mind, and over the next few days and nights he pressed the replay button time and time again.

A short head is always desperately hard to take. I invariably believe I should have been able to do something that would have swung the result the other way. It's even harder to take when you want something really badly and, boy, did I want to win the Irish Derby. My immediate reaction was the same as the critics, that I should have held on to Definite Article a bit longer. But Annus Mirabilis was the reason I didn't. I also considered I might have followed Winged Love down the inner. But, the more I thought about this, the more convinced I became that I wouldn't have got there in time if I'd done that. Maybe I could have won if the race was run again but I eventually came to the conclusion that could, not should, would have been the operative word.

This was not the only big race in which Mick Kinane's luck seemed to desert him. On Singspiel he was second in the Grand Prix de Paris, the Eclipse and the Great Voltigeur. In the last of the three the margin was not much bigger than the thickness of this page. And on Swain in the Arc he was only third. Frankie Dettori, Walter Swinburn and Willie Carson all lodged greater claims to the title of big race king than did Kinane.

It might have been different if Sheikh Mohammed had not transferred several of his most promising two-year-olds into the name of Godolphin at the end of the 1994 season and taken them to Dubai. When they returned to Britain in 1995 they remained in the ownership of Godolphin and were trained, not by their original trainers, but by a little-known bearded former policeman called Saeed bin Suroor and it was Dettori, not Kinane, who rode most of them. However any sense of frustration he might have felt was nothing compared to that suffered by Henry Cecil who was powerless to do anything except look on in anguish as former Warren Place inmates like Vettori won the French 2,000 Guineas, Moonshell the Epsom Oaks and Classic Cliche the St Leger.

When Cecil started to lose some of his 1995 two-year-olds to Dubai in September that year, his wife Natalie mentioned her husband's disappointment to a racing journalist. Sheikh Mohammed took exception when this appeared in print and made a scarcely veiled attack on the second Mrs Cecil at a press conference he held at Ascot not long afterwards :

> Henry Cecil is one of the best trainers in Europe but I want him to train my horses, not somebody else, and not someone who knows very little about the thoroughbred racehorse . . .
> I have nothing against Henry Cecil. Indeed I have great respect for him. I shall continue with him as long as he wants, and as long as he trains the horses. But if he allows people with hardly any knowledge of horses to interfere with him, that's bad.

Needless to say this was hardly well received in the Cecil household and at Goffs Sales in Ireland ten days later Cecil was told that Sheikh Mohammed was transferring all the 40 horses he had with him to other yards. Anthony Stroud said that, when one of the two-year-olds (Mark Of Esteem) arrived in Dubai, a veterinary examination revealed a knee condition that could require surgery.

He added: 'Sheikh Mohammed expressed considerable disappointment that Cecil had not kept him fully informed of all the facts and had misled him.'

Mick Kinane's view of the arrival of Godolphin and its all-conquering season was rather different:

> Classic Cliche was never going to be one of my rides and, although I lost out on Moonshell and Vettori, I was by this stage part and parcel of the whole Sheikh Mohammed racing operation. He had adopted a new policy and it was upto me to work within it and do the best I could. It was much the same with the Irish jockeys' championship. I just wasn't able to hold on to it in 1995 because, in addition to missing the beginning and the end of the season, I was riding in England so much. But you can't have it all ways and, frankly, I was lucky to be champion in 1994.

One of the star performers of 1995 was Blue Duster who swept all before her in the top English two-year-old fillies races. She was trained by David Loder who is related to the late Major Eustace Loder, the breeder of Pretty Polly who was one of the most famous race and broodmares in history. A distant cousin, several times removed, is Edmund Loder who owns the Eyrefield Lodge Stud where Pretty Polly is buried and where many of her best descendants have been bred.

David Loder, a tall, likeable Old Etonian who is showing signs of going prematurely bald, was meant to go to Bristol University and then into the City to make his fortune but he persuaded his parents to let him spend a year in Australia first. He put his love of horses to good use on a stud in New South Wales and, when he returned to England, he turned his back on university to work for a point-to-point trainer. Little more than a year later he graduated to racing proper as a pupil-assistant at Newmarket with Sir Mark Prescott. After a year with English-born champion American jumps trainer Jonathan Sheppard, he temporarily succumbed to his father's wishes and joined a firm of stockbrokers in London. But it wasn't for him. He became assistant to Geoff Wragg in the days when Edmund Loder's Marling was hitting the highspots and at the age of 28 he took over the Sefton Lodge Stables on Newmarket's Bury Road. Two months earlier he had been invited to join Sheikh Mohammed's entourage at the big Keeneland yearling sales in Kentucky and the

Sheikh was one of his first owners. The Sheikh also owned Blue
Duster who struck Mick Kinane as something special the first time
he rode her.

She was still a few weeks off her first race when I partnered
her in a gallop at Newmarket at the beginning of May and she
was terribly impressive. When I returned home I said to Katie
[as he sometimes calls his wife in private] that this was a
marvellous filly and she was sure to be my Ascot banker. She
was favourite for her debut at Sandown at the end of the
month but it was a messy race and I had to take it up on her
too early. She still won comfortably but she was looking
around at everything. In the Queen Mary she jumped the
road but she had so much talent that she was able to get back
onto the bridle once I sat still and gave her a chance. After
that it was a doddle.

Her next race was also at Ascot in the Princess Margaret
Stakes on the day of the King George VI and Queen Elizabeth
Diamond Stakes. She jumped the road once more but she still
won terribly easily. She was then put away until the Cheveley
Park more than two months later. Up until then she hadn't
been in a true run race and I was looking forward to this one
because I thought they would go a proper gallop right from
the start. I was convinced that nobody had yet seen the best
of her.

I was drawn on the rails and I wanted to tuck in behind the
leaders. There were only five runners and I knew full well
there was a strong possibility that one of them would come
up on my outside and try to keep me boxed in behind the
horse in front. I felt that Michael Hills on My Branch was the
danger and that it was he who would probably try to trap me.
Sure enough, he did just that and I was hemmed in behind
Walter Swinburn on Dance Sequence. I couldn't afford to be
made to look silly by staying where I was, so I decided to pull
out and pass the leader. This meant making my move a fair
bit earlier than I wanted but it made little difference to Blue
Duster. She was a star and she won like it too.

13

Melbourne Glory

For a horse who was to go down in racing history Vintage Crop made an inauspicious start. He was so weak and backward as a two-year-old in 1989 that Dermot Weld eventually gave up and sent him back to the County Kildare Gilltown Stud of Bert and Diana Firestone who had bred him. He recommended castrating the colt and leaving him to mature until the end of the following season when he could be returned to Rosewell House.

In fact he stayed at Gilltown until he was four and by this time a Japanese businessman called Yoshiki Akazawa had bought him together with all the other horses the Firestones had in Ireland and, so he thought, the stud as well. In fact the Aga Khan maintained that he had already made a verbal agreement with Bert Firestone to buy back the stud he had inherited from his grandfather. There was a famous legal battle in the High Court in Dublin in 1991 and 1992. The Aga Khan won and Akazawa had to move his horses out of Gilltown.

But it was Akazawa from whom Weld purchased Vintage Crop in 1991. He bought him for Michael Smurfit who was looking for a prospective hurdler with the potential to go to the top. His company sponsored the Champion Hurdle at Cheltenham and one of Smurfit's ambitions was to win the race. Weld decided to give the gelding an outing in a two mile flat race at Thurles in October before sending him jumping.

He also ran Padiord in the same race. Some trainers don't care if the outsider beats a better fancied stable companion. Weld does. He feels that this is letting down the betting public and implying that he does not know what he is doing. As a result 'the wrong one' at

Rosewell House wins only once in a blue moon. That blue moon shone at Thurles on 17 October 1991 and Mick Kinane was every bit as surprised as the trainer.

> Padiord had a bit of form and started second favourite, whereas Vintage Crop had not even done a proper piece of work. Dermot intended to work him beforehand but, as he was such a light-framed horse, he felt doing that and racing him could be asking too much of the horse. The Thurles race was intended, basically, as part of his education. Pat Shanahan rode him and I was astonished when he loomed up at the seven furlong pole, even more so when he cruised to the front soon afterwards. That was the last I saw of him that day. He went on to win by four lengths and I never got in a blow.

Vintage Crop was then sent over hurdles, winning at Fairyhouse and Leopardstown, but Weld decided he was still immature – too much so to be trained for the Cheltenham Festival. That, and his owner's ambition, were to be put on hold for another season.

> I rode him on his return in May, in a mile and three-quarter handicap at Gowran Park. He only had 8 st 5 lb so you can imagine what a certainty he was, and he won like it too. His next race was not until Leopardstown in August. Pat took over because I was riding Sharp Review and he stayed on to finish third to me. Vintage Crop then absolutely hacked up under 9 st 10 lb in a handicap at Tralee and it was decided to run him in the Irish St Leger which was sponsored by the Smurfit Group. I know he was only fifth – Steve Cauthen won the race on Mashaallah, trained by John Gosden – but he put up a hell of a performance considering he'd had training problems and didn't finish 100 per cent sound. His next outing was in the Cesarewitch at Newmarket but the race was run only a few days after I had left for Hong Kong. It was the first time I'd gone out there for six months and I felt it would not be right for me to either delay my departure or to fly back for the race. I discussed it with Dermot and he seemed happy enough for Walter Swinburn to ride the horse. Vintage Crop started favourite and won by eight lengths – a huge margin.

Weld had entered Vintage Crop for the following month's Melbourne Cup. He'd had his sights set on Australia's most famous race for some time and had wanted to run Rare Holiday the previous year. He got as far as getting the horse handicapped but the quarantine requirements proved insuperable. The Australians insisted that Rare Holiday must spend a month in England and almost as long again in Australia. 'I also encountered travelling difficulties,' Weld recalls, 'and there seemed to be a general lack of co-operation. I came to the conclusion that at that stage the Australians did not want overseas runners.'

The attitude of the Aussies was to change in a big way in 1993 but, before that historic year was even reached, Weld ran into serious difficulties with Vintage Crop:

> In December 1992 I ran him in a schooling hurdle at Punchestown and afterwards he was intermittently lame. I thought it was a slightly torn muscle or ligament high up in the horse's quarters or in his back. Every time he did any fast work he aggravated it. Eventually we diagnosed arthritis at the end of his back in the lumbar sacral joint and surrounding muscles – and that can be extremely painful. Anybody who suffers from a bad back will realise just how painful.

Vintage Crop ran in the 1993 Champion Hurdle but, even though he did well for an inexperienced novice, he came nowhere near fulfilling his owner's ambition. He was then prepared for a tilt at the Ascot Gold Cup and, when that failed to come off, he was aimed at both the Irish St Leger and the Melbourne Cup. He had physiotherapy almost daily.

> Despite his problems with arthritis, he improved considerably that year and the reason he was so comprehensively beaten in the Gold Cup was because he couldn't handle the soft ground. I then rode him to win the Curragh Cup on Irish Derby day and he was impressive.
>
> He returned from a short break to run in the Meld Stakes at the Curragh in August and it was that race that really brought home to us just how good he was. The distance was only ten furlongs, much too short for Vintage Crop – or so we thought. As it was the year I had an agreement to ride for the Aga Khan, I said I would ride his filly Takarouna instead. She

started favourite and I thought she would win. Pat Shanahan again rode Vintage Crop and I was really surprised when he came cruising up on the outside. The horse had not done much work and he was beaten only half a length. To show so much ability in a Group Three after being dropped considerably in distance suggested that he was a really classy horse.

The Jefferson Smurfit Memorial Irish St Leger came next. The opposition included Drum Taps, who was also Melbourne Cup bound and had twice won the Ascot Gold Cup, the Paul Cole-trained Snurge who needed only to finish in the first two to become the leading British trained money earner of all time. Assessor, second in the Gold Cup, and Irish Derby third Foresee were also in the line-up. The diehard traditionalists have tended to knock the Irish St Leger since it was opened up to older horses in 1983 but this was a hot race. Vintage Crop, plunged on at all prices from 8-1 to 9-2, was never far off the pace.

> When I was weighing up the race beforehand I thought the gallop might be slow and, if it was, I'd made up my mind to make my move quite early. Frankie Dettori sent Drum Taps straight into the lead but the pace he set was too steady for some of us and just under halfway Johnny Murtagh took over on Shrewd Idea. I went past him early in the straight and I reckoned that, if I could get a length or two clear of the rest, Vintage Crop would be hard to catch – and that's just how it proved.

The Melbourne Cup is not just Australia's famous race. It's a national carnival, the Down Under equivalent of rather more than the Grand National, Cheltenham and Royal Ascot rolled into one. If you added the FA Cup and the World Cup, you would be nearer the mark. Just about everybody has a bet or a sweepstake ticket and the legend that the whole country comes to a halt while the race is run is true.

Dermot Weld's perseverance, and a major change of approach by the Victoria Racing Club, saw the quarantine period cut to a far more acceptable fortnight in Ireland and the same period in

Australia. The weights were calculated in late July, i.e. after the Ascot Gold Cup but before the Irish St Leger, with Vintage Crop set to receive 7 lb from Drum Taps who had finished virtually ten lengths behind him at the Curragh.

However this considerable advantage was thought to be outweighed by all the weight Vintage Crop had lost on the 38-hour journey. He also suffered from dehydration and, while Drum Taps was able to impress the local work-watchers in his gallops, the other raider had to be confined to comparatively light exercise. Frankly, the Australian trainers thought they did not have much to fear. Neither horse could possibly be fit enough. The traditional method of preparing a horse for the Melbourne Cup is to give him a succession of tough races, each time increasing the distance. Over two-thirds of the other 22 runners had their final outing during the week before the Cup.

There were also doubts expressed about Vintage Crop's jockey. He might be a big name in the rest of the world but what did he know about Australian race-riding? And what did he think he was doing not arriving until the day before the race? At least Dettori had taken the trouble to fly out in time to get some first hand experience by riding in a race on the course three days earlier. Shades of the Belmont Stakes perhaps?

In a way the locals were right to question Kinane's ability to cope with their great race. Australian jockeys ride tight and, for someone not used to it, dangerously so. In Europe jockeys don't get so close that the horses are actually jostling each other. Apart from anything else, the stewards would stamp on them if they did. But in Australia the jockeys ride elbow to elbow as a matter of course. It's also a matter of pride to go the shortest way round. Any newcomer, no matter how good he might be in Europe, was clearly going to have trouble holding his own. At best he would be squeezed. More likely he would suffer interference. Little wonder then that Vintage Crop, despite his apparently lenient handicapping, started a 14-1 chance. Significantly, though, the Irish champion's legion of fans in Hong Kong resulted in the horse being backed down to 4-1 on the Tote there.

> I was very much aware that the Australian way of race-riding was going to be a problem, not for me but for the horse. I was reasonably confident I could hold my own but Vintage Crop had encountered nothing like this at home. Nor would he be

expecting it. He can be a bit timid at times and this would obviously not help him in all the hurly-burly.

I did a lot of preparation for the race beforehand, including studying videos of the previous 20 runnings of the Melbourne Cup. I also discussed the whole thing with several of the Australians in Hong Kong. One was Geoff Lane who is now a trainer and used to be a top class jockey in Australia. Another was Darren Beadman who was then riding in Hong Kong. They all chatted quite freely about the race and how it is run. As a result I was able to build a pretty good picture. Despite Vintage Crop's lack of experience of Australian racing, I thought I had a major chance of winning. He appeared to have 7 lb in hand and I knew he was quite a different type of horse to many of those that traditionally run in the two mile race. Basically he was a proper stayer and a lot of the opposition were not.

I couldn't go out any earlier because of my Hong Kong commitments. I was riding at Sha Tin on the Sunday. The Melbourne Cup was on the Tuesday. It's always on the first Tuesday in November. Catherine stayed in Hong Kong and I travelled on the overnight flight with Robin Parke who writes for both the *South China Morning Post* and the *Racing Post*. It's normally an eight hour flight but, as we went via Sydney, it took a bit longer and we arrived in Melbourne at lunchtime on the Monday.

I went straight to the Victoria Racing Club office to meet Les Benton who is one of the organisers and promotes the race in Europe. With his help, I dealt with the necessary paperwork and got my helmet cleared for use the next day. I then went to Flemington to have a look at the course and walk round it. What struck me most was how firm the ground was. I knew immediately it was too firm for Vintage Crop. Possibly because of his arthritis, he cannot cope with extremes of going.

I was booked into the Hilton on the Park and in the very early hours of Tuesday I was woken up by all the noise. As you know, I normally sleep like a log so this shows you just how loud it was. It was rain and it was absolutely milling down. I don't think I have ever been more pleased to be woken up! Vintage Crop might not like it soft but the ground had been so firm the previous day that I knew, no matter how much rain fell, it wasn't going to make it soft by English or Irish standards. Almost certainly it would make the going just right for him.

But in the race we ran into problems right from the off. Vintage Crop started slowly and was crowded almost immediately. He didn't like it and laid his ears back showing he didn't. I had to ride him and give him a slap down the shoulder to tell him he'd got to fight his way back into it. To his credit, he got stuck in and made his way through the worst of it. By the time we'd passed the winning post for the first time, I'd got him into a decent position.

I then came off the rails and tracked Frankie on Drum Taps, partly to give me a bit of cover in case the Aussie jockeys had decided to take me out. I'd figured there was a possibility some of them might but they would find it harder with Drum Taps immediately in front of me. Also, being off the rails, I could move in or out if anybody tried anything. Thankfully, though, none of them did.

On the final turn we were going well and, although we were some ten lengths off the leaders, I felt pretty certain I could make it up. Then a sod of earth flew up from beneath the hooves of one of those in front and hit Vintage Crop in the face. He jinxed and faltered. But he got over it pretty quickly and, once I was sure he had done so, I knew I had it in the bag. He took off when I asked him to quicken and he hit the front inside the final furlong to win, going away, by three lengths from the New Zealand horse Te Akau Nick.

People crowded round, shouting and cheering, as we were led in and Dermot Weld handed me a tiny Irish flag to hold as we made our way towards the winner's enclosure. Then the TV interviews started.

Kinane has never minded reporters' questions or requests for interviews after big race wins – 'I am always happy to share my successes' – but nothing he had encountered in the rest of the world had prepared him for the massive media interest shown by the Australians in the man who had just ridden the history-making winner.

I was followed by TV cameras the minute the race was over and they hardly let up until I got into bed that night. There was a seemingly endless succession of interviews and these continued at the Melbourne Cup Dinner. This is a traditional affair attended by over 500 people. Part of the tradition is that the winning connections should be guests of honour. There were presentations on the rostrum, more TV cameras and more interviews. It also seemed to be traditional that we should go on to a nightclub afterwards. There were even TV cameras there!

I had a fair bit to drink and I woke up with a terrible hangover and the phone ringing. I was due to do another interview, this time for a radio station. I couldn't face it. The whole world seemed to have gone crazy and I'd had enough. I took the phone off the hook.

14

Aussie Aggro

Vintage Crop had three major targets in 1994 – the Ascot Gold Cup, the Irish St Leger and the Melbourne Cup. In the first he started favourite but was beaten three-quarters of a length by the unconsidered Arcadian Heights. However at the Curragh on 17 September he became the first horse to win the same classic in successive years, even though the traditionalists were quick to claim that the race was no longer entitled to be called a classic.

But disaster struck in Melbourne. A week before the race Vintage Crop shied at an empty Malteser bag blown along by the wind as he was led out for morning exercise. He whipped round and gashed his off-fore against a jagged aluminium rail. He had to have 14 stitches and it was touch and go whether he would make the race. Amazingly he started favourite despite his injury, and despite the handicapper taking no chances by giving him top weight. But the race had no fairy-tale ending, just a barrage of abuse and criticism not experienced by a visiting sportsman since Larwood and his body-line bowling some 60 years earlier.

The Australian media could hardly have lambasted Ireland's big race king more if he had refused to speak to them and, by the time they had finished with him, he felt like doing just that. His tactics were pilloried, his judgment dismissed and his ability ridiculed.

Les Carlyon of *The Age* was typical:

> The strangest ride was Ireland's Mick Kinane on Vintage Crop, last year's winner. He rode the horse hard out of barrier 17 to try to find the rail. The strategy backfired. In the end,

Kinane couldn't get across either by going forward or going back. For most of the race he was seven and eight wide. Few horses have covered so much extra ground in a Cup and finished so close. Vintage Crop simply refused to stop trying. Before Vintage Crop was saddled in the Birdcage an Irish voice in the crowd yelled to David Phillips, Vintage Crop's strapper, 'Make Gerry Adams the jockey and we'll cheer you all the way to the winning post.' The Sinn Fein president wouldn't have sat as pretty as Kinane but he could hardly have covered more ground.

The same paper employed several other critics who laid in unmercifully. Tony Bourke wrote:

Vintage Crop ran valiantly to finish seventh under his 60 kilograms, considering his interrupted preparation and a ride by Michael Kinane that beggared description for one of the world's leading jockeys.

Patrick Smith added:

Michael Kinane rode Vintage Crop as though he were out on a scouting party looking for Shane Dye on Veandercross. The route to Tipperary is shorter than the one he plotted for last year's Melbourne Cup winner. Vintage Crop is a mighty animal to have finished seventh.

Jockey-cum-journalist Alf Matthews, who rode in the race, weighed in with with this lengthy insight into what he claimed the rest of the jockeys' room was saying and thinking:

It's Michael Kinane and Vintage Crop that have become the talking point. We jockeys have a little code – when a fellow rider looks bad on one, it takes only a glance or even a roll of your eyes to know they've got it wrong. Just 12 months ago Kinane was the toast of international jockeys, and yet yesterday he performed so dismally in our own back yard breaking some cardinal rules on, of all days, Cup day.

He started on the inside of me and 30 strides later I'm one off the fence and Kinane is six wide. I'm not looking for bouquets, but rather a genuine explanation. The room's filling now with more Aussie jockeys letting down and the Irishman's ride on Vintage Crop is becoming a hot topic. Willie Carson [who finished 22nd of 24 on Weld's other runner, Cliveden Gail] moves into the room quietly but with his usual confidence.

I ask: 'Willie, what the hell was Kinane doing out there at this point?' I take a step back and prepare not only for a sermon but I can detect that the gap between our style and theirs is widening rapidly. Willie starts, not concerned who listens, 'Better ground out wide, Alf'.

I replied: 'Sixty kilos and he's six wide. If I did that, I would be riding at Port Lincoln next Cup day, not Flemington.'

Carson returns fire: 'You Aussie blokes jump, push and bustle. Look, the ground out there was hard and fast. Mick Kinane and Dermot Weld felt to be out there was a better option. Flemington is one of the biggest racecourses you'll find and keeping your mount comfortable and happy is half the battle. Have a look at Jeune [who won the race]. He's pushing and pulling. You don't do that. You have to keep your horse comfortable. Look at you (he pointed at me) pushing your way into an inside position. If that happened at home, you and ten other blokes would get time.'

But it's clear our riding cultures are poles apart. Whether it's right or wrong to sit three, four and five wide in a race, the stark difference between our styles was never more highlighted than yesterday at Flemington. But I still remain puzzled at Kinane's ride and his tactics. One thing I'm certain of is that international horses may well be superior in some areas, but their riders are certainly not.

The insults and criticisms hurt Mick Kinane:

They bothered me, particularly the extent to which they went on and on about my riding and my tactics. I was subjected to an awful going-over, particularly for being on the outside and off the track as some of them called it. They seemed paranoid about their own way of race-riding and about expecting visiting jockeys to conform to this. They also seemed to be taking their revenge on me for winning the race the previous year. At least Alf Matthews can now claim he is famous for the way he laid into me. He is hardly famous for his riding ability.

Vintage Crop still had all the stitches in on the day of the race and Dermot Weld wanted him ridden towards the outer so that there was less risk of him being bumped or knocked. But the fact is that the horse was in nothing like the same form as he had been 12 months earlier. Indeed he was slow and sluggish. As a result he was soon at the back and, as we passed the winning post with a circuit to go and turned towards the back straight, I pulled him out to see if I could make up a few places and then get back in. But I wasn't able to get back. Then, on the far side of the course, there was a bit of interference. A horse dropped back sharply, straight into my path, and I had to pull Vintage Crop out to avoid clipping heels.

I had to make some sort of a bid to try and win and I had to do it from the outside because I still couldn't get in. Maybe the critics felt I should have dropped in behind and waited on the off-chance that I would be able to find a way through. But that's not my way of doing things. Obviously it was a bitter disappointment for things to work out so badly after the fabulous race the previous year but that's often the way it goes in racing. In any case the crowd didn't seem to be complaining – I never heard any boos or jeers. It was just the press.

Vintage Crop's back problems worsened in 1995. Early on in the year Dermot Weld was on the point of scrapping a third Ascot Gold Cup bid and sending the gelding, then eight years old, to a specialist X-ray unit in England for a deep-set bone scan to try and find out why the intermittent lameness was becoming more frequent. A sparkling reappearance at Leopardstown in early June persuaded Weld to go ahead with the now customary big race targets of the Ascot Gold Cup, the Smurfit-sponsored Irish St Leger and the Melbourne Cup. But the physiotherapy was stepped up to keep the muscles from stiffening and the horse was also given laser treatment to increase the blood supply to the area around the arthritis-affected lumbar sacral joint. Weld admitted, however, that he was counting on the adrenalin produced by the big race atmosphere to overcome the pain Vintage Crop so often showed when worked on the Curragh.

No longer was it possible to set your watch by the reliability of his work. Possibly as a result of lying awkwardly at night, he frequently seemed to feel something and he tended to save himself in his home gallops. We were unable to help him by treating him with bute or similar medications because these are banned and would result in his being disqualified.

Vintage Crop's Ascot Gold Cup run, though, was disappointing. He managed only a well-beaten fourth behind Double Trigger, Mark Johnston's tough stayer, who was also Melbourne Cup bound. Vintage Crop gained some compensation in the Curragh Cup on Irish Derby day but this was only a Group Three race and, after an effortless warm-up at Leopardstown, his attempt to win a third Irish St Leger proved a depressing anti-climax. His fourth place behind Strategic Choice and Moonax was a bitter pill to swallow and for a time it looked as if the Down Under trip would be scrapped. But the horse's jockey soon realised his initial impression was the wrong one.

> I came in from the race thinking that time had caught up with him but the following week showed he just wasn't right. A few weeks later, though, he was. We put him through a fair bit of work before we made up our minds to send him to Melbourne but, once the decision was made, I felt he had a good chance of being in the money if he remained sound and on song.
>
> I again arrived in Melbourne on the day before the race. As in 1994 Catherine went with me – we flew out after racing at Sha Tin on the Sunday – and the press were waiting for us when we arrived at the airport. I'd more or less decided I wasn't going to say much to any of the Australian media after the way they had treated me the previous year. But I answered all the questions put to me at the airport.
>
> However there was a lot of rain – it started on the Saturday evening and an inch fell in the first 24 hours, rivers flooded and some of the main roads became impassable – and it made the ground far softer than it had been in 1993. It was officially heavy and, although it wasn't heavy by Irish standards, it was really too soft for Vintage Crop. Down at the start he got a bit warm and, although I felt it was nothing to worry about, he became narky once he was loaded. He

played up and got his leg onto the side of the stall. Maybe he tweaked something in the process.

Whatever it was, he was struggling right from the off. The Australian jockeys ride the start of the Melbourne Cup as if the race was a six furlong sprint and Vintage Crop became detached almost immediately. For the first three furlongs I had to drive him along just to stop him falling even further behind. I was worried, I thought we were being run out of the race.

I was a bit happier once we passed the winning post and started to turn towards the back straight. He began to come onto the bridle and I said to myself that I must sit still and give him a chance to get it together. Mind you, I thought I hadn't a prayer. I was still plum last. However, once he was back on the bridle and settled into his stride, I knew he was going to run a race and come home. The rest had gone hard – too hard for such testing ground. They had to come back to me.

Six and a half furlongs out I started to make a bit of progress. Half a furlong later some of the others began to come back. A gap appeared and I knew the time had come to begin moving through the field. But, no sooner had I started my run, than one of those in front came back into me. I had to check to miss his heels. Vintage Crop soon got going again and at last I felt I had a chance – not of winning, I still didn't think that was possible – but of getting into the money. At the very least, he was going to run a big race.

As we turned for home, he was really motoring. I was still only halfway through the field but they were dying in front of me. For a few glorious strides, I was hopeful that the whole lot were going to cave in. As I thought, they had gone too hard from the start. I had to really put it up to Vintage Crop at this point. He was beginning to get set into his rhythm and I had to ask him for more. I hit him again, and again and again. Maybe I was too hard but he had to be made to do it. He may not be the best I have ridden but he is one of the gamest and he is my favourite. He gave me everything he had but, because of that sluggish start, it wasn't enough. We were only third. In another two strides we might have been second but we wouldn't have beaten the winner, Doriemus ridden by Damien Oliver. He was one of the few who hadn't gone too hard. When we passed the winning post first time round, he was only one in front of me.

A number of journalists came up to me afterwards. I spoke to all those who had questions to put to me but, when a race official asked me to go along to the press conference, I said 'The press seemed to manage pretty nicely without my help last year. They can do so again.' He was surprised!

Alf Matthews was in full flow in *The Age* the following day. Not a word about most of the Australians riding their horses into the ground. All the criticism was reserved for Jason Weaver on 7-2 favourite Double Trigger and Frankie Dettori on Bullwinkle – although Kinane did not exactly get away scot-free:

> People were bemused and surprised at the riding performances of the international jockeys. There was much talk like 'It's the last time one of those jocks will ride a favourite in a Melbourne Cup.' But the performance of Kinane can be defended to such a degree that, had he ridden the horse in the same manner last year, he would have won.
>
> The effort of Jason Weaver on Double Trigger was confusing, to say the least. Weaver attempted to start a run on the stallion at the 1,800 metres, of all points of the race. He then ended up having a duel for a short distance with the renowned breakaway leader, Coachwood, and 400 metres later the English visitor punctured to finish near the rear. And Frankie Dettori bewildered many with his effort on Bullwinkle, a horse known to have a short sprint that needs to be well timed. Instead Dettori chose to take off 800 metres from home and was disappointed after the race that the horse appeared to struggle in the straight.
>
> I know it's easy to criticise these three riders but I believe that the Victoria Racing Club, if it is genuine about having international riders in Melbourne for the Cup, should ensure that they are here well before the 48 hours that they arrived before this race. How can these jockeys be expected to fly into a foreign country, then ride against foreign riders, tackling horses they have never heard of, on track surfaces of which they have little or no knowledge? Shane Dye [second] and Oliver gave all of them a lesson, not only in the skills that they displayed, but in their homework and the

other facets, such as studying form and videos that are
impossible to absorb in two days.

Most of the other journalists acknowledged the problems Kinane
encountered with his mount in the early stages of the race but Clive
Galea, writing in Australia's *Sunday Telegraph*, was determined not
to let the facts affect his prose. This is what he had to say:

> Any number of hoops were well in contention for the prize
> which most got up my nose, with Damien Oliver on Pontal
> Lass and his imitation of a zipfastener in the Derby my first
> thought. But even a howling nark like me would have to
> concede that would be churlish after his great ride on
> Doriemus.
>
> And so the prize goes to Michael Kinane who must have
> thought it was an eight-day bike race, he got so far back on
> Vintage Crop. Last year the Irishman covered more ground
> than the early explorers and this year he wasn't much better.
> In fact those two efforts were so bad I'm beginning to believe
> his win in 1993 must have been a fluke.

15

The Dark Tiger

Nearly six million people live in Hong Kong and more than half of them are gambling mad. But there are no football pools or bookmakers, or at least not legal ones. The only form of gambling, apart from the lottery, that the law allows is racing and the Hong Kong Jockey Club runs, not just the racing, but the betting as well – and that includes the lottery! Its statistics show that a million people have a bet – many of them several bets – on each race day. Over 600,000 have telephone betting accounts and there are 125 off-course betting shops, all owned and linked into the Club's Tote monopoly.

Only a small proportion of the gamblers actually go racing, even though the basic admission price is less than £1, but attendances are still the envy of the rest of the world. The average crowd at the two racecourses, Sha Tin and Happy Valley, is nearly 50,000 and up to 15,000 of these are not present at the meeting but at the other course where they watch everything on television screens! It's not uncommon at Happy Valley, which is on Hong Kong island and close to the most densely populated part of the country, to have so many racegoers that the gates have to be shut before racing even starts. More than £10 million is bet on each race. The Club creams off six per cent from the turnover and, even though it donates a lot to charity, most of the money goes back into the industry to make Hong Kong the richest racing country in the world. The facilities for the public are unbelievable and so is the prize money for the horses. Even a minor race is worth between £35,000 and £40,000.

To the purist, racing in Hong Kong might seem a bit

purposeless. There is no breeding industry to link one equine generation to another – all the horses are imported – and the steady build-up towards the classics is largely lacking. Indeed most of the races are handicaps but this matters not one iota to the racegoers who cheer every race home as if it was the Derby. They are avid students of both form and the times clocked at the pre-dawn trackwork. They also take other factors into account, factors which in Europe would be dismissed as the prerogative of the ignorant. But to a Chinese gambler the horse's name and the colours it carries are considered things of tremendous relevance. Some names, when translated into Chinese, are considered lucky. Others are not. It's the same with the colours. A lot will also depend upon whether the punter considers his omens are favourable and whether the Fung Shui – the luck doctors who claim to know how to improve your chances of enjoying good fortune – have told him that his luck is going to be in. If all these "signs" are right, the punter will bet as if he could not lose. When he does he will limp away cursing the trainer and the jockey, particularly the jockey, but determined to fight again. Tomorrow is another day and the fortune he seeks is, unlike the pot of gold at the end of the rainbow, something he just might reach if he sticks at it long enough.

Jockeys who win for the punters are treated like film stars and their faces are as widely known to the man in the street as the most popular figures on television. They are just as well paid. They get ten per cent of the winnings and five per cent of the place money. The best of them are also paid handsome retainers, while the owners – who bet in huge amounts – are renowned for the size of the presents they give to their jockeys when their horses land gambles. Little wonder that Hong Kong is the favourite destination for European jockeys during the winter. Demand for licences, though, far outstrips the supply. The country allows only 33 jockeys and one-third are Chinese apprentices. A further third are also locally born and the Europeans have to compete for the remaining places with the top jockeys in Australia and South Africa.

Mick Kinane has been one of the favoured few in recent years and the Hong Kong gamblers have looked upon the Irish champion as a lucky omen. His name, translated into Chinese, means dark tiger – and that's considered lucky and therefore punter-friendly.

After going out for two meetings in the 1986–87 winter, I

spent a month riding in Hong Kong the following season. I had 20 rides and several placed horses but I didn't crack any winners. My next trip there was in December 1990 when I went out to ride Milieu for Dermot Weld in the Invitation Cup at Sha Tin. The horse disappointed and, although I had four other rides, they produced no winners. Twelve months later, though, I won the Invitation Bowl at Sha Tin on Dermot's Additional Risk. It was the first time a European-trained horse had won in Hong Kong and it caused quite a stir. I had already fixed up a month's licence for the following February [1992] when I clocked up 11 winners. At the time it was the highest monthly total for a visiting jockey. That was also when I made an arrangement with David Oughton to ride for him for six months starting in October 1992, and I did the same for the next two winters.

I soon came to love the life out there. Jockeys start the working day early. I get up at 4.00 a.m. four days a week to ride trackwork at Sha Tin but I normally manage to catch up on my sleep with a couple of hours when I return to the apartment we have in Wanchai on Hong Kong island. Racing only two days a week means that life is nothing like as hectic as it is in Ireland and England, and it gives me the chance to do all the things I just don't have time for at home. I am able to spend much more of my life with Catherine, I play plenty of golf, go to restaurants and enjoy a much more relaxed way of life. I often don't realise just how much I enjoy it until I get out there. Of course there are drawbacks, there are everywhere, and to begin with Sinead and Aisling had to leave their schools in Ireland, and their friends, to spend half the year at a school in Hong Kong. They adapted pretty well but it was far from an ideal arrangement. It was a lot better when they moved to a boarding school in Ireland and spent their Christmas holidays in Hong Kong.

Mick is noticeably more relaxed in Hong Kong than he is in Europe, despite being continually on call via his mobile phone. Driving with him to Sha Tin – he has a white Honda provided by the stable – it seems as if half the population has his number. The phone rings repeatedly. Owners tell him such-and-such is fancied, or ask him if he has heard that so-and-so's has been working like a dream. Each caller is greeted with a grin and cheerfully given the jockey's opinion as he happily puts up with traffic jams that would drive him mad at home. When he reaches the racecourse, there is no rush to change and weigh out. Instead he and Catherine go to the flat of David and Jane Oughton next door to the course for a leisurely chat. He doesn't join the other three in a drink – the weight still has to be watched – but he has time to relax in a comfortable chair.

The Oughtons live in the same block of flats as Patrick-Louis Biancone who surprisingly turned his back on a glittering training career in his native France – he won two Arcs, the French Derby and the Washington International – to move to Hong Kong. Most of the other European trainers also live in this building. Many of the officials are housed in a nearby complex and all the country's 900-plus racehorses are in stable blocks no more than a stone's throw away. It's a close-knit, claustrophobic community which, if you let it, could get on your nerves. But most of Hong Kong is constructed on the same over-crowded principle.

David Oughton has become almost as used to it as he is to the racing blood that courses through his veins. His father was a jump jockey – and finished in the frame in the Grand National three times in four years – until a bad fall forced him to turn to training. David's mother, Diane, was the daughter of Lewis Bilbie Rees who rode Music Hall to win the 1922 Grand National. LB was the brother of FB (Fred) Rees who won the big race on Shaun Spadah the previous year and who in 1924 became the first jump jockey to ride 100 winners in a season in Britain. In the dining room of the Sha Tin apartment there is a photograph of the two Rees brothers, another of LB on Music Hall sailing over Becher's for the second time in the 1922 race and one of Alan Oughton clearing the same fence on Tiberetta 35 years later.

David, tall, handsome and slim with black wavy hair going grey at the edges, was a month away from his 18th birthday when his father died of cancer at the age of 43 in June 1972. Diane took over the Findon stable and David, not light enough to follow in the family footsteps, rode as an amateur. He is an English gentleman in the best sense of the word. Educated at Hurstpierpoint, he is courteous and considerate and, at the same time, an engaging conversationalist. It was not long before mothers of marriageable daughters in Sussex began to look upon him as something of a catch. The one who struck lucky was Mrs Hardy Gillingham whose husband was a prosperous farmer and also the master of the Crawley and West Horsham Foxhounds. Jane, their dark-haired daughter, had little interest in racing but all that changed when she started going out with David. They were married in 1979 and three years later Diane Oughton handed over the licence to her son.

I knew Gordon Smyth (for whom Michael Jarvis acted as head lad when Charlottown won the 1966 Epsom Derby) and he started training in Hong Kong when he left England. He said that I should go out and have a look if ever a position came up. One winter, when there was a lengthy spell of bad weather with no racing, Gordon rang. He thought the Jockey Club would soon be looking for a new trainer. I ought to fly out. I stayed for a fortnight and Gordon's information proved correct. I was offered a position training ten horses. I had 50 at Findon and was getting winners, on the flat as well as over jumps. It didn't seem to make much sense to give up 50 to train ten but Gordon convinced me I would make more money in Hong Kong. I wasn't doing much more than making a living at Findon and I had two young children I wanted to educate at public school. I couldn't see how I was going to be able to afford the fees if I stayed put, so Jane and I decided to make the move. That was in 1987.

I miss England and, if I'm honest with myself, I have to say I would rather be training there but I simply could not afford to turn my back on Hong Kong. I now have a stable of almost 50 horses and all the bills are paid by the Jockey Club. They get most of the training fees – only a small proportion goes to me – but the bulk of my income comes from my prize money percentages and that can be considerable. Training horses in Hong Kong is very different from my days on the Sussex downs. All the work is done on Sha Tin racecourse under the critical eye of the racing correspondents and the other work watchers. My working day starts at 4.30 a.m. and the owners expect me to go into Hong Kong to have lunch with them. In theory I should be able to get in a nap like the jockeys in mid-morning but it seldom works out like that so I have to go to bed early. The social contact with the owners is considered extremely important and trainers also have to fax them their tips for each meeting.

Oughton has done well out of Hong Kong. His educational ambitions for his children have been achieved. Chloe is at Benenden, best known as Princess Anne's old school, and Charlie is at a prep school in Sussex. Their father drives a Porsche ('cheaper than a mistress and more fun') and he has become one of the most successful trainers in the country. He has also employed some of the best jockeys. Tony Murray and Philip Robinson preceded Mick Kinane.

> When Mick came out to ride Additional Risk in December 1991, I put him up on one of mine and he finished second. He rode a few more for me when he returned in February and, as Philip Robinson's Hong Kong lifespan was coming to an end, I was looking for a top jockey to take his place. Mick and I discussed the matter at length and we came up with an agreement that he would ride in Hong Kong for six months of the season. Philip and Tony Murray were really good jockeys – and I was lucky to have them – but Mick is in a different class. Indeed I think he is the best in the world and, without any shadow of doubt, he has been my greatest asset in recent seasons. We have also become close friends. To begin with, I was struck by the occasional moodiness that people talk about but I soon discovered that there was a big heart beneath it all. Also that he is an intensely private person who does not suffer fools gladly.

The six-monthly contract had to be approved by the Hong Kong Jockey Club which rules racing with a rod of iron that it is not afraid to bring down hard. Philip Johnston is the Director of Racing and, as such, one of the key figures entitled to wield the rod. Tall and grey-haired, he comes from Kelso in Scotland and was born in 1940. He was educated at Winchester and Trinity College, Dublin, and his first Hong Kong racing post was back in 1968.

> We don't like having European jockeys in Hong Kong for too long. It's a difficult place for a jockey to keep out of trouble and, in order to preserve their reputations, we have decided that five years is just about the maximum for a continuous stay, or a succession of visits. Often we tell jockeys we don't want them after much less than this. We don't normally accept a jockey riding here for six months at a time. We

usually insist they come as short term Jockey Club jockeys – riding for anyone who wants them – or that they are retained for the full season. We are not totally happy with the Kinane arrangement because it means Oughton is using Club jockeys at each end of the season and then there is a shortage. But we decided to make an exception with Kinane because he is world-class.

On the final day of that sensational February in 1992 Mick Kinane won the Hong Kong Derby on Sound Print trained by Brian Kan, and it was largely due to his friendship with Ambrose Turnbull that he got the ride. Turnbull, a hard-living character from Lurgan in Northern Ireland, first met Mick in Phuket in Thailand at the poolside bar of the Meridien Hotel where he was breaking the journey on his return from riding in the World Jockeys' Series championship in Japan. Turnbull recalls the moment in his distinctive tones which still bear the unmistakable traces of the land of his birth:

> I thought the fellow's face was familiar and I said 'Is your name Kinane?' He seemed happy to talk to a fellow Irishman and we had a drink together. We had become friends by February 1992 and he spent that month at my house. He was an amazing guest. On the days he was riding trackwork he would be back in bed before I got up and I never once heard him either leave the house or come back in again. Early on that month we talked about the Derby and he said he had been offered a ride in the race. I told him not to take it, Sound Print was the best horse in the field and he should try to get on him. I gave him Brian Kan's number and told him to ring it. When Kan said 'He's yours,' Mick promptly rode him to win the Hong Kong Classic Trial and little more than three weeks later he rode a peach of a race to follow up in the Derby.

Turnbull, until early 1996 the marketing director of the *South China Morning Post*, is an avid racing enthusiast. He flew to Australia for the 1993 Melbourne Cup, talked the bookies into giving him 20-1, backed the horse to win A$100,000 and then persuaded Mick to join him and journalist Robin Parke in the impromptu celebrations he held in a racecourse bar. He turned the photograph of the three of them into a Christmas card and sent it round the world. He is also fond of telling the story of how he preserved the Irish champion from an over-ardent female admirer:

> Jockeys are treated like gods in Hong Kong and one young air hostess fell for Mick in a big way when he stayed with me that February. I am not sure that she actually met him – if she did it was only briefly – but she found out where he was staying and she rang up repeatedly. I had to keep making all sorts of excuses why she couldn't speak to him. Fortunately, just when I thought I wasn't going to be able to fend her off any longer, Catherine arrived and I was able to hand over the protection to her!

16

Riding for a Fall

The early morning trackwork under floodlights at Sha Tin is one of the most intriguing, and closely watched, aspects of Hong Kong racing. Mick Kinane normally drives into the car park reserved for the jockeys shortly after 4.45 a.m. It's one of the few times of the day that there is little traffic on the roads and the journey from Wanchai, despite stops at the two tunnel entrance toll booths, takes little more than 20 minutes. He locks the car, takes his whip and orange helmet out of the boot and ducks under the rails, across the course, to the trainers' stand. This three-storey affair is used by the stipendiary stewards on racedays – it commands a good view of the straight – and is the hub of the trackwork activity.

Hardly anyone else has arrived and the jockey – dressed in red short-sleeved shirt, navy breeches and black riding boots – goes straight to the spartan kitchen on the ground floor to make himself a cup of tea. Five minutes later David Oughton arrives, clipboard in hand, wearing jeans, a brown jacket and brown shoes. On the clipboard is the work schedule – who is riding what and at what time. The stable jockey is down to partner six horses between 5.00 a.m. and 6.40 a.m. He is to ride work with Winnie Chung, a pretty dark-haired apprentice who is highly regarded by Oughton and who was the first girl to ride a winner in Hong Kong.

Mick Kinane disappears down the tunnel which leads to the stable blocks. Five minutes later he reappears, this time on the back of the first of the six horses he is to exercise. Following him is Winnie, her long hair tied with a rubber band just beneath her silvery blue helmet 'silk' which is set off by a pink tassel. She too wears breeches and riding boots. But she feels the cold morning air more than the Irish-born jockey and wears a navy short-sleeved anorak over her grey cotton blouse. As the horses reach the equitrack – the expensive all-weather surface which can stand up to the workload of over 900 horses galloping on it every day – she moves her mount up alongside Mick's and the pair break into a gallop. Up in the trainers' stand David Oughton presses his stopwatch. At the very top of the grandstand a long window is lit up. Behind it are 30 faces, each with a stopwatch in one hand and binoculars in the other. For the racing journalists what happens in the next two hours is almost as important as the twice-weekly racemeetings and could have a big bearing on them. Unlike the work-watchers at Newmarket, they have identification made easy for them. Every horse in Hong Kong has a number and the letters attached to the numbers signify the year of importation. So too do the different-coloured number cloths which protrude beneath the saddles. Attempting to deceive the onlookers by switching cloths is a serious offence.

Watching proceedings in the trainers' stand is one of the stipes, Christopher Lee. With grey hair, glasses and black wellingtons, he looks rather like a benevolent headmaster on his day off. He spent six years of his working life with Paddy Mullins, the shy man who was many times Ireland's champion jumps trainer. Lee is more talkative than his former boss and recalls that he has also worked as a racing official in South Africa, Malaysia and Singapore. He is on duty, he explains, in case any of the trainers want an informal chat about a problem horse and to see that none of the short-term Club jockeys have stayed in bed.

Mick Kinane and Winnie Chung come thundering up the straight. Mick's watch is picked out by the floodlights and its reflection throws out a glare like a mirror caught by the sun. The lights show up the line of skyscraper flats behind the stands and on the other side of the course the far longer line of similarly built high rise buildings that stretch all the way into Kowloon. David Oughton clicks his stopwatch again as the pair pass the post and mutters 'The Sir Gaylord has worked better today, thank goodness. Should give the jockey a bit of confidence. He wasn't too keen on him last week.' Oughton looks down at his clipboard to check who is next to work. His former colleagues in England would have a fit if they saw what was written on the schedule. He has listed his horses not by name but by their numbers!

Standing on the balcony of the trainers' stand is a curious-looking bald man in a blue tracksuit with a white top and wearing trainers. Lawrie Fownes, now in his 60s, used to be the leading trainer in Calcutta. His unusual garb has 'graced' Hong Kong for several years. He calls out his instructions to his jockey as he rides past – 'One and a half, and half, Jim'. Jim nods. The indecipherable seemingly means something to him. As Fownes peers down the straight to watch somebody else's horses, he is joined by another man in a tracksuit. But this is a smarter tracksuit, almost respectable by local standards. The top and the trousers are navy and actually match. Written across the back is Heads Sportswear. The wearer is David Hill, a brown-haired Englishman in his 30s who also used to train in India.

David Oughton says a polite good morning to the pair before hurrying off down the tunnel. He walks briskly to the four-way interchange to speak to the riders of those returning to the stables. This equine crossroads is one of the most dangerous places on earth. There are horses coming from all four directions. Some of those who have just worked are still very much on their toes. Many of the ones going out for exercise are in an even more excited state. They have been cooped up in their boxes for the past 23 hours, they know exactly where they are going – and they can't wait. They jig and prance, some lash out, others swing their hocks round and continue their fever-pitched path to the track almost sideways on to the direction they are travelling. They take up nearly all the space between the walls of the tunnel and are the most dangerous of the lot. In the tunnel the only safe place is on the back of a horse. The pedestrian runs the risk of being kicked, trampled or crushed – or all three, as Oughton recalls as he walks up the ramp towards safety:

> I was down here one morning in November 1992. There were horses everywhere and, unknown to me, one of them got loose. The first I knew about it was when I heard Mick shout 'Look out!' I glanced over my shoulder and saw this riderless horse coming straight at me at a flat-out gallop. There were horses between me and the wall. To the runaway horse, I looked more likely to give way than the other horses. I still had my back to him when he crashed into me. I was knocked flat, and all the air was crushed out of me. I ended up in hospital with a punctured lung, a broken shoulder and several cracked ribs.

Back in the trainers' stand he watches a batch of former English and Irish horses walking out onto the small cantering circuit on the inside of the main work track. One of these is Adjalabad who was trained by John Oxx for the Aga Khan to finish second at Leopardstown as a two-year-old. Ron Carstairs, the banking executive and Hong Kong Jockey Club steward who bought him, had been to the cinema only a few days before he did so. He renamed him Braveheart.

As daylight takes over from the powerful floodlights, three magpies can be seen pecking away at the worms just beneath the surface of the grass course on which the horses race. For the work-watchers, now to be seen scattered all over the stands, the morsels they have picked up through their binoculars are every bit as tasty. Thousands more will watch the trackwork when it is shown on television that evening. Below the trainers' stand Lawrie Fownes is being interviewed for the programme. The camera is concentrated on the bald head. Viewers will miss out on the garish tracksuit.

The reporters are beginning to come down from their eyrie in the stands to get a few quotes to fill out their reports. But they will have to wait a little longer for David Hayes. The former Australian champion trainer – tall, dark-haired and casually dressed with jeans and brown jodphur boots – is still watching the last of his string as they come pounding up the straight. As he clicks his stopwatch, he is joined by a blonde in a pink knee length blouse and white trousers. She is the wife of Piere Strydom, a visiting South African jockey. She is also his agent. Hayes means rides and almost certainly winners.

Down below her, the fair-haired Strydom is talking to Ivan Allan who owned the 1984 Doncaster St Leger winner Commanche Run in the days when he was training in Singapore. Allan, a bulkily-built colourful figure with dark hair combed forward, is leaning against the rail and keeping a watchful eye on what he regards as the over-eager attentions of the media.

> This is a great place to train. The facilities are fantastic and there are so many big names here. The atmosphere is so good that every raceday is like Derby day but the trouble is there is too much press interest. If you get yourself a cup of coffee, your picture is in the paper drinking it. Normally I watch the trackwork from further up the course and I keep away from

the reporters by going backwards and forwards on my
bicycle.

He looks across to where Mick Kinane is talking to David
Oughton:

> The great thing about Mick is that he has kept his nose clean
> for so long. But he has left a big hole in my heart. Back in
> 1989 I had a good colt with Henry Cecil called Citidancer
> and we decided to run him in the Phoenix Champion Stakes.
> I listened to the commentary on the radio and I got more and
> more excited as I heard how he and Steve Cauthen were
> leading up the straight. When I heard Mamaluna challenging
> him and being beaten off, I thought my horse was going to
> win a Group One. He was still in front at the furlong pole and
> I was just thinking victory was mine when along comes Mick
> on Carroll House and robs me. I should have got some
> compensation by backing Carroll House in the Arc but I was
> so pissed off I didn't bother.

Happy Valley is where Hong Kong racing began. On the night of 2
February 1994 it was where Mick Kinane's career nearly ended.

Originally built on the site of a drained, malaria-infested swamp,
Happy Valley is one of the most exciting racecourses in the world.
The stands run along the side of the short straight and the rest of the
track is almost completely surrounded by apartment blocks which
go right up to the edge of the course and turn it into an
amphitheatre. The turns are tight and, on the wrong horse, they can
be dangerous.

But any thought of danger was far from the Irish champion's
mind as he turned for home on House Honour in the third race on
the card. He had already won the first two and was in the sort of
inspired form that can make jockeys unbeatable. It can also make
them force their way through minimal gaps that normally they
might think twice about. There was one of these between On The
Double, the blinkered horse in the lead, and the rails. House
Honour's jockey decided to go for it. But the packed stands uttered
a collective gasp of horror as they saw the horse stumble and lurch
violently left, sending his jockey flying over his head. They

continued to watch as Kinane was thrown into the path of two of the three horses immediately behind him, and as he was kicked and pounded like a human football beneath the flailing, aluminium-tipped hooves, each one pile-driving into him with the force of half a ton behind it. When the unfortunate rider was eventually slammed into the rails by one final sickening blow, and lay slumped and lifeless, the crowd's attention remained riveted. But this time they watched in a silence that was almost funereal.

As the ambulance team rushed towards him, Mick Kinane could remember every painful moment:

> I had gone for a run on the inner but, just as the two horses in front started to come back to me, House Honour chickened out. I knew I was taking a risk in the first place but I would have got away with it if he had gone through with his effort. I would still have been alright if he had banged against the rail and bounced back off it. Instead he baulked and clipped the hind heels of the horse in front. He went down, not all the way but enough to dislodge me, and I was thrown forward over his head. We were travelling at a good 35 mph and the surface of the equitrack is like a road, but it was the kicking that did the real damage. The hooves hammered into me and the first kick I got was across the top of my chest just below my throat. After that I was kicked repeatedly. The blows seemed to land all over my body as I tried, desperately, to protect my face. Some of the worst kicks landed on the area around my hips and, just to add insult to injury, House Honour virtually finished me off by kicking me himself. As I lay there against the rail, struggling to breathe, I felt pretty near dead. Except for the pain. I didn't know what was broken. It felt more like a question of what wasn't.

David Oughton was among those in the stands:

> I saw it as clearly as anybody, probably clearer than most because it was my horse he was riding. When I saw him lying there, after taking that terrible pounding, I feared the worst. At best he was really badly hurt. Mind you, he should not have been poking up the inner like that. However he was riding like a demon and his inspired riding would almost certainly have snatched the race if House Honour had gone

through with it. It would have been quite a night because he'd
won the first two for me, I won the fourth on a horse he was
due to ride and his replacement was beaten a short head in
one of the other races. Mick would have won on the horse. I
rushed down to the medical room by the side of the weighing
room. I was surprised to find he was conscious and what
happened next was the one moment of light relief in the
whole thing. I asked him how he was and all he said, in that
low deadpan tone of his, was 'I've felt better!'

I immediately rang Catherine. She was in the apartment in
Wanchai getting ready to leave for Thailand the next day. It
was Chinese New Year and we had booked a holiday at the
Phuket Yacht Club. Catherine and Jane were to fly ahead, and
Mick and I were to join them after the racing on Saturday.
Catherine had been watching the race on television and she
was in a dreadful state when I got through to her. She went
straight to Canossa Hospital where Mick was being taken. I
went there too so I missed my third winner.

Astonishingly the X-rays revealed nothing worse than fractured
ribs and severe bruising, although nothing worse is a relative term
which did little to alleviate the pain and suffering of the patient.

For a fall that had broken so little, I was desperately sore. The
first kick, the one just below the throat, made the whole area
go black with bruising and for two days it was so painful that
I couldn't even swallow. The bruising around my hip joint
was just as bad. It was to be nearly five weeks before that
came anywhere near right. I was teribly lucky not to have
broken more bones, or even suffered some form of permanent
damage, but I felt dreadful.

Catherine and Jane cancelled Thursday's flight and they were
about to do the same with Saturday's when David Oughton put an
idea into their heads.

The weather in Hong Kong had become cold and damp. It
was no place for a man with bruised muscles and bones,
whereas we knew it would be warm and sunny in Phuket. The
problem was getting him out of hospital and onto the plane.
I spoke to his doctor and he said 'No way.' But Mick thought

it a good idea. He was loaded with painkillers, and he creaked and groaned a fair bit, as we helped him onto the plane. The effect of the painkillers didn't last the journey but three days later he was well enough to get on a jet ski.

However getting on a horse proved a far more formidable obstacle and, ominously, a far more frightening one. Two and a half weeks after the fall, Mick rode work at Sha Tin. But he had to give up. The pain was too great. And it was more than mere pain. Retired jump jockeys will know all about this. It's what usually ends their careers. To ride racehorses, and to go on riding them day after day, calls for a special breed of courage – particularly when you have taken painful, bone-breaking falls and know you are going to suffer more of them. Eventually these falls take their toll on the mind. No longer will it allow the thoughts of the pain that is bound to come to be shrugged aside. The reverse happens. The mind, previously so strong, becomes filled with images of falls and broken bones. The images turn to fright, even terror. The jockey can't ride in a race without these images overpowering all else. Jump jockeys have an expression for this. It's known as losing your bottle – and it forces you to give up.

Flat jockeys do not normally suffer this fate. But they do not normally suffer the sort of fall Mick Kinane had. After riding that piece of work, he confided in David Oughton.

> I was made very much aware of the inner tortures he was going through with his nerves. Normally when you have a bad fall, you are knocked out and you remember little about it. The fact that he was able to remember every moment of this one caused the problems and the whole thing had a profound effect on him. He told me the fact that it was all so clear in his mind was the most frightening aspect of all. I remember him telling me that, as he was on the ground beneath the horses' hooves, he looked up and saw this foot coming down at him. It was impossible for him to get out of the way. He just had to wait while it hammered into him. This really seemed to get to him. He was desperately worried and it made for a long passage back.

Even now, hundreds of rides later, Mick can remember all the agonising detail of that long passage back:

I never thought a fall would affect me mentally. None of the previous ones had any effect on my nerve, not even the one at Gowran Park in 1985 when I was kicked in the face and broke my jaw. Naturally you feel a bit apprehensive on your first ride back after injury but it's often partly because you are still in a bit of pain. The after-effects of this fall, though, were different and it really got to me. For a start, I could remember every goddam bit of it. I had to force myself to ride again but, after that first bit of work, I had to take another week off.

It was nearly four weeks before I was able to resume race-riding. I had a winner on my return [the former Kevin Prendergast-trained Ready at Sha Tin] and that was a big boost to my system. But it took me another two months to really get over it. Whenever I was riding tight I would tend to think that my horse would clip the heels of the horse in front, just like House Honour did, and I would come down – and be kicked and battered all over again. Up until this I had never thought about anything like that happening in the course of a race. Eventually I was able to get through it and ride that way once more but I wouldn't like another fall like that. I also wouldn't like to suffer a second time the mental agony I went through.

17

The 13 Million Dollar Question

Early in 1996 two events at Sha Tin rocked Hong Kong racing. In the first race on the second Sunday in February Walter Swinburn, riding a blinkered newcomer called Liffey River, ended up in the intensive care unit of the Prince of Wales Hospital with fearful injuries that were to keep him out of action for months.

His mount, drawn on the outside of the field, veered to his left as he came out of the stalls. He then went right, careered across the course behind the other runners, and smashed himself and his rider into the rails. Most of the damage was done when Swinburn was hammered into the stanchion supporting the aluminium rail. He broke his collar bone and several ribs. But the battering and the bruising he suffered proved far more serious. He had to undergo an operation to have fluid drained from his skull, and it took several days to clear all the blood and all the mucus out of his lungs.

This appalling accident, and the subsequent bulletins on the jockey's progress, made the papers all over the world but only in Hong Kong was the Benji case treated as high drama. Benji, a four-year-old with a chequered medical history, made his debut in the World Channel Handicap over seven furlongs at Sha Tin four weeks after Swinburn's fall. He started little fancied at 12-1 in a field of 14 for the seven furlong race and what little support he did have was largely due to his rider being on a roll after uncharacteristically going without a winner from mid-November to early January.

Only a fortnight earlier he had sprung a 20-1 surprise when getting up only yards from the line on Che Sara Sara in the Hong

Kong Derby. Che Sara Sara was trained by David Oughton whose horses were also firing on all cylinders. Oughton was the trainer of Benji.

The gelding made little impression for much of the race. Mick Kinane felt he wasn't moving quite right, possibly as a result of the injuries he had suffered earlier in his life, and he was not hard on him. When Benji did start to switch on in the final furlong, the race was as good as over. His rider, still a bit concerned, saw no point in doing much more than nurse him home as he ran past some of the beaten horses to finish fifth and over seven lengths behind the winner, Money Horse ridden by Darryll Holland.

When a horse runs on at the finish like this, with the rider seemingly taking it easy, suspicions are invariably aroused. Sometimes these suspicions are justified. The jockey, knowing he is on a horse whose connections believe had little chance of winning, dare not get down to work and win – or even go close to doing so – if he is riding for a stable that bets. Whether he wins or not, the horse will be no price the next time he runs and the jockey may well lose the ride.

Normally it's only horses who show unexpected improvement who put their riders in this sort of predicament. If the jockey knows from the outset that he is not to try, he will deliberately lie a little too far out of his ground and, when the horse does start to pick up, he will make sure that it keeps getting pocketed behind those in front.

The Sha Tin stewards pride themselves on missing very little and it took them no time at all to decide to hold an inquiry into Benji's running. Many in the crowd also took a poor view of the apparent lack of effort on the part of the horse's jockey. They began to bay for blood.

The stewards listened carefully as David Oughton explained all about the horse's problems and as Mick Kinane stated that he felt all was not well for most of the race.

> He just wasn't moving properly. He'd had chips of bone taken out of his knees at one stage, and I felt he wasn't right. Only inside the final furlong did he seem to get it together and run on. The stewards accepted our explanations. Then, for the whole of the next week, the horse was lame. Unfortunate for the horse, but it provided the post-race veterinary back-up to substantiate what we'd said at the inquiry.

The stewards may have accepted the evidence but many of those writing for the Chinese language papers did not. The critics lambasted Kinane for not trying and the stewards for not suspending him. The newspapers continued in much the same attacking vein for days. Then Benji's owner, Howard Liang Yum Shing, took the horse away from David Oughton and sent him to Patrick-Louis Biancone. The doubters in the press took this as vindication of what they had written. The attacks took off again and, when Benji won on his first start for Biancone, the momentum increased fourfold. And the reputation of the stewards nose-dived.

Mick Kinane flew back to Europe after riding at Sha Tin on 6 April. He had forgotten all about Benji. So too had the Chinese language papers. They had something new to get their teeth into. Several of Biancone's horses had been tested positive.

It was not until six weeks later that the spectre of Benji returned to haunt Kinane. He had just returned from a highly successful York when he received a telephone call from David Oughton. There was a hitch with the licence application that Oughton had lodged on Kinane's behalf for the 1996–97 season. Jockeys' licences are difficult to get in Hong Kong. But for years Kinane's application had been a formality. Apart from anything else he had that commitment, made at the height of the Sheikh Mohammed saga early in 1993, that he could ride in the colony until it was transferred to China.

Oughton faxed to Kinane's Curragh home the letter he had received from the Hong Kong Jockey Club. The Club then faxed Kinane a letter saying much the same thing, namely that his application would be considered by the Licensing Committee on 31 May and it would be necessary for him to appear at the hearing. Soon afterwards a second fax arrived saying why he was being asked to fly a third of the way across the world. The Hong Kong Jockey Club's Security Department had some questions that they wanted to put to him.

Mick was livid:

> My initial reaction was to let them get on with it. If they wanted to be difficult about my licence, they could bloody well hold the hearing without me. If they had questions to put to me, they should have asked them before I left. They must have known it was virtually impossible for me to get away at such a busy time in the season.

By this time Benji had won again, and it wasn't just the Chinese language papers that were making the connection. Philip Johnston was quoted in the *Racing Post* strenuously denying that the licence referral had anything to do with the 10 March incident. You didn't have to read too much between the lines to suspect there might well be fire lurking beneath the smoke.

> I rang David Oughton and discussed the matter at length. He was extremely annoyed about the whole thing but he said that he was very keen for me to fly out for the hearing, and so were his owners. I talked it over with Dermot Weld and he also thought I should go, if only to clear my name. Frankly, the Hong Kong Jockey Club had put a slur on it.

Mick rang Philip Johnston and asked why the questions could not be sent to him by fax. If so, he could answer them by the same method. 'Communications have made great strides in recent years,' he informed the Director of Racing, adding with more than a hint of sarcasm 'even in Ireland.'

> In fact Philip was very good about it. I don't think he was too pleased about my application being treated in this way. But he explained that he felt I should go back. He pointed out that it wasn't the sort of thing that could be done over the phone and that I was well able to stand up for myself at a hearing. But I did say that I would look a real fool if I travelled all that way only to be told I couldn't have a licence. Don't forget, the Hong Kong Jockey Club can do just what it likes. It doesn't even have to give a reason.
>
> However everybody's advice seemed to be that I should go to Hong Kong and clear things up. Frankly I didn't feel that I had anything to clear or that there was anything they could ask that could possibly have any bearing on me, or on me getting a licence. But, if I elected not to go, somebody was bound to say I'd chickened out because I had something to hide. Therefore I decided I had to go and face whatever they were going to throw at me.

The next question was when to go. The 31 May was a Friday and only two days before the French Derby. He would be entitled to ask for an alternative date. But the calendar was crammed. The dual

Irish Guineas meeting was only days away, and he was riding Deadly Dudley in the National Stakes at Sandown on 28 May. Asking for the hearing to be brought forward was clearly out of the question. But having it deferred also seemed to pose problems that were looking increasingly insuperable. The Epsom Derby was on 8 June. He was riding Dr Massini and he simply couldn't afford to be out of contact, and unable to snap up alternatives, if this accident-prone colt was the subject of another injury scare. And then there were his commitments in Ireland to Dermot Weld. The more he looked at it, 31 May seemed the only option. At least it was if he was prepared to go without proper sleep for two nights, put up with jet lag and subject his system to a punishing ordeal that would have any doctor throwing up his hands in horror.

Catherine went through all the relevant airline timetables. Her husband plumped for a flight from Dublin to Heathrow on Thursday, 30 May – he was riding at Fairyhouse the previous evening – and the 2.30 p.m. British Airways direct flight to Hong Kong that arrived in the colony at 10.30 a.m. on the Friday. He would fly out again at 10.30 pm the same day, arrive in Heathrow at 4.45 a.m. on Saturday and fly on to Dublin in time to ride at Naas that afternoon. With a bit of luck he would get a decent night's sleep at home before flying off to Paris early the next day. As in January 1993, he forked out £4,000 to travel first class.

Flight BA031 touched down at the busy Kai Tak airport a few minutes early. David Oughton and a couple of his owners drove Mick to his Wanchai apartment where they had a drink and he had a cup of tea before going off for a refreshing shower. They then went next door to the Grand Hyatt Hotel for a light lunch. Robin Parke joined them and, somewhat understandably, the main topic of conversation was the hearing scheduled for 3.00 p.m. in the stewards' room at the Happy Valley racecourse. There were two other hearings taking place that afternoon. Darryll Holland was in the same boat as Mick Kinane. Earlier in the month, when Kevin Darley, Paul Eddery and Richard Quinn had been granted their licences, Holland was told that he would have to appear before the Licensing Committee. Lawrie Fownes's application on behalf of his nephew, Wendyll Woods, had been refused. He had lodged an appeal and this was also on the agenda.

Kinane did not have to wait long before he was ushered into the stewards' room. He nodded politely in the direction of the three men who were sitting as both judge and jury. This was no ordinary rubber-stamping committee. The three were all stewards of the Jockey Club and were prominent figures in the community.

The chairman of the Licensing Committee, Wong Chung Hin, known to his friends and colleagues as CH, was a justice of the peace and had been honoured with a CBE. He was also the deputy chairman of the Jockey Club. Sitting with him were Alan F.S. Li, a fellow of the Institute of Chartered Accountants, and the Honourable Andrew K.N. Li. He too was a Commander of the British Empire and a JP. He was also a Queen's Counsel and a doctor of law. The fourth member of the Licensing Committee was absent. Michael Thornhill had horses with David Oughton and he felt that, as a result, it would be wrong for him to act at the hearing.

As Mick Kinane took his seat, he decided he didn't like the way things were shaping up – 'I had an uneasy suspicion that the balance was tipped unfairly against me. I felt that two of the three sitting in judgment would not be on my side. Indeed I suspected that it was they who had instigated the decision to defer my licence application to this hearing.'

Also present was David Twynham, the Jockey Club's Security Controller. It was he who did most of the questioning – and it was questioning that Kinane didn't like.

> The security people were definitely looking for something and the line of approach seemed to be aimed at trying to pin something on me. They started by going back to 1993. They mentioned all sorts of people I was supposed to have met that year and the following year. I couldn't recall meeting any of them but in Hong Kong you tend to meet a lot of people and you haven't a clue who they are.
>
> Some of them might come up and say they would like you to ride a horse for them. But you would have to check them out if you wanted to find out if they were who they said they were. Twynham kept asking if these people had approached me for tips. I felt that, if I said yes, the Committee would use that as a reason not to issue the licence. They would say 'Why didn't you make the officials aware of the fact? You know you have a responsibility to report the matter to the Jockey Club if somebody does approach you for a tip?'

In Europe jockeys being asked for tips is treated by the authorities as an occupational hazard, and the days when it was forbidden to reply are long gone. Indeed some are paid by the newspapers to give their views. Kinane's opinions, for example, appear in the *Daily Mirror*. But in Hong Kong passing on such information is a serious offence in the eyes of the Jockey Club.

The Security Controller then dropped his bombshell. He mentioned the name of a man suspected of being an illegal bookmaker and added 'Mr Kinane, according to our confidential sources, you met - - - - and, according to our sources, he paid you 13 million American dollars in February 1994.' As his disbelief registered, Mick Kinane's grim-set expression gave way to a broad grin.

> I felt like replying that, if I had been paid that sort of money, did they really think I would be sitting there listening to all these questions? Somehow, though, I didn't think that would be an appropriate answer!
>
> Once we had established that I had never met this man, or received any money from him, they asked me about two of my friends. I was amazed that they were asking about one of them because he is a member of the Hong Kong Jockey Club. They asked me if he bets. I said I didn't know. But it would be quite easy for them to find out. Certainly a lot easier than for me to do so. Eventually we moved on to the two most recent years. The questions were all silly stuff. The whole session lasted about an hour and I left the room convinced they were simply going through all this in an attempt to save face over the Benji affair.

Mick was then kept waiting while the Licensing Committee heard Lawrie Fownes's appeal. They decided Fownes had a valid case and ruled that his nephew could ride in Hong Kong during the 1996–97 season. They then asked for Kinane to be brought back into the room. Again he was asked to sit down. 'Mr Kinane,' Wong Chung Hin began. 'We have considered your application carefully and we have decided that we will give you a licence for next season. A little reluctantly, I might add, in the light of some of your answers.'

Mick Kinane looked directly at the three men sitting opposite him. Now that he was going to be given his licence, he could afford to let rip. 'Gentlemen,' he informed the Licensing Committee trio, 'this hearing has consisted of some of the most pre-fabricated rubbish that I have ever heard in my life.'

> I left them feeling none too pleased. But I was annoyed and I
> gave them what they deserved.

When Mick walked out of the stewards' room he was confronted by a barrage of questions from the waiting media. One of them asked him if he was happy about the outcome. It seemed a reasonable question. At least it did if you had not been present at the concluding stages of the hearing. 'It's not a question of being happy,' the pressman was bluntly informed. Darryll Holland fared less well. He was told he could not have a licence. No reason was given. He later lodged an appeal but this was turned down. So too was Biancone's appeal against the HK$250,000 fine slapped on him over the prohibited substance cases.

The high hopes held out for Blue Duster – the One Thousand Guineas was widely considered to be a match between her and the Henry Cecil-trained Bosra Sham – were dashed when Mick rode her in a gallop after racing at the Newmarket Craven meeting. David Loder had been bullish about her progress but Mick Kinane gave her a poor report.

> Because the ground was so fast, David didn't want me to do all that much with her. We went six furlongs and, although she moved well and was clearly in great nick, she made a rattling noise in her throat when I was pulling her up. I told David that she shouldn't be doing that after such a light piece of work. Either she had a good bit to go fitnesswise or there was something wrong with her. There was. She was forced to miss both the Guineas and Royal Ascot, and she was sent out to Dubai in a bid to get her right.

In the Two Thousand Guineas Mick struck lucky – not with his own mount, Danehill Dancer, who never looked like winning – but with the stewards. They hit Frankie Dettori with an eight-day whip ban. The ebullient Italian was also fined £500 for jumping off his horse before reaching the winner's enclosure and embracing the colt's stable lad in his delight at getting the photo-finish verdict. Eight days ruled him out of York and Kinane, who picked up several of his rides, turned the meeting into a personal benefit winning on seven of his 13 mounts. His victories included the Yorkshire Cup on Classic Cliche and Mick promptly recommended to the winning Godolphin team that the four-year-old should have a crack at the Ascot Gold Cup. He assumed, as did everybody else, that Dettori would be back on board. Another of his York winners was Dr Massini who immediately became one of the favourites for the Epsom Derby but, despite surviving one setback, he went lame again three days before the race. Mick was snapped up by Henry Cecil for Storm Trooper but there was no happy ending.

> Dr Massini was a good ride to have but, after things went wrong with him the first time, I felt there was a strong possibility he might not make the race. It was a long way from being a total surprise when he was ruled out. Storm Trooper was disappointing. He is not very big, the Derby turned into a rough race and he didn't enjoy it at all. I thought I was going to get some compensation that day, though, on Singspiel in the Coronation Cup when Frankie Dettori set only a moderate pace on Swain. I knew from riding him in the Arc the previous season that he stayed well whereas my fellow was really a mile and a quarter horse. Halfway up the straight I felt I was sure to be able to beat Swain for speed but Frankie kept asking him for more and he kept finding it to hold us off by a neck.

The margin in the French Derby six days earlier was even closer:

> I was fully recovered from the Hong Kong trip by this time, although I'd been pretty tired at Naas the previous day. Peter Chapple-Hyam, though, fell ill and had to rest before the start of the Prix du Jockey-Club in which he ran three. John Reid, who is Peter's stable jockey, opted for High Baroque, Pat Eddery rode Astor Place and I was on Polaris Flight who was the least fancied of the trio according to the betting.
>
> But Peter was hoping for a big run from him and I was told to try to ride him from mid-division. I popped out well and close to the favourite, Helissio, ridden by Dominic Boeuf. I decided to track him but after only a furlong just about everybody else was trying to do the same. At Chantilly you go on one side of the course early on and then switch to the other, close to the paling. The centre can get rough and I was

in danger of being knocked over. There was simply no room, they were all going hard and everybody was fighting. I decided to ease back. I started to ride early in the straight and Polaris Flight soon began to make up enough ground for me to think that I was going to be placed. I tracked Gerald Mosse on Ragmar but he left me when he quickened. Then Ragmar ran a bit to the left and stalled. My horse was really travelling by this stage and we almost got there. In another stride I would have won. Mind you the third horse, Le Destin, was finishing even faster and if there had been another two strides he would have won.

The interference Ragmar caused us was only slight but, when I asked Peter if he wanted me to object, he said I should. I knew my chances of getting the race were pretty slim. Then the stewards announced an inquiry which confirmed that they also thought there had been interference. Once I saw the film, though, I knew I was going to get nowhere.

Five days before the start of Royal Ascot, Frankie Dettori broke his elbow in a freak fall at Newbury. Mick Kinane, already hot favourite to be top jockey at the meeting, went odds-on. He rode five winners to become the first since Lester Piggott in 1979 to win the Ritz – now London Clubs – Trophy three years in a row.

Two of his winners would have been partnered by Dettori – Charnwood Forest, and Classic Cliche in the Ascot Gold Cup for which Double Trigger started at 2-1 on. There was considerable doubt about Classic Cliche getting the trip.

All the jockeys knew that Jason Weaver would try to make it throughout as he had done 12 months earlier but the pace was not as strong as I'd expected. In fact we didn't do much more than saunter until we got to Swinley Bottom and so my horse had hardly had to work at all. But, as we turned for home, I knew Double Trigger would keep pulling out more once I took him on. I had made up my mind to creep there and then run at him quickly. When we straightened up Classic Cliche came off his stride for a second but he was really doing no more than change legs and he soon got back into gear. Then, when I asked him to go on and win his race, he hung in a bit. Possibly the ground was a little bit firm for him, possibly he was feeling the pinch of the two and a half miles. For a stride or two, I was concerned. But he then knuckled down to it.

Weaver was widely criticised in the following day's papers for not going fast enough. Ironically, only two days earlier, he had been praised to the hilt for his riding of Bijou d'Inde in the St James's Palace Stakes. This time it was Kinane who came under attack for going too soon on Ashkalani and Alain de Royer-Dupre commented bitterly 'I have to thank the stewards of France-Galop for this. They cost me the race.'

Gerald Mosse, Royer-Dupre's stable jockey who had won the Poule d'Essai des Poulains on the Aga Khan's colt, was sitting out a suspension and the France-Galop stewards had rejected his appeal. Mick Kinane was also brassed off with the result.

> The really disappointing part of it was getting beaten because I hadn't been told to hold the horse up for a late run. I asked a lot of questions beforehand and I probed as much as I could. Alain does not speak English that well but the language was not a problem because I was asking the questions through Ghislain Drion, the Aga's Irish stud manager. I asked them if Ashkalani would get the trip really well and they said he would. In fact all the answers to my questions were positive. There was nothing negative except that I was to make sure that he settled early on. Then make progress gradually. This I did and in the straight I was travelling so well I felt the time had come to go. But, when I headed Bijou d'Inde, my fellow tried to hang in towards him. I had to pull my whip through and give him one. But I still thought I was going to win. Not until inside the last 20 yards did I have any reason to think differently. Then he suddenly lost his concentration. He ran a bit to the left, then a bit to the right – and the world fell apart!

It did so again 12 days later when Kinane's Irish Derby hoodoo struck him a savage and humiliating slap across the face. Dermot Weld's main Irish Derby hope early in the season was a colt called Zagreb, a son of Theatrical, the horse who went within half a length of giving Mick Irish Derby victory on only his third attempt back in 1985. Zagreb looked the part when he ran out an impressive winner of his debut in a maiden at the Curragh in April, particularly when subsequent races proved that several of the 26 who finished behind him were pretty smart.

But things then went wrong with Zagreb. He picked up a heavy head cold and had to be treated with antibiotics. These can have quite a lasting effect on horses who often appear to have made a full recovery only to run lifelessly on their return to action. Dermot Weld, concerned about this, kept putting off Zagreb's next race and, when the colt finally did reappear, he was beaten. Mick Kinane, aware that there was a slight doubt about Zagreb's fitness, held him up and had only one behind him turning for home. He was beaten a head and was widely criticised for giving his mount too much to do. Pat Shanahan, who had ridden the colt in a lot of his work, was to say this quite bluntly after the Irish Derby.

The Irish Derby looked like going by without Zagreb when he was ridden by Kinane in a gallop eight days before the race. Zagreb, although the relevance – or rather lack of it – was not fully appreciated at the time, had two ways of working. Some days he sparkled. Some days he didn't. This was one of the latter and Kinane, already offered the mount on a supposedly fully-recovered Dr Massini, knew which one he wanted to ride in the Curragh's big race.

Zagreb worked better the following Tuesday but still not well enough and Dermot Weld agreed to release his stable jockey for Michael Stoute's colt. He promptly announced that Zagreb was a doubtful runner and said that Pat Shanahan would be on Touch Judge – 'if he runs, but he is more likely to go for the Curragh Cup on the same card.'

When it rained in the early hours of Friday morning, Weld changed his mind. He told Shanahan that Zagreb would run and that he would ride him. Shanahan was pleased just to have a mount in the big race. He had fallen so far out of fashion, and so much out of favour, since the heady days of 1984 when he won the Irish Oaks on Princess Pati at the age of 21, that three years before he got the Zagreb call he was seriously considering leaving Ireland to try his luck in Macau. This is Hong Kong's poor relation and widely regarded by the jockeys as a real last-chance saloon.

Needless to say nobody held out much hope for Zagreb. It never occurred to any of the 27,500 racegoers at the Curragh that Mick Kinane could have got it wrong. Indeed they all seemed to know how keen he had been to ride Dr Massini and Kinane's 15th Irish Derby mount started second favourite. It was quite early on in the race that Kinane knew that Ireland's premier prize was going to elude him yet again – Dr Massini was simply not travelling – but, when Zagreb swept into the lead and galloped clean away, Kinane could have been forgiven for wishing the earth would open and swallow him up. This was the race – by now the race above all others – that he wanted to win, and the horse he had so happily rejected was handing him the ultimate humiliation in full view of everybody, not just in the land of his birth but on TV all round the world.

Extenuating circumstances there might have been but, so far as the pundits were concerned, he had made one of the biggest mistakes of his life. This one was on a par with the penalty kick missed by Gareth Southgate at Wembley only four days earlier. It knocked England out of Euro '96 and earned the hapless Southgate a place in football history for all the wrong reasons. Ironically the headline splashed across the front page of *The Sporting Life* proclaimed KINANE OWN GOAL. Like Southgate, and for as long as he lives, Kinane will never forget – or be allowed to forget – what had turned out to be a dreadful decision. From that moment on, whenever his name is mentioned in connection with the Irish Derby – whether on television, in print or in person – he will be reminded of the day he picked the wrong one.

Every big race jockey's nightmare is finding he has gone for the wrong horse and the fact that it had in the past always happened to his rivals – often with him being the beneficiary – made it hurt even harder.

I was gutted. I had turned down Zagreb because I was disappointed with him that night at Leopardstown and because I didn't think he was mature enough to win the Irish Derby. But I made the wrong call and it cost me dear. They say this game is a great leveller. Some days, like that one on 30 June 1996, it feels an awful lot tougher than that.

18

The Method

This book would not be complete without an in-depth examination of why the subject has been so successful. People often try to answer this question with other top sportsmen but I suspect few ever really get to the roots. With a jockey, it is doubly difficult because he is only half the equation. The other half is the horse, and the best jockeys have not only to beat their rivals with superior tactics but also to persuade their mounts to produce more than the opposition.

Mick Kinane, when quizzed on the reasons for his own success, is able to reach only parts of the answer:

> To a certain extent, in my case at least, it's breeding. I inherited a lot of my riding ability from Dad and my determination from his mother. She was a really tough lady and Dad often says that I have a lot of her qualities. Confidence also plays a big part. When you have it you ride better because you don't feel under any pressure and, almost automatically, everything you do turns out right. Confidence comes from riding winners but to start with, or when you are having a bad run, you have to instil confidence in yourself. That means believing in your own ability. I would never claim that I am better than the other jockeys – I am not, not all of them anyway – but I have to believe I can be better if I do everything right. It's this belief that carries me through the days when the winners just won't come.

In an attempt to find out the rest of the answer I asked some of those who have reached the top in racing, and who have had reason to study Kinane, either as a rival or as an ally.

Lester Piggott was, by common consent, one of the greatest jockeys the world has ever known. Despite having severe weight problems until well into his 40s when he found that his metabolism had stabilised at not all that much more than his usual riding weight, he was champion jockey in England 11 times and won 30 classics including the Epsom Derby an incredible nine times. He also won 16 Irish classics, three Arcs and countless other big races all over the world. He is convinced that the principal reason for Kinane's success is the way he uses his brain.

> Whenever I see Mick Kinane, he is thinking. He is going through the next race, or races, in his mind. He does this over and over again, and he's always doing it. He's what I call a thinking jockey and it's his greatest asset.

Steve Cauthen, who has seen Mick successfully step into the breach in the Sheikh Mohammed colours he was at one stage entitled to regard as his own, has carefully studied the Irish champion's methods:

> In addition to being very strong, Mick is a real stylist – he keeps low and he keeps close to his mounts. He has also become tactically excellent – he knows exactly where to put his horse in a race and when to make his move. As a result he is an all-round top class jockey, as good as there is anywhere in the world.

One champion who does not ride against Kinane, but who has watched him closely, is Richard Dunwoody. The triple National Hunt champion is one of the best, and certainly one of the most stylish, jump jockeys I have ever seen. He has this to say:

> Mick Kinane's strength in a finish, and his ability to use his whip equally effectively in either hand, almost goes without saying in a man who has been champion so often but I am convinced that what enables him to nick all those big races is that he somehow always manages to have his horses in the right place at the right time. It's rare to be able to fault him tactically.

Richard Hannon, like Lester Piggott, has been struck by the extent to which Mick works everything out in his mind beforehand:

> He is a very quiet man who thinks a lot about what lies ahead. He then goes about his job and gets it done economically and efficiently. In addition, he is a strong jockey who can power his mounts home. Furthermore, he is totally dedicated to his profession.

Henry Cecil has been impressed as much by Kinane's character as by his riding ability:

> He is strong and he is good but it's one thing being good and it's another being able to take being good. To my mind there is nothing worse than turning into a bad winner. But Mick is not in the least bit cocky. Indeed I find him modest and I wouldn't think that he has changed throughout his whole career.

On the Curragh Liam Browne has watched with a certain amount of pride the man he taught hitting the headlines around the globe:

> He always wanted to become the best and he was so determined to succeed. He is rather like a horse that has kept on improving right up to Group One. Most of my apprentices, with the notable exception of Tommy Carmody, have only made it to Group Two but Mick is the equivalent of a Derby horse. Mark you, he didn't always look as if he was going to get to the top but he has made it by being totally dedicated. He is also extremely strong and he has a great racing brain.

This last part is seized on by Dermot Weld:

> The most important reason of all for Mick Kinane being a top jockey is because he is so intelligent. Indeed, it's not a question of him being a jockey who is intelligent but much more a case of being a highly intelligent person who happens to be a jockey. I know he sits well on a horse, keeps them balanced, is very determined and is a skilled tactician. But a

lot of other jockeys have the same qualities. What sets him apart is his brain. He is more intelligent than any jockey I have ever come into contact with. I firmly believe that he would have been a success at almost anything he chose to do.

I am far from convinced about this last point. Virtually all those who have reached the top of their particular tree have done so partly because they wanted, above all else, to succeed in their particular sphere. They also love what they are doing. Put them in another environment and they would be both unhappy and unsuccessful. Mick Kinane might have made the grade as a boxer or as a professional golfer if his build had been bigger but he would not have got far, for example, as a politician. Nor, even by his own admission, does he have what it takes to be a successful trainer. Tommy Carmody is much nearer the mark when he says:

> The reason Mick is so good is that he is so hungry for winners. He will do anything he possibly can to win a race and that extends to every detail of his life. People say that good horses make good jockeys – and they are quite correct. But Mick has made sure that he has put himself in the right places, and done the right things, to get on those good horses. In order to achieve his aims, he has tightened up every single aspect of his riding including his tactics and his style. He looks so good on a horse because he is almost part of the horse and he does everything right to get the best out of his mounts. In short, he has made himself good and it's his hunger to ride winners that has done that. He also hates to get beaten but that is all part of the same thing.

This is a thought-provoking assessment and I am convinced that what lies behind the achievement of Kinane's aims is a complex mixture of dedication, skill, aptitude and an overriding, all-consuming will to win.

Let's begin with his preparation which, even in the case of the most minor race, is more detailed than that of any jockey I have ever come across.

> I would never dream of going to the races without having done my homework. I like to be fully prepared and that

means finding out all I can, not just about my own horse, but about all the others in the race. I spend hours studying the racing papers and the form books. It might sound hard work but it's not for me because I love doing it. All this preparation helps me to work out the strengths and the weaknesses of the opposition, what sort of pace there is likely to be, how the race should develop and how the dangers are likely to be ridden. From there I can get a fair idea of what sort of race I need to ride.

When he is at home this detailed study is sometimes done on the kitchen table, sometimes in the small sitting room at the back of the house where he studies the videos of past races but mostly in the sauna. This is the last room in the wing at the side of Clunemore Lodge. If you drive past and look over the electronically-controlled heavy wooden gates, that keep unwelcome visitors at bay and help to preserve the privacy he values so highly, you won't see it because it is hidden from view by the main part of the house. There is a small bathroom in there – he is mentally running through the day's races even when he is shaving – and three large framed pictures. One is of Marilyn Monroe, another is of a grossly overweight lady riding a bicycle and the third is of a gorilla gazing longingly at a huge club sandwich. This is the only one of the three that has a caption. It reads: 'Diet – what diet?' On the row of shelving where the jockey lies are piles of newspapers.

> I lock myself away in this sauna, I know I won't be disturbed and I like the isolation. Although it's a sauna I don't do that much sweating and I only have the temperature between 60 and 70 degrees fahrenheit. If you go into saunas at leisure centres you will find it much hotter, often in the 80s or 90s. Really, this is too hot and, as a result, you can't relax.
>
> Virtually all jockeys prepare for races in their minds but everybody has a different way of doing it. I find that there is much more mental than physical effort involved in race-riding. The physical part is easy because you are already fit from riding so much work and riding in so many races.

When jockeys are going down to the start they often seem to be relaxing and happily chatting to each other. Not Mick. His determination to win means that he is working on the race all the time.

Even what happens in the parade ring can be important and I always make a point of talking to the lad or girl who is leading me round. The trainer will know how the horse should be ridden and normally he will tell you 95 per cent of what you need to know. But that other 5 per cent can be vital. The person who looks after the horse knows him best and what he or she has to say can often prove invaluable.

I don't talk to the horses all that much but I like to build up their confidence by being as quiet on them as I can. I will give them a pat and try to make friends with them. If they are a bit hyped up going down to the start I try to calm them down. I find that, if you can get the relationship off to a good start, it can be a big help when the race gets underway. If the horse is happy with you when you go down, and he begins to trust you, he will be in the right frame of mind for the race and he will run for you.

Horses are individuals. No two are the same. When I haven't ridden a particular horse before, I find I can assess a great deal of his mental make-up during that canter to the start. How he is taking things in, how he is moving – whether he is fighting or is settled and relaxed – all contribute to giving an idea of what he is going to be like in a race, and of how I need to ride him.

Once we are down at the start, I sit quietly and I don't bother him if he seems happy. When we are in the stalls, though, I do talk to him. I want him to listen to me and pay attention. I will pat him to keep him standing quietly. I want him relaxed but not too relaxed. I want him ready to respond to me when the time comes to jump out. My main preoccupation, though, is getting him to stand square so that he jumps straight and on the right leg.

At this stage I have hold of the mane, not the reins. If it has been plaited, I will have already undone the last couple of plaits so that I have something to get a grip on. When the gates open I lean forward onto my hands. Obviously if he jumps to the left or to the right I have to correct him but, assuming he has been standing square, he will normally jump straight. Because I have hold of the mane, rather than the reins, there is no risk of me jabbing him in the mouth. Not only is this painful for the horse, it stops him pushing himself forward and making the maximum use of his hind-quarters to

project himself out of the stalls. I learnt about this when I
made that first visit to the States at the end of 1978. I watched
how the American jocks left the stalls and I soon came to the
conclusion that they are the best in the world at getting their
mounts smartly and quickly away from the gate.

Like many of the top jockeys in Britain and France, Mick has
changed to the American method of riding with his toes balanced on
the irons. This is far less secure than the traditional method
employed by the likes of Lester Piggott, Pat Eddery, Willie Carson
and Michael Roberts. These jockeys, all champions, ride with their
feet 'home', i.e. with the base of the stirrup under the instep and
pressed against the edge of the heel of the riding boot. They prefer
this style because they can kick their mounts without risk of their
feet slipping out of the irons. They are also far less likely to lose their
irons if their horses should stumble. So why the switch?

I decided to try it because I felt I was beginning to look
untidy, possibly as a result of riding so much work. I
experimented with it on the gallops and then, when I got the
hang of it, I began to use it for race-riding. I now find it more
comfortable and, although I am sure it doesn't bring me any
more winners or make the horses go any faster, it does keep
me lower and closer to the horse.

In one respect Kinane's style is slightly different, even to the
others who have adopted the American stance. If you stand by the
rails, a few yards along from where the horses leave the paddock
and go out onto the course, you will see the jockeys rise up into
their normal crouch as the horses take hold and break into a
canter. They all ride too short for their knees to grip the saddle but
they all, to a greater or lesser degree, make contact with the horse
and the saddle with their calves. Their legs below the knee form an
inverted V. Some even ride with their knees almost touching at the
point of the V. The exception is Kinane. His knees are so wide
apart that the lower part of his legs go almost straight down. His
legs make no contact with the horse other than at the ankle. His
balance is wholly dependent on his toes precariously balanced on
the irons.

But back to the race:

I am a firm believer in getting into a good position early on. Dermot Weld taught me that. If you can do it, you will not have to use your horse up so much at a later, more vital stage. What decides that good position, more than anything else, is the pace at which we are travelling. If it's a good pace, and the horse can be ridden close to it, then I will settle him a few lengths off the leaders and stay there until the race begins in earnest. If the pace is slow, I will also want to be handy but this time so that, when it quickens, I don't run the risk of giving the leaders a start. If, on the other hand, the pace is too fast it's no good me burning up my horse to stay in touch. What also plays a big part is how the horse needs to be ridden to give of his best, i.e. whether he likes to come from behind or whether he prefers to be up there.

What I also have to do is work out whether or not I should be on the rails, and that depends to a great extent on what is happening in front and on what I think is going to happen – whether the leaders are going to fall back when they tire, or drift to one side or the other. Hopefully my homework will have told me what they are likely to do. Obviously nobody wants to get boxed in and, while there are obvious advantages to sticking to the rails and so going the shortest way round, I have to weigh up the risks of not getting a clear run. And I have to keep weighing them up as the race progresses. Once I am in the position I want, I try to switch the horse off and just let him lob along behind those in front so he does not feel he is racing. I want him to conserve his energy, mental as well as physical, so that he has as much as possible left in the tank when the time comes to call on it.

When I start to ride the horse, I am not so much kicking him with my heels as squeezing him. I'm also pushing my fists into his neck, even punching him, to urge him on to pull out more. It's the feedback you get from your legs and hands that tells you whether a horse has more to give. You also get a good idea from how quickly he responds when you start to ask him. Supposing, for example, there is a gap three or four furlongs out and you need to go for it. If he moves there the second you push him, you know you are going to have a fair bit left when the time comes to race in earnest.

When that moment comes the powerful, rhythmic, relentless yet supremely polished Kinane finish seems to galvanise his mounts and time and time again those who have backed him are treated to the sight of the Irishman cutting down the opposition and driving hard for the line. When he is in full flow on a horse that is responding, there can often be an aura of almost invincibility about his performance. And that look of grim determination and desire for victory, that so delights younger brother Jayo, never leaves him.

> I am conscious of this refusal to accept defeat and also that I am somehow instilling the same attitude into my horse. It's all part and parcel of what I am. The horse invariably gets the message and he will respond accordingly. He will also give his all if that is what I have to call upon him to do. With most of them that means first showing them the whip and then giving them a few smacks. Horses, although bred to race and to try to beat each other, will often only exert themselves to the maximum when they see and feel the whip. Usually when you wave it at them, they quicken. But most of them will quicken again when you hit them.

It is at this point, of course, that the whip controversy starts to rage and Mick has on occasion found himself at the centre of a storm. Surprisingly, though, he had never had so much as a caution concerning the whip in England until April 1994. He received one in Ireland in 1988 but he had no further problems in that country until July 1995. That first English caution came at Newmarket after he had finished third on Bobzao in the Jockey Club Stakes. The stewards had him in and asked him to explain why he was raising his arm above shoulder height when he was using his stick. This is expressly forbidden by the rules to ensure that horses are not hit with undue force. He was warned about his future use of the whip. On the opening day of Royal Ascot little more than six weeks later, though, he threw both caution and the rule book to the winds – and this time the stewards were harder on him. They pointed out that he had again broken the shoulder height rule and had hit the colt with unreasonable force. They punished him with a two-day suspension.

The colt was Grand Lodge, owned by Lord Howard de Walden and trained by William Jarvis, and he needed every last ounce of Kinane's power-packed finish to get up in the last stride of the St James's Palace Stakes. It was, by common consent, one of Mick

Kinane's greatest rides. Lester Piggott, when talking to me about Kinane, said: 'Of all the races I have seen him ride, that one on Grand Lodge stands out. I thought he was absolutely superb that day. It was a tremendous piece of riding.'

Timeform echoed similar sentiments in its *Racehorses of 1994* annual:

> Skill, strength and determination have made Kinane one of the best jockeys in the world and it's safe to say that Grand Lodge wouldn't have won the St James's Palace Stakes without an inspired ride. He rode a tremendous race on a very game horse who responded to every call, battling all the way to the line to get the better of Distant View. Kinane's reward: a two-day suspension for 'using his whip from above shoulder height with unreasonable force.' Applying an absurd rule in censure of an almost universally-praised exhibition of jockeyship was, for British racing, like rubbing salt into a self-inflicted wound. As in many similar instances, the Kinane case served to leave the way the authorities have sought to deal with a relatively-insignificant problem open to ridicule. Kinane himself put it in a nutshell 'I had to give Grand Lodge what I did to get up and win . . . it was a classic example of where the rules come into conflict with winning.' The ill-advised tight whip guidelines have done more, through the publicity given to cases, to caricature racing as a cruel sport than the actions of any whip-happy jockey. No good jockey hits a horse any more than necessary and it is ridiculous to tell an internationally-acclaimed rider like Kinane that he can't ride properly.

At the time Mick was upset about the suspension – not about the two days but about the criticism of his riding that it implied – but he now looks on it rather more philosophically.

> Having been cautioned at Newmarket for the same offence earlier in the season, a suspension was automatic. On the other hand, if I'd stayed within the rules on Grand Lodge, I would almost certainly not have won. The Jockey Club and its stewards are doing their best to make racing look good from a visual point of view and they have decided that one of the things they don't want to see is jockeys raising their whip

arm above the shoulder. They are in charge and, if that's the way they want to do things, then that's fine by me and I will do my bit by trying to abide by their rules.

The Jockey Club stewards came under fire when they first issued the six-stroke rule – the acting stewards have to consider holding an inquiry whenever a jockey uses his whip six times or more – and to begin with I, like many of the other jocks, was convinced they had got it all wrong and they were very hard on a lot of riders. From 1994 on, though, the stewards have been more flexible and have taken a more sensible approach to the rule. As a result you will often see a horse being hit six or seven times, often more, with no action being taken because the horse has been responding all the time. This is a much more practical way of interpreting a rule which, in any event, was never meant to be totally black and white. I just wish the Irish stewards had shown as much sense in 1995.

At Killarney in July that year Kinane hit Political Domain, the 5-2 favourite for the Heineken Handicap, 11 times and his three-day suspension ruled him out of much of the following week's big Goodwood meeting. Kevin Manning was also suspended at Killarney and the jockeys were so incensed by what they regarded as two cases of blatant injustice that they called for a meeting with the stewards. But it didn't do Kinane much good. At Fairyhouse the following month he was given another three days for excessive use of the whip, this time on the Tommy Stack-trained Madaraka. It was too much for the Kinane temper. He flared up and told Richard Teevan, the senior stewards secretary who had also been on duty at Killarney, exactly what he thought of him! In racing, letting fly at officials – with or without justification – is considered a serious offence and Mick avoided collecting a far longer ban only when Dermot Weld persuaded him to apologise. But even today he is still furious about the two incidents:

> Both suspensions were solely the result of poor stewarding. Madaraka and Political Domain were running lazily and were responding each time I hit them. I wasn't hitting them that hard, just enough to let them know there was a race to win and that they had to keep trying. In the circumstances it's ridiculous to say that my use of the whip was excessive, let

alone that it merited a suspension. There is a further point that the stewards chose to overlook. Before the Killarney incident there had not been so much as a caution for a whip offence on my official record sheet in Ireland for seven years. A jockey can expect to receive a caution for the first offence after such a long period unless it is a particularly serious one. Only for the second and subsequent offences, do you get a suspension. That's another reason why I say it was bad stewarding.

Mick Kinane is convinced that many of those who are the most emotive over the whip issue are on the wrong tack and fail to understand either the mental make-up of the racehorse or how well treated the vast majority actually are.

I often think that people who criticise jockeys for hitting a horse during a race somehow equate this with whipping horses in some sort of gruesome punishment. Using the whip in a race is totally different to cornering an animal in, say, a stable and hitting him. That is cruelty and I would never condone it, or anything like it. It would invoke both panic and fear in a horse, whereas hitting him in the course of a driving finish does not make him afraid and nor does it cause him much in the way of pain. I agree it stings but to the horse who is already exerting himself quite a bit, it's simply a signal that he must exert himself more. His blood is up and so a smack does not register as real pain. If it did he would stop, swerve or try to get rid of the person who was hurting him. What must also be remembered is that racehorses are pampered from birth. They get the best food money can buy, they are exercised like international athletes, they are groomed as expertly and as caringly as if they were visiting the most expensive masseurs in a London gym and they are housed in the equine equivalent of the Ritz. Their feet are manicured every month and the minute they get the slightest thing wrong with them, the doctor is summoned. The staff who look after them are nothing like so well fed or so well treated. It costs an enormous amount of money to keep racehorses in such luxury and so it's surely not too much to ask that, when they do what they are bred to, they should be expected to give their maximum. If I was told there was a next life, and I was asked what I wanted to come back as, I wouldn't have much hesitation in saying a racehorse.

However Kinane is convinced that both the Jockey Club and the Turf Club have got it badly wrong with the rule that makes it illegal for a jockey to hit a horse down the shoulder with the whip in the forehand position.

I believe both bodies were right to stop jockeys picking up their whips and hitting horses with force down the shoulder but to rule this out altogether, particularly in cases where safety is involved, is a big mistake. If, for example, you are involved in a finish and you already have your whip in the forehand position you are in trouble if you suddenly sense that the horse is about to swerve or jinx. The only way to stop him is to hit him down the shoulder on the side he is going to swerve towards. He then knows where the whip is and he will keep straight. But if you hit him without changing your grip on the whip you will be in trouble with the stewards. If you change your grip to the carry position that will take you a fraction of a second, and you will be too late to stop the horse swerving. You will cause interference and you could cause an accident, even injury, by failing to take action in time to stop your horse moving off a straight line. The Jockey Club rule does suggest a dispensation in exceptional circumstances but the Turf Club one does not. In any event they are both courting disaster by keeping the rule in its present form.

19

Moods, Meals and Money

Mick Kinane's perpetual planning ahead – repeatedly running through future races in his mind – has an unfortunate side effect on his relations with other people. Only elder brother Thomas is brave enough to pull his leg about it. Everybody else either wonders what they have done to offend him or recognises that the frowning appearance may not necessarily signify that he has got out of bed the wrong side.

He is not always like this, of course. On other occasions he is fond of making little witticisms – often they are not much more than a play on words – but they are enough to make him burst out laughing, and on such occasions his humour is infectious. But its Kinane's darker side that makes the most impression and Tommy Carmody, even though he has known the champion since he was a teenager, admits that he is still put out when he meets Mick in one of his pensive periods.

> So often when I see him he is frosty. I am made to wonder whether I should say hello to him or whether I would be better off saying nothing at all. He's also moody. We all are at times but few of us are as moody as he is!

Mick admits he is at fault:

> I *am* moody – many professional sportsmen are – and I know I can sometimes appear to be in a terrible frame of mind. Often it's no illusion The boys in the weighing room have

long got used to me. They know that, while I can be in great form some days, I can also be grimly serious. I tend to repeatedly toss over everything in my mind and I get lost in my thoughts. I am far from perfect. Nobody knows this more than me but it's just the way I am and at this stage I can't change myself into somebody I am not.

The boys in the weighing room sometimes refer to him, somewhat irreverently, as Mickey Joe. To Catherine and to his parents he is always Michael but to racegoers around the world he is Mick. His surname also has three different versions. Many of the commentators in England say Kin-aine. The Irish course commentator says Kin-arne. So does the one in Hong Kong. The correct pronunciation is Kin-anne. He never complains when people get it wrong but, when he is in a bad frame of mind and somebody says something he doesn't like, the determined jaw is apt to jut and the white-tipped eyebrows, which somehow look out of place beneath the short reddish-brown hair, add to the fearsome frown. Dermot Weld often has to bear the brunt of Kinane's moods and it is sometimes assumed that relations between the two are bad when his stable jockey is not allowed to get off one of the Rosewell House horses to ride in a big race for Sheikh Mohammed. But, according to Weld, these are not the worst moments:

> We had far more problems in the early days than we now do over the Sheikh Mohammed contract, basically because there is a fair bit of give and take on both sides. Sometimes other trainers ask me why I let him off my runners so much but I consider the 'You are my stable jockey, you ride my horses' approach an outdated one. I also believe that, in the long term, it doesn't really work. We've had a few rows over the years but nobody ever hears about them. We have great respect for each other and as a result we are always able to sort out our differences.

Mick agrees:

> In many ways the reason why we have remained together so long is that Dermot is such a good negotiator. If he had forced my hand and said 'It's either my job or the other one', the partnership would have broken up some time ago. He does

not have my services as much as he used to but he still has me
on his horses when he most wants me. The way it works is that,
if Dermot does not have a horse in a Group One or Group Two
race on a particular day and Sheikh Mohammed does, then I
can be released to ride for the Sheikh. Furthermore, as not all
the Rosewell House owners now contribute to my retainer, the
stable's first call on me only relates to horses belonging to
owners who pay a share of the annual fee.

The person who has to put up most with the moodiness and
frostiness is Catherine. Slightly taller than Mick, she is an attractive
woman with clear complexioned, rose pink cheeks that are the envy
of several of her female friends. In many ways she is the perfect foil
for her husband. She is outgoing and invariably cheerful, pleasant
and polite. But she has long been determined to keep out of her
husband's limelight and she invariably turns down all requests for
interviews. My attempts to get her views on the better known half
of the partnership failed completely!

> Catherine is a bit funny about media attention. She is not at
> all easy with it and she has decided that she doesn't want to
> get involved. My view is that, if this is the way she wants it,
> fair enough. She has been a great help to me and she has
> always been most supportive. It can't be easy being married
> to somebody who is away from home so much but she has
> been extremely understanding about this and the other
> aspects of a jockey's life.

One of the things Mrs Kinane has had to be most understanding
about is the way her husband's mood can change from inner
euphoria to near despair, depending on whether he has won or lost.

> Trying to switch off after race-riding, particularly when
> things have gone well, is something I find extremely difficult.
> I think it's because the adrenalin gets so pumped up that it
> takes several hours to return to normal. I never punch the air
> when I win a big race, or stand up in the irons and wave at
> the crowd. Just because other people do it, doesn't mean that
> I have to. It also doesn't mean that winning excites me any
> less than those who do. Indeed I suspect that it may even thrill
> me more than most jockeys.

However a narrow defeat in a big race can be particularly hard to take. The old saying that 'It's how you play the game that counts, not whether you win or lose' has never cut any ice with me. I aim to win and, when I don't, it shows. I am no good at hiding my emotions – certainly not when I get beaten – and people in racing have to take me as I am.

What most people in racing do not see is the drained, seemingly exhausted Kinane after he has been in the sauna or has had a particularly tiring day at the races. Sometimes the latter comes after a morning's work session and is followed by riding gallops on the racecourse after the last race is finished. By the time Mick gets back to the jockeys' room on such occasions he looks as if he is finished too. All he seems able to do is slump down onto his bench and, with great effort, lift up his legs for the valet to pull off his boots.

In addition to the physical effort of all those gallops, riding a lot of fancied horses and being involved in one finish after another can take its toll. So does all the mental preparation involved. But, although I may look and feel knackered, I recover quickly. It's the same after a sweat which, as I have said, I don't like doing. However at certain times my weight can shoot up a couple of pounds for no apparent reason. It's sod's law that this often happens when I am trying to ride at my normal minimum, 8st 4lb, and so I have no choice but to sweat it off.

Smoking, or rather trying to give it up, simply accentuates the weight problems. Dermot Weld made it plain very early on in our relationship that he thought I shouldn't be smoking and after my first season with him I did give up. I managed to stay cigarette-free for a couple of years but it proved a hard habit to break and trying to do so can make you bad tempered – although I can be that without giving up smoking! I have given up cigarettes many times since but, when I did so in Hong Kong during the 1994/95 winter, my weight went right up to nine stone. As Dad said all those years ago, I should never have started smoking in the first place. At the time I thought it was smart and I've had to learn the hard way that it's not.

His weight has to be watched constantly. Like most jockeys, Mick can never afford to tuck into food without calculating the calories and he has to repeatedly turn himself away from temptation. The knowledge of what the scales will tell him is enough to keep him on the straight and narrow – that and past experience that the punishment for any breach is a session in the sauna.

> I keep my eating habits pretty much unchanged throughout the year but I don't starve myself. I have a cup of tea when I get up, my breakfast can be a bowl of cereal or a piece of toast and for lunch I will have another cup of tea plus a couple of sandwiches. Dinner is my main meal – meat or fish plus potatoes and other vegetables – and I will often wash it down with a glass of wine. But it's only the one course. No soup or puddings. However, even with that diet, I still have to keep an eye on the scales and, whenever the weight starts to creep up, I have to reduce my intake.

It was his ability to sleep almost at will that Tommy Carmody so envied when they were both apprentices. These days it has no bearing on Mick's diet but it fits in well with all the travelling he does.

> When I am flying I am normally asleep before the plane takes off and, if I'm making a long car journey with Catherine doing the driving, I invariably sleep for at least an hour. It's a help to be able to switch off like this, particularly with me spending so much time running through the races in mind. It has also been a help with the Sheikh Mohammed job. After the first year Anthony Stroud said he wanted me to ride more work on their horses and build up more of a working relationship with the trainers. That has meant a lot more travelling, particularly in the early part of the season, and so I decided I would take the odd day off whenever I had the chance as well as become more selective about the Irish meetings. When you are young you can dash here, there and everywhere just for a ride but now, particularly as I aim to stick at this game for several years to come, I feel there is no point in travelling halfway across the country to ride a horse that is not going to win.

The golf course gets the benefit of most of those days off although his handicap remains stubbornly fixed at 17 and there are accusations that he tries too hard.

> I started playing when I was 19 but I don't have enough time to practice and my busy schedule means that I can sometimes go for a fortnight without getting in a game. I play a lot with Pat Shanahan, and also fourballs involving Thomas and Catherine although she sometimes criticises me for my approach to the game, saying 'You take it far too seriously!' But that's me. I'm competitive with everything I do although, unlike race-riding, it doesn't really hurt if I get beaten when I should have won. I really enjoy the game and I have many friends among the top Irish professionals, particularly Christy O'Connor jnr, Des Smyth and Eamon Darcy. Sometimes I play with them too. I also have a great passion for hurling and I support Tipperary but it's impossible to find the time to go and watch a match. When I do have a few minutes to spare, I enjoy working in the garden and looking after my Charolais heifers.

Sinead and Aisling also get plenty of attention and, although neither daughter showed much interest when they were younger – the pony that was bought for them had to be sold when they couldn't be bothered to ride it, they are now keen on both riding and racing and they have a pony once more. Sinead, born in 1983 and three years older than her sister, delighted her grandfather recently by informing him that she was going to become a jockey – 'Somebody,' she pointed out, 'has got to keep up the family tradition!'

The top jockeys make a lot of money and Mick is by far the wealthiest in Ireland. He is also one of the best paid in the world. Anthony Stroud calculates that his percentages in his first year with Sheikh Mohammed came to more than those of any other rider in Europe, and that was without taking into account his Hong Kong earnings plus his English and Irish retainers. But Mick has to suffer a harsher tax regime than his rivals in the other major racing countries. In Ireland a married man with two children reaches the top 48 per cent tax rate when his income hits £24,000. He also has to pay a 2¼ per cent social insurance contribution so he is soon at the stage where the State claims over half his earnings.

Taxation is my biggest burden and it means that I pay a high
price for my decision to remain in Ireland. I am not
complaining – I have done well out of racing – but I have to
retire a lot earlier than people do in most other jobs and there
is always the risk that injury could bring my career to a
premature end. As part of the investment for my retirement,
and as an insurance policy against the consequences of a bad
accident, I have bought land around me at Clunemore
whenever any has come up for sale. Money is important to
me when I am negotiating retainers – that's business – but not
in the day-to-day race-riding. When I win a big race, I never
think in terms of the percentages I have earned. All I am
concerned about is trying to do things right and, in the
process, win the race.

When the time does come to hang up his boots he has already
decided that he will not follow in his father's footsteps and become
a trainer:

To succeed in that you have to want to train very badly
indeed. I just don't have that ambition and nor do I have the
right temperament. I will probably dabble in farming – I love
the idea of working on the land – and buy and sell a few
horses. But I plan to go on riding for as long as I'm still
enjoying it, provided people still want me to ride for them.

When he sits down in the evening, after enjoying that small dinner
and his glass of wine, he occasionally muses over one major
ambition that still remains unfulfilled. Surprisingly it does not
involve a big race but it's an ambition that seems to be slipping
further and further from his grasp.

Believe it or not, it's to ride a winner over hurdles. I thought
I was going to achieve it when Fortune And Fame had his first
race over jumps at Thurles in November 1991 but Dermot
Weld chickened out and put up Brendan Sheridan instead. I
only want to do it once, just to get a taste of what it's like to
be a jump jockey. After all, that's what I was bred to be.

Appendix A

Mick Kinane's winners

Year	Ireland	Britain	France	Germany	Hong Kong	Italy	India	Japan	Australia	Austria	Spain	Switzerland	Saudi Arabia	USA	Total
1975	2														2
1976	28														28
1977	40	1													41
1978	46														46
1979	42						3								45
1980	58						9								67
1981	28						14								42
1982	41	1					6								48
1983	54						2								56
1984	88					1	8								97
1985	105		1			2	17								125
1986	80					1	18								99
1987	86	1			1	1	13								102
1988	113					7	12								132
1989	112		1			2	19								134
1990	80	3	1			2	3	1						1	91
1991	111				1	2					1				115
1992	100	4	1	1	22	1							1		130
1993	115	4		2	26	1			1		1				150
1994	84	23			28	1		2				1			139
1995	72	28	1		14	1									116
1996	67	29		2	35	1		1		1					136

Appendix B

Mick Kinane's Group and other Big Race Wins

YEAR	COUNTRY	GROUP	RACE	HORSE	TRAINER
1976	Ireland	III	Ballyogan	Reelin Jig	L. Browne
1978	Ireland	III	Mulcahy	Enid Calling	M. Kauntze
1980	Ireland	III	Athasi	Etoile De Paris	M. Kauntze
		III	Park	Lone Bidder	M. Kauntze
1981	Ireland	II	Nijinsky	Young Kildare	L. Browne
		III	Larkspur	Sharp Singer	A.J. Maxwell
	India	III	AC Ardeshir Gold Cup	Ipi Tombi	D.N. Adenwalla
1982	Ireland	I	Irish 2,000 Guineas	Dara Monarch	L. Browne
		III	McCairns Trial	Dara Monarch	L. Browne
		III	Park	Countess Candy	L. Browne
	Britain	II	St James's Palace	Dara Monarch	L. Browne
1983	Ireland	I	Heinz 57 Phoenix	King Persian	L. Browne
		II	Gallinule	Carlingford Castle	L. Browne
		III	Seven Springs Sprint	Jester	A. Redmond
		III	Ashford Castle	Without Reserve	L. Browne
	India	I	Calcutta 1,000 Guineas	Wheels	S. Charan
1984	Ireland	III	Glencairn	Castlemartin King	D.K. Weld
	Italy	II	Legnano	Vers La Caisse	D.K. Weld
	India	I	Golconda Derby	Deccan Star	M. Khan
		I	Indian 2,000 Guineas	Eversun	A.U. Khan
1985	Ireland	II	Derrinstown Derby Trial	Theatrical	D.K. Weld
		II	Beresford	Flash Of Steel	D.K. Weld
		III	Ballyogan	Committed	D.K. Weld
		III	Royal Whip	Kamakura	D.K. Weld
		III	Park	Gaily Gaily	D.K. Weld
		III	Glencairn	Kings River	D.K. Weld
	Italy	I	Premio Parioli	Again Tomorrow	D.K. Weld
		II	Legnano	Easy To Copy	D.K. Weld
	France	I	Prix de l'Abbaye	Committed	D.K. Weld
	India	I	Indian Oaks	Revelation	B. Chenoy
		II	Breeders' Produce	Sir Bruce	J. Dalal
		I	Indian 2,000 Guineas	Sir Bruce	J. Dalal
		III	Maharaja Jiwajirao Scindia Gold Trophy	Wisdom	V.M. Lad
1986	Ireland	I	Irish 2,000 Guineas	Flash Of Steel	D.K. Weld
		III	Tetrarch	Flash Of Steel	D.K. Weld

YEAR	COUNTRY	GROUP	RACE	HORSE	TRAINER
1986	Italy	II	Legnano	High Competence	D.K. Weld
	India	III	RR Ruia Trophy	Solitary Splendour	I. Fernandes
		I	Indian Oaks	Silver Haven	U. Singh
		I	Indian Derby	Sir Bruce	J. Dalal
		I	Indian 1,000 Guineas	Nauvkhal	U. Singh
1987	Ireland	I	Moyglare	Flutter Away	D.K. Weld
		II	Tattersalls Gold Cup	Cockney Lass	D.K. Weld
		III	Tetrarch	Big Shuffle	D.K. Weld
		III	Railway	Flutter Away	D.K. Weld
		III	Park	Trusted Partner	D.K. Weld
		III	Leopardstown	Careafolie	D.K. Weld
	Britain	III	Cork and Orrery	Big Shuffle	D.K. Weld
	Italy	II	Melton	Ginny Binny	V. Zuco
	India	III	RWITC Gold Trophy	Paper Tiger	U. Singh
1988	Ireland	I	Irish 1,000 Guineas	Trusted Partner	D.K. Weld
		III	Gladness	Careafolie	D.K. Weld
		III	Greenlands	Big Shuffle	D.K. Weld
		III	Futurity	Phantom Breeze	D.K. Weld
		III	Killavullan	Sedulous	D.K. Weld
		III	Ballymacmoy	Executive Perk	D.K. Weld
	Italy	I	Premio Roma	Welsh Guide	M. Osthaus
		I	Premio Parioli	Gay Burslem	D.K. Weld
		II	Melton	Edy Bedy	V. Zuco
		III	Dormello	Marina Duff	A. Colella
	India	II	CN Wadia Gold Cup	Commander In Chief	D. Todywalla
		I	Indian Derby	Cordon Bleu	R.R. Byramji
1989	Ireland	I	Irish Oaks	Alydaress	H.R.A. Cecil
		I	Phoenix Champion	Carroll House	M.A. Jarvis
		II	Derrinstown Derby Trial	Phantom Breeze	D.K. Weld
		III	Royal Whip	Beyond The Lake	D.K. Weld
		III	Meld	Slender Style	D.K. Weld
		III	Concorde	Executive Perk	D.K. Weld
		III	Futurity	Teach Dha Mhile	D.K. Weld
		–	Cartier Million	The Caretaker	D.K. Weld
	France	I	Arc de Triomphe	Carroll House	M.A. Jarvis
	India	III	Moghul Monarch Super Mile Trophy	Northern Star	B. Chenoy
		III	Maharaja Jiwajirao Scindia Gold Trophy	Enrico	B. Chenoy
		III	Royal Hong Kong Jockey Club Trophy	Sea Jade	B. Chenoy
		III	RWITC Gold Trophy	Icelandic	B. Chenoy
1990	Ireland	III	Phoenix Sprint	Northern Goddess	I.A. Balding

YEAR	COUNTRY	GROUP	RACE	HORSE	TRAINER
			Cartier Million	Rinka Das	D.K. Weld
	Britain	I	Two Thousand Guineas	Tirol	R. Hannon
		I	King George VI and Queen Elizabeth Diamond	Belmez	H.R.A. Cecil
	USA	I	Belmont	Go And Go	D.K. Weld
	India	I	Indian Oaks	Golden Treasure	B. Chenoy
		III	Gool Poonawalla Trophy	Speculate	B. Chenoy
1991	Ireland	III	Meld	Sardaniya	J.M. Oxx
		III	Flying Five	Flowing	D.K. Weld
		III	Killavullan	Misago-Togo	D.K. Weld
	Italy	III	Citta di Napoli	Riverullah	B. Grizzetti
	Hong Kong	I	Invitation Bowl	Additional Risk	D.K. Weld
1992	Ireland	II	Gallinule	Brief Truce	D.K. Weld
		II	Pretty Polly	Market Booster	D.K. Weld
		III	Concorde	Rami	D.K. Weld
		III	Curragh	Tropical	D.K. Weld
		III	Meld	Market Booster	D.K. Weld
		III	Park	Asema	D.K. Weld
	Britain	I	St James's Palace	Brief Truce	D.K. Weld
		II	King Edward VII	Beyton	R. Hannon
	Italy	I	Derby Italiano	In A Tiff	D.K. Weld
	France	II	Maurice de Gheest	Pursuit of Love	H.R.A. Cecil
	Germany	I	Aral Pokal	Tel Quel	A. Fabre
	Hong Kong	I	Hong Kong Derby	Sound Print	P.C. Kan
		I	Stewards Cup	Sound Print	P.C. Kan
		III	Hong Kong Classic Trial	Sound Print	P.C. Kan
1993	Ireland	I	Irish St Leger	Vintage Crop	D.K. Weld
		II	Gallinule	Massyar	J.M. Oxx
		III	Phoenix Sprint	Tropical	D.K. Weld
		III	Desmond	Asema	D.K. Weld
		III	Royal Whip	Rayseka	J.M. Oxx
		III	Anglesey	Keraka	J.M. Oxx
		III	Flying Five	Tropical	D.K. Weld
	Britain	I	Derby	Commander In Chief	H.R.A. Cecil
		I	Eclipse	Opera House	M.R. Stoute
		II	Queen Anne	Alflora	C.E. Brittain
	Germany	I	Bayerisches Zuchtrennen	Market Booster	D.K. Weld
		I	Aral Pokal	Monsun	H. Jentzsch
	Australia	I	Melbourne Cup	Vintage Crop	D.K. Weld
	Hong Kong	I	International Bowl	Winning Partners	N. Begg
1994	Ireland	I	Irish Champion	Cezanne	M.R. Stoute
		I	National	Definite Article	D.K. Weld
		I	Irish St Leger	Vintage Crop	D.K. Weld

YEAR	COUNTRY	GROUP	RACE	HORSE	TRAINER
		III	Gladness	Ridgewood Ben	J.M. Oxx
		III	Derrinstown Derby Trial	Artema	D.K. Weld
		III	Flying Five	Tropical	D.K. Weld
		III	Matron	Eternal Reve	F. Boutin
	Britain	I	St James's Palace	Grand Lodge	W. Jarvis
		I	Coronation	Kissing Cousin	H.R.A. Cecil
		I	King George VI and Queen Elizabeth Diamond	King's Theatre	H.R.A. Cecil
		II	Queen Anne	Barathea	L. Cumani
		II	King Edward VII	Foyer	M.R. Stoute
		II	Champagne	Sri Pekan	P.F.I. Cole
		III	Craven	King's Theatre	H.R.A. Cecil
		III	Brigadier Gerard	Chatoyant	J.W. Watts
	Hong Kong	II	Queen Elizabeth II Cup	Deerfield	N. Begg
1995	Ireland	II	Tattersalls Gold Cup	Prince of Andros	D.R. Loder
		II	Blandford	Humbel	D.K. Weld
		III	Derrinstown Derby Trial	Humbel	D.K. Weld
		III	Greenlands	Nautical Pet	D.K. Weld
		III	Curragh Cup	Vintage Crop	D.K. Weld
		III	Meld	Needle Gun	C.E. Brittain
		III	Beresford	Ahkaam	D.K. Weld
	Britain	I	Cheveley Park	Blue Duster	D.R. Loder
		III	Chester Vase	Luso	C.E. Brittain
		III	Queen Mary	Blue Duster	D.R. Loder
		III	Queen's Vase	Stelvio	H.R.A. Cecil
		III	Princess Margaret	Blue Duster	D.R. Loder
	Italy	I	Derby Italiano	Luso	C.E. Brittain
	France	II	Prix de Royallieu	Russian Snows	J.M. Oxx
	Hong Kong	I	Queen Elizabeth II Cup	Red Bishop	H.A. Ibrahim
1996	Ireland	I	Irish Oaks	Dance Design	D.K. Weld
		II	Tattersalls Gold Cup	Definite Article	D.K. Weld
		II	Pretty Polly	Dance Design	D.K. Weld
		III	Greenlands	Lidanna	D. Hanley
	Britain	I	Ascot Gold Cup	Classic Cliche	S.b. Suroor
			Fillies Mile	Reams Of Verse	H.R.A. Cecil
		II	Yorkshire Cup	Classic Cliche	S.b. Suroor
		II	Queen Anne	Charnwood Forest	S.b. Suroor
		II	Hardwicke	Oscar Schindler	K. Prendergast
		II	Falmouth	Sensation	Mme. C. Head
		III	Earl of Sefton	Luso	C.E. Brittain
		III	Palace House	Cool Jazz	C.E. Brittain
		III	Ormonde	Oscar Schindler	K. Prendergast
		III	Musidora	Magnificient Style	H.R.A. Cecil
		III	Queen Mary	Dance Parade	P.F.I. Cole
		III	Queen's Vase	Gordi	D.K. Weld
	Germany	I	Aral-Pokal	Luso	C.E. Brittain
	Italy	III	Melton	Beat Of Drums	G. Botti
	Hong Kong	I	Hong Kong Derby	Che Sara Sara	D.A. Oughton

Index